The Trail of the Huguenots

The Trail of
THE HUGUENOTS
in Europe, the United States
South Africa and Canada

G. ELMORE REAMAN

Baltimore
GENEALOGICAL PUBLISHING COMPANY
1 9 6 6

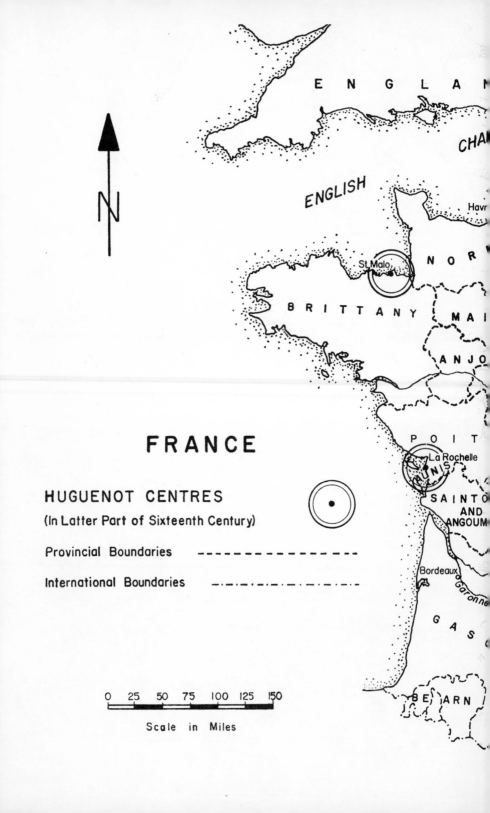

ENGLAND

CHA

ENGLISH

Havr

St Malo

NOR

BRITTANY

MAI

ANJO

FRANCE

POIT

La Rochelle

UNIS

HUGUENOT CENTRES

(In Latter Part of Sixteenth Century)

SAINTO
AND
ANGOUM

Provincial Boundaries ----------------

International Boundaries -- -- -- -- -- --

Bordeaux

Garonne

GAS O

0   25   50   75   100   125   150

BE ARN

Scale   in   Miles

Contents

PART SEVEN

References

PART EIGHT

Appendices

Foreword

The Huguenots, descendants of French Protestants in days when it was criminal to be Protestant, now are a submerged people. In France they survive only in a small measure. In the Dispersion, however, unlike other *émigré* groups, Huguenots voluntarily and even eagerly lost group identity by accepting assimilation.

It has been estimated that almost two million Huguenots fled France. For the most part they did not establish large French-speaking culture islands within other peoples. Only here and there did a refugee congregation continue to worship in French. They did not form large and homogeneous groups like the Dutch in South Africa, the Germans in eastern Pennsylvania or even like the Roman Catholic French in eastern Canada. Rather the Huguenots chose to let themselves merge with the cultural and economic life of their newly adopted lands, accepting the ways and modes of their new homes with eagerness.

The first reason for this Huguenot readiness to be assimilated comes from the nature of the migration itself. It was not a mass movement of people. Rather it was a steady flow of individuals and families. During the period of this migration it was illegal to flee France; capture meant the galleys. So the border was crossed in secret, not by large conspicuous groups, but by families and individuals; and sometimes even families were broken up.

Another reason for the eagerness to forget France and its corroding ways comes from the character of the Huguenot movement itself. It was basically a protest against a corrupt civilization. Rightly or wrongly the Huguenots were seeking to revive French life by putting moral fibre back into French character. And when France exiled them their attentions were centred, not with the old culture, but with the new life that lay ahead. This made them entrepreneurs, adventurers, and good material for colonization.

This astonishing trait of the Huguenots to accept and even to welcome assimilation with the countries which received them has made a historian's nightmare. Even the descendants of the Huguenots themselves are unaware of their background. How shall this migration be told? How shall the movement of these two million people into new cultures and new lands be chronicled? What did they contribute to their new homes? These questions must be raised, but the historian's task is not easy because there are no records, no source materials, no fundamental documents to record this migration. Only here and there, as in London, Berlin, Charleston, and New York, did French-speaking churches continue. Here the task was simpler. But most of the evidence must begin, as Dr. Reaman does in this work, by recording the families which came from France to become part of a larger community.

This historical task has been going on in Western Protestant lands since the end of the nineteenth century. Huguenot Societies have been forced to ferret out family background because this was the one sure way to come to grips with the historical problem. Who would suspect, for example, that behind the Anglo-Saxon Virginia background of George Washington lay the Gallic character of Nicholas Martiau, his first American forbear? Indeed, when my father, Dr. John Baer Stoudt, founder of the Huguenot Society of Pennsylvania, first suggested that many Pennsylvania German families had Huguenot backgrounds he was laughed at. Yet my mother's maiden name was deLong, an ancient Huguenot family from Dauphine, and my father's forbear was the Kieffer whom Dr. Reaman mentions as changing his name from Tonnelier when he settled in Zweibrücken. Perhaps if he had settled in London he would have called himself Cooper.

While this digging out of family roots of Huguenots has been taking place in most lands of the Western world, Canada has remained strangely silent, unaware of the part that these French refugees played in her history.

It has remained for Dr. Reaman to ferret out this information, to gather it together and to present it in this present work as the first coherent account, along with information about the Huguenots of the Dispersion generally, of the discovery, conquest, settlement, and development of Canada and of the part that the people of Huguenot background played in that story. This is a pioneering accomplishment and is as far, perhaps, as we may go due to the circumscription of the evidence. As in his former work, *The Trail of the Black Walnut*, wherein he showed the large part the Germanic groups played in the settling of Ontario, so in this work, too, Dr. Reaman gives us a rememberably reported and significant account of the part the Huguenots played in the history of Canada.

Norristown,   JOHN JOSEPH STOUDT
Pennsylvania   *Ph.D., D.Theol.*

Author's Preface

History requires to be rewritten from time to time because new facts come to light and new points of view need to be taken. This applies to French Huguenots. As so frequently happens, history is looked at regionally, with the result that whatever is discovered is made available for but a small number of people. I found this to be true of the historical facts assembled in *The Trail of the Black Walnut*. It was discovered that Ontario's earliest settlers had located in five general areas: The Niagara Peninsula; the counties of Essex and Kent; the counties along the St. Lawrence River from Glengarry up to Prince Edward; York County; and Waterloo County. Each of these areas had an excellent knowledge of its backgrounds but not a single one knew anything about the history of any other. It was as if each section of the province and each individual group were little islands separated by time and distance with no historical relationship.

This is particularly true of French Huguenots. France, the British Isles, and the United States are quite aware of their Huguenot ancestors. But what of Canada? The term Huguenot is almost unknown here and when known is often not understood. Among the earliest settlers in Upper Canada (Ontario) we find families whose names are Secord, Nelles, Ryerson, Rousseau, and Ruttan, names that are definitely French in origin. If you were to ask a member of the foregoing families if he has any knowledge of his Huguenot ancestry, he would likely be at a loss to tell you. Even if he were aware of it he might not know whether to be proud of or sorry for it. Then again, if he learned that there were Huguenots among the first settlers in Nova Scotia and Quebec, he would not see any connection between his ancestors and those who were among the earliest founders of Canada.

It is a generally accepted point of view in Canada that Frenchmen have always been Roman Catholics and that Protestantism has had little or no relationship with France. It has been further accepted that there was no connection between Protestant French and the exploration of Canada by the French. A careful study of both of these points of view will show that they are untenable. It may come as a surprise to learn that historians of this period state on good authority that, if it hadn't been for the business enterprise of Huguenots in France and their desire to found a colony where they could remain loyal to the King of France and yet enjoy freedom of worship, it is doubtful if there would be many French in Canada today. Furthermore, it is quite possible that had the French allowed Huguenots to migrate to Canada in the seventeenth century, England would have stood a slim chance of conquering Canada.

Such information does exist in authentic sources, but few persons in Europe or America—and that includes Canada—have any knowledge of it. French Roman Catholics have naturally advanced their point of view and Protestants have never thought it worth while to investigate it. Huguenot Societies in France, England, and the United States are not aware that from 1534 until 1633 Canada was practically Huguenot controlled nor do they know that many of the earliest settlers in Upper Canada (Ontario) were descendants of *émigrés* from France, some of whom first went to the British Isles, then to the United States, and finally to Ontario.

To gain any adequate or comprehensive understanding of the Huguenots who settled in Canada, one must study them in France, follow them to the lands that first gave them asylum, and, lastly, assemble as much genealogical data about them as is available after they settled in Canada, especially in Ontario.

In covering such a long period of time and space one is reminded of James Bryce's remark : "The secret of historical composition is what to neglect." Although no effort has been made to give a complete history of Huguenots either in the country of their origin or in later settlements, I have tried to select what I have considered the salient facts to give an overall picture of their problems and migrations. I have found that Europeans have little knowledge of the widespread character of the Huguenot settlements in the United States and vice versa. Furthermore, neither Europeans nor Americans realize the part that the Huguenots have played in Canada—nor, indeed, do Canadians, themselves.

Certainly, a study of these wonderful people is highly rewarding and, because they have played such an important part in the colonization of Canada, it is high time they received credit for it. This book is an effort to make the general reader aware of their importance.

Acknowledgments

This study could not have been undertaken had it not been for the co-operation of the Huguenot Society of London, which put their Huguenot Library at my disposal. Mr. C. F. A. Marmoy, the Hon. Librarian, gave me unstinted advice and assistance; Miss Irene Scouloudi, Hon. Secretary; Mr. Peter Minet, Hon. Treasurer; and Mrs. Grace Lawless Gwynn, Research Assistant, were always most encouraging and helpful with suggestions.

Major J. S. P. Armstrong, Agent-General for Ontario, London, was most generous of his time in making contacts for me both in London and on the Continent. M. René Garneau, when Counsellor for the Canadian Embassy, Paris, France, made possible rewarding interviews with Professor Emile G. Léonard, Directeur d'études à l'école des Hautes Études, and M. le Professeur Philippe de Félice, Secretary of the Société de l'Histoire du Protestantisme Français, both of Paris, France.

For the United States, I should mention Dr. Samuel B. Sturgis, Past President, National Huguenot Society; Dr. John Joseph Stoudt; and Royal A. Mabee, for orientation to the Huguenots in the United States. A special word of thanks should go to Dr. Arthur D. Graeff for many valuable suggestions.

In Canada I am indebted to Mrs. Esther Clark Wright, Ottawa, for little known facts about the Huguenots in the Maritimes. Pastors of Huguenot Churches, the Rev. J. E. Boucher, of Ottawa; the Rev. André Poulain and the Rev. Jacque Beaudon, of Montreal; and the Rev. A. Jossinet, of Quebec City, because of their Huguenot backgrounds, checked my characterization of Huguenots. The Geography Department, University of Waterloo, kindly drew the map of France for me.

The discovery of persons now living in the Province of Ontario

—and there are many, many more, not included in my biographical sketches—would have not been possible except for the fine co-operation of a hundred and fifty daily and weekly newspapers who published my request for information of Huguenot ancestry. I must also thank the hundreds of persons who replied, many of them over eighty years of age, who wrote, "At last, someone is giving recognition to these wonderful people."

Much time and energy was spent in typing the manuscript by Mrs. Jean Ingram, Mrs. Vera Youngman, and Mrs. Victor (Agnes) Hill. Finally, I owe a debt of gratitude to my wife, Flora, and daughter, Elaine, for advice, encouragement, and assistance of various kinds.

Waterloo, Ontario   G. ELMORE REAMAN
November 10, 1962

PART ONE

Religious Upheavals

BACKGROUNDS OF PROTESTANTISM

An American and his wife were visiting Rotterdam, Holland, for the first time and came across the statue of Erasmus. As the former from college days had been an ardent admirer of this great humanist, he did obeisance to the statue to the wonderment of the passersby. A few evenings later these two were exploring the city, and becoming lost wandered about for some time until they came to the square containing the statue of Erasmus. Their delight was intense, for it seemed that this Renaissance figure was still capable of giving direction to human beings.

After the Second World War these same Americans were re-visiting Rotterdam and betook themselves to the Erasmus square, but this time there was no statue; it had been dislodged from its base during the blitz, they were told. However, they were directed to another location near the harbour, and here they found the Erasmus statue. This time it was facing the western sea; this time it was looking toward America, and the American, who had Huguenot blood in his veins and whose ancestors both French and German had been religious refugees in response to the free-dom of thought advocated by Erasmus, realized how appropriate it was that his statue was facing the western world and that he could still bring light and encouragement to it.

This incident suggests how a personality can embody so timeless a spirit that it can project itself into all subsequent generations. Here was a twentieth-century scholar acknowledging his debt to a sixteenth-century thinker because the latter was representative of a group of religious leaders who provided motivation for the thousands of religious refugees who, during succeeding centuries, fled from Europe to North America to provide its first settlers.

Calvinism was an important part of this motivation because of its pioneering, rugged individualism, modern stoicism, dedication, and sublimation. It inspired Presbyterians from Scotland, Walloons from the Netherlands, Evangelicals from Germany, Reformed from Switzerland, Puritans (Congregationalists from England and New England), and Huguenots from France, the latter cementing all these cultures together and acting like a leaven with an integrating, articulating, complementing, and ennobling result.

Strangely enough wherever the French Huguenots have settled they have allowed themselves to be assimilated, content to make their contribution in business, industry or the arts without emphasizing their nationality. Nevertheless, although the fleur-de-lis flag may have lessened in its importance at Versailles, it has increased elsewhere, and so the flag of Henry of Navarre is the official flag of the Province of Quebec and the Huguenot Cross is known far and wide as signifying the Erasmian spirit of Humanism so much needed in a world where emotion rather than intellect rules and where world brotherhood is not only desirable but essential if civilization is to continue to exist.

Let us try to understand the spirit of the Renaissance as expressed by the religious thinking of the French Huguenots and see what answers can be found for the Zeitgeist of our day.

Protestantism, as we know it today, is usually thought to have been initiated by such reformers as Luther, Zwingli, Calvin, and Melanchthon. Certainly these were the men who crystallized the thinking of their times, set up the opposition to the Roman church and gave direction to the movement. Nevertheless, for several centuries before their time, there had been "protests" against many of the practices common to the Roman Catholic church, some of these offering bitter opposition but in the end succumbing to the power of Rome.

In the early years of the twelfth century we find a group called the Waldenses, named, it is said, after Peter Waldo, a wealthy French merchant in Lyons, France, who took upon himself the vow of poverty and gave leadership to them until he died in Bohemia in 1217.

This group, which sought individual perfection apart from the Roman Church, rejected the official clergy, abstained from oaths and the use of force, and attempted in general to reintroduce primitive Christian fellowship and apostolic simplicity of living. They were able to carry on with these ideas as a sect because of their remoteness, since they lived in the Vaudois valleys or the valleys of the Piedmont. Because of their location, they are frequently referred to as Vaudois and come into the Huguenot story with their massacre during the reign of Francis I.

Claiming that they were converts of the faith preached by St. Paul—proof of which can neither be proved nor refuted—their beliefs came to be widely accepted; in fact, members of this sect still exist, showing its vitality. They accepted and taught doctrines of the apostles and acknowledged the Bible, particularly the New Testament, as their guide.[1] The tenets of their religion were: (1) that oaths are forbidden by the Gospels; (2) that capital punishment is not allowed to the civil powers; (3) that any layman may consecrate the sacrament of the altar; and (4) that the Roman church is not the church of Christ but the enemy of Christ.

The Waldenses carried on active missionary work among the barbarians to the north of them. "Their Pastors were designated 'Barbas' (a term meaning uncle). It was in the almost inaccessible solitude of the deep mountain pass that they had their school. . . . They were required to commit to memory the Gospels of St. Matthew and St. John, the general epistles, and a part of those of St. Luke. They were instructed, moreover, during two or three successive winters, and trained to speak in Latin, in the Romance language, and in the Italian. After this they spent one year in retirement, and then were set apart to the holy ministry by the administration of the Lord's Supper, and by the imposition of hands. They were supported by the voluntary contributions of the people.

"These missionaries always went forth two and two, to wit, a young man and an old one . . . they traversed Italy, where they had stations organized in many places, and secret adherents in almost all the towns. . . .

"Each pastor was required to become a missionary in his turn. . . . Besides this, the Barbas received instruction in some trade or profession. Some were hawkers, others artisans, the greater part physicians or surgeons, and all were acquainted with the cultivation of the soil, the keeping of flocks, to the care of which they had been accustomed in their early years."[2]

As the See of Rome became supreme, the isolation of the Vaudois Church ceased to exist and for several centuries the Waldenses were bitterly persecuted yet never completely conquered. The ideas for which they stood spread into Hungary, Bohemia, France, and England, and provided the groundwork for the Reformation leaders. Even the Roman church itself was influenced by them when actively promoted. The Albigenses are one example. Here we have one branch of the Cathari, considered one of the most active heretical sects of the Middle Ages against whom in 1208 a crusade was sent by Pope Innocent III and during which thirty thousand perished. This happened in Languedoc, a section later to figure prominently in Huguenot opposition. "The influence of Catharism on the Catholic Church was enormous. To counteract it, celibacy was finally imposed on the clergy, and the great mendicant orders evolved; while the constant polemic of the Cathari teachers against the cruelty, rapacity, and irascibility of the Jewish tribal god led the church to prohibit the circulation of the Old Testament among laymen. The sacrament of 'extreme unction' was also evolved by way of competing with death-bed *consolamentum* (removed original sin, restored to immortality)."[3]

Let us now turn to England in the fourteenth century and to John Wyclif (1320–1384). A theologian and a very successful teacher at Oxford University, Wyclif became critical of the existing evils of the church and wrote and spoke against them ; moreover, he was supported by John of Gaunt and also by the common people against the threats of the pope whom he branded as Anti-Christ. The Peasants' Revolt, although not directly connected with Wyclif, drew some of its incentive from his teachings. Wyclif chose two means of advancing his beliefs, both based on the thesis which he had long maintained : the supreme authority of Holy Scripture, as the great charter of the Christian religion. The first means was his institution of the "poor" or "simple" priests to preach his doctrines throughout the country. (This was much like John Wesley's preachers in the eighteenth century). The second was the translation of the Vulgate, the Latin version of the Bible, into English. This version of the Bible, and still more his numerous sermons and tracts, established Wyclif's now undisputed position as founder of English prose writing. He and Martin Luther in Germany hold the same importance in their respective countries in this particular.

Wyclif retired from active duties and died from a stroke while hearing mass in his own church. A study of his life shows him to be sincere and to have emphasized the immediate dependence of the individual Christian upon God, a relationship which needs no mediation of any priest, and to which the very sacraments of the church, however desirable, are not entirely necessary. His ideas were carried on by adherents to a religious movement known as Lollards. Lollardy flourished most during the ten years following Wyclif's death and was endorsed by many of the nobles. The lay preachers were among the people and were very well received ; however, the Church, backed up by Richard II, Henry IV, and Henry V, did its utmost to suppress the movement but, as always happens, persecution only made for increased interest and it continued to exist until Henry VIII's reign, when the writings of Luther began to appear in England. Actually, Lollardy, which continued down to the Reformation, did much to shape the movement in England. The subordination of the clerical to lay jurisdiction, the reduction in ecclesiastical possessions, the insistence on a translation of the Bible which could be read by the "common" man, were all contributions passed on by the Lollards.

But Wyclif's influence was not restricted to England. During Richard II's reign, some nobles who came to the English Court along with his wife, Anne of Bohemia, took up the beliefs of Wyclif and through them they were carried back to Bohemia. Here John Huss, on the staff of the University of Prague, was doing some thinking on his own as a philosopher, and here he became familiar with Wyclif's theological theories. In Bohemia, there was the same effort as elsewhere to obtain money for the Roman Church, coupled with the same immorality of the priests.

The Hussite movement was a democratic and national movement. John Huss got into difficulties because he advocated the doctrines of Wyclif, although he was more interested in the moral aspects than in theological theories. Huss gained at first some government support but this dwindled as soon as the Pope took action against him. Finally, Huss was tried for heresy, condemned and burned at the stake (1415). He is remembered for having been the chief intermediary in handing on from Wyclif to Luther the torch which kindled the Reformation and for having been one of the bravest of martyrs to die for his religious beliefs.

Out of the defeat of the Bohemian movement, however, a definite sect, the Moravians or *Unitas Fratrum* (1415–1648) emerged, which reverted to the tenets of the Waldenses. A number of Huss's followers took up a doctrine which was generally broad and radical. In 1495 at a synod of Reichenau, they accepted the Bible as their only standard of faith and practice. They taught the Apostles' Creed, rejected Purgatory, the worship of saints and the authority of the Roman Catholic Church; practiced infant baptism and confirmation. Nevertheless, the Brethren laid their chief stress on conduct rather than doctrine. In 1501 they edited the first Protestant hymn-book and in 1502 published a catechism which circulated through Switzerland and Germany and fired the catechetical zeal of Luther. Thus we see Europe generally was ready for what came to be known as the Reformation.

One more factor needs to be mentioned because of its import-ance in the dissemination of knowledge : Printing. Gutenberg of Mainz, *c.* 1456, and Fust and Schaeffer, printed folio editions of the Bible in the Latin Vulgate. In 1462 a second edition appeared and a number of copies were taken to Paris. Soon translations appeared in German, Italian, Bohemian, Dutch, French, and Spanish, but copies were few and the Roman Church placed the printers under penalty of excommunication and death. England's Wyclif's translation was prohibited and Tyndale's translation of the New Testament was first made in Antwerp in 1526. Yet it must not be thought that the Bible was an unknown book until Luther's time. Although the interpretations were mutilated, copies were scarce, but from time to time they came into the hands of persons who created trouble for the Roman Church.

And now we come to the period that is generally associated with the beginnings of Protestantism—the early years of the six-teenth century. Professor Emile G. Léonard in his *Histoire du Protestantisme* [4] discusses the different reasons advanced to explain the origin of the Reformation. "The Catholic writers," he says, "give political reasons for it, also moral reasons (desire for in-dependence on the part of unworthy clerics). Protestants, without overlooking political causes, stress moral causes which they found in the bad habits of the clergy and even in the Holy See. Neutral historians give economic reasons and point to the sufferings and troublous times. However, Lucien Febvre states that the great religious reformers commencing with Luther were interested above all in spiritual problems and not so much in reforming the church but saving sinful man who is lost. First of all, they sought salvation for themselves. During the latter part of the Middle Ages there was a new interpretation of religion because of the struggles of the church itself to solve its own problems. Following the Hundred Years War there was a scarcity of clergy and churches and this was a fertile field for Protestantism. The need for help did not go unheeded and the first response came from what we now call humanism, that is, the exalting of man, a characteristic of the Renaissance."

A word about the Renaissance of New Learning. In many respects the Renaissance prepared the way for the Reformation since its most noted features were an awakening of the mind and a thirst for knowledge.

Before the fifteenth century educated people were to be found only in the church. With the fall of Constantinople, when captured by the Turks in 1453, many learned men came from the East to Western Europe bringing literature and other treasures. The Middle Ages had had a civilization and culture all its own but this culture was imprisoned by ancient customs and numerous wrong notions. The Renaissance upset these traditions at many points and gave birth to many new ideas which did not so much change the subjects of study but did set up a new view-point from which well-known facts might be considered, thus laying the foundations of modern science. Languages, philosophy, art, government, and religion were all approached, as it were, with an open mind with the result that many errors and opinions which had been current for even centuries were rejected.

For our purpose the coming into being of Humanism is most important because new ideas about human nature and man's place in society and his relationship to God brought about a revolution in thinking among the more educated class of people. It had a peculiar fascination for the French nobility because it brought inspiration and new ideas which fostered adventure.

This atmosphere of exalting man spread rapidly. Perhaps Petrarch (1304–1374) in Italy can be considered one of the first Humanists for he was one of the first to devote himself to the study and imitation of Roman and later of Greek literature which, in the sense of literary appreciation, was considered to be the basis of culture. In Germany there was Rudolph Agricola (1442–1485) who proposed that the works of antiquity should be translated into German. Humanists increased in numbers in Germany and their ideas soon invaded the universities, where they attacked the methods employed by the theologians. Reuchlin, an eminent Hebrew scholar, set up a new standard for a study of the Scriptures by emphasizing the importance of a knowledge of Hebrew.

The acknowledged prince of humanists was Erasmus. Born in Rotterdam in 1466, he became a citizen of the world, for he lived in England, France, and Germany and left his mark on the thinkers of those countries. Like most northern humanists he was deeply interested in religious reform of the Roman Church, for he had had first hand contact with the monks as he had been forced into a monastery when a boy. Erasmus felt that the first thing to do in order to promote higher ideas of Christianity was to purify the sources of the faith by preparing a correct edition of the New Testament. Up to that time the only version available was the Vulgate (Latin) into which many mistakes and misapprehensions had crept. Accordingly, in 1516, he published the original Greek text, with a new Latin translation which exposed without question the mistakes of the great body of theologians. He wanted the New Testament to be in the hands of people, men and women of all classes, but of course the masses were not familiar with Latin. Because his aim was to reform the Church, he was opposed to a revolt against the Pope and the Church, believing that such a disturbance would result in more harm than good. For him culture, especially the classical studies, was to be the chief agency in religious reform. His hopes were doomed to failure and he died an embittered man in 1536.

In Germany there was widespread discontent with the condition of the Church. The rulers were dissatisfied because the Pope enjoyed the right to fill many important offices in Germany and frequently appointed Italians. (This possibly explains why the rulers later supported Luther against the Pope.) The peasants eked out a living, most of their earnings being claimed by the clergy; consequently, the times were ripe for a leader to put the Pope and his clergy in their places.

Martin Luther, of peasant origin, proved to be that person.

Born in the Harz Mountains of a father who was a miner, Martin knew what poverty and superstition were. As he was to be a lawyer he attended a school at Erfurt but decided July 17, 1505, very much against his father's wishes, to enter a monastery. But here, since he had an enquiring mind, though not always sublimated, he became dissatisfied with his observances of the rules, for they failed to give him peace. He felt himself a hopelessly corrupt sinner. Then he turned to a study of the Bible and eventually came to the conclusion that good works were not enough, that man could only be saved by faith in God's promises.

In 1508 he began to teach at the University of Wittenberg and in 1511 he journeyed to Rome but returned shocked by the impiety of the Italian churchmen and the scandalous stories about Popes Alexander VI and Julius II.

Up to this time Luther had no idea of attacking his Church, but after his visit to Rome he encouraged his students to defend his favourite beliefs in debate, to rely upon the Bible, Paul's writings above all, and upon the Church fathers, especially Augustine.

Because Tetzel, a Dominican monk, began in October, 1517, to sell indulgences in the neighbourhood of Wittenberg, Luther wrote a series of ninety-five articles in Latin and posted them on the door of the Chapel of the University, yet without any idea of attacking the church. However, they created a sensation, were translated into German and scattered throughout the land. The reception of these theses was such that Luther was summoned to Rome, but he refused to go. Luther from then on was a centre of controversy. He wrote many pamphlets, until finally he was excommunicated in 1520, but defied both the Pope and Emperor Charles V. Summoned to Worms by the Emperor, he was outlawed by the Edict of Worms in 1521.

On his way home from Worms, he was abducted by the Elector of Saxony and hidden from the action of the Emperor. During this time he finished his translation of the New Testament into German. For the next few years Luther continued to be the centre of controversy and at one point the peasants rose in revolt to avenge their wrongs and establish their rights. He tried to reason with them and urged the government to put down the insurrection. This it did with terrible rigour, some ten thousand being killed, many of them with utmost cruelty.

Briefly, Luther's greatest contributions were made by his defiance of the Roman Church, his translation of the Bible into German, his polemical writings, and his revival of the essential gospel of salvation by grace, and justification by faith. He believed that the Church should be closely linked with the State; and his natural conservatism led him to retain most of the ceremonies, the vestments and the uses of lights on the altar, which had existed at the Roman Church, although he was careful to explain that their retention might be dispensed with if necessary. He insisted in the use of the vernacular and the supreme place assigned to preaching. Also, the people partook of the bread and wine in the sacrament of the Lord's Supper.

Luther was not the only reformer to challenge the Pope. In Switzerland Zwingli[5] had advanced many of the same ideas. The Anabaptists[6] (those who believed in adult baptism) in Switzerland and Holland were gaining many followers. Charles V then took a hand in the matter and ordered that the "Evangelical" princes restore the Mass. "As they formed only a minority in the diet, all that they could do was to draw up a *protest*, signed by John Frederick, Philip of Hesse, and fourteen of the imperial towns (Strasburg, Nuremberg, Ulm, etc.). In this they claimed that the majority had no right to abrogate the edict of the former diet of Speyer for that had passed unanimously and all had solemnly pledged themselves to observe the agreement. They therefore appealed to the Emperor and the future council against the tyranny of the majority. Those who signed this appeal were called from their action *Protestants*." [7]

Charles V of Spain, in an effort to reconcile the warring religious factions, called the Diet of Augsburg in 1530 at which time Melanchton drew up the Augsburg Confession, which eventually became the creed of the Lutheran Church. However, it was not until 1555 that the Peace of Augsburg was signed which gave each German prince and each town and knight immediately under the emperor the right to make a choice between the beliefs of the Roman Catholic Church and those found in the Augsburg Confession.

There were two noteworthy weaknesses in the Peace of Augsburg which were destined to make trouble : only one group of Protestants was included in it; the numerous followers of Calvin and Zwingli were hated alike by Roman Catholics and Lutherans. In the second place, the clause which decreed that ecclesiastical princes converted to Protestantism should surrender their property could not be enforced, for there was no one to see to its execution. Nevertheless, this Peace of Augsburg was a milestone in the history of the Reformation ; it gave state recognition.

It is very difficult for us in this age to understand the universal and deep-rooted horror of heresy which prevailed from the twelfth to the eighteenth century in Europe. Too much stress cannot be laid upon the fact that heresy was considered treason against an institution which, practically all, learned and unlearned, agreed was not only essential to salvation but was also necessary to order and civilization. Frank criticism of the evil lives of the clergy, not excluding the Pope himself, was common enough. But this was not heresy. One might believe that the Pope and half the clergy were bad men, and yet in no way question the necessity for the Church's existence or the truth of every one of its dogmas, just as nowadays we might consider our rulers inept and dishonest without repudiating the system of government altogether. The heretic was the anarchist of the Middle Ages. He did not simply denounce the immorality of the officers of the Church ; he claimed that the Church was worse than useless. He sought to lead people to throw off their allegiance to it and to disregard its laws and commands. Here we find the reason for the Church and the state teaming up to dispose of him as a menace to law and order. Besides, heresy was a contagious disease which spread rapidly and unobserved so that, to the rulers of the times, even the harshest measures appeared justifiable in order to stamp it out.

When it was found that attempts at internal reform of the evils in the Church and efforts to exterminate heretics by the sword failed, a third and what proved to be a permanent defense against heresy was the establishment, under the headship of the Pope, of a system of tribunals designed to ferret out secret cases of unbelief and bring the offenders to punishment. The unfairness of the trials and the cruel treatment to which those suspected of heresy were subjected, through long imprisonment or torture—inflicted with the hope of forcing them to confess their crime or implicate others—have rendered the name of the Inquisition infamous. Because of the frequent success of these methods, they were practiced to the end of the eighteenth century; it might be a different agency employing them but the purpose and results were the same. It would seem that the end justified the means, no matter how terrible the means might be. In passing, it might be remarked that such brutalities exist even into the middle of the twentieth century.

PART TWO

The Trail begins

HUGUENOTS IN FRANCE FROM FRANCIS I TO LOUIS XVI

Matriarchs and mistresses who determined
the rulers' attitude to the Huguenots

Throughout the rise and fall of the Huguenots in France there were three institutions that either singly or in combination were their inveterate enemies; they were in time of origin the Sorbonne, the Parlement, and the Jesuits and they worked hand in glove with the Papacy to further Roman Catholicism. In order to understand why they exercised so much influence, one must know something of their origins.

The Sorbonne owes its name and origin to Robert of Sorbon near Reims (1201–1274) who went to Paris to qualify for priesthood, attained high repute by his sanctity and eloquence and became confessor for Louis IX. Assisted by the King, he started a small school to teach theology which in 1259 was declared "useful to religion" by Pope Alexander IV. At first destined for poor students, the Sorbonne soon became the meeting place for all students of the University of Paris where they might hear the most outstanding theologians lecture. Ultimately, it acquired almost legal standing and the professors were referred to by the clergy of France as well as the whole Roman Catholic world. During the Reformation it was the animating spirit of all the persecutions directed against the Protestants. Without having advised the massacre of St. Bartholomew, it did not hesitate to justify it and it inflamed the Roman Catholic League against Henry III and the King of Navarre. It declined after 1682 and was suppressed in 1792 but reorganized on a non-sectarian basis in the nineteenth century to become the chief French centre of learning.

The Parlement at Paris had nothing in common with the Parliament of London—the latter was a representative assembly, the former a company of hereditary magistrates. It came into being in the latter half of the thirteenth century as a permanent court of justice. Besides judicial functions the Parlements—for there came to be more than a dozen in the provinces—possessed political rights. With a wide power of administration they could make regulations having the force of law within their province upon all points not settled by law. They could address injunctions to officials and individuals. From time to time they opposed those who espoused the cause of Protestantism.

Jesuits was the name given to the members of the Society of Jesus, a religious order in the Roman Catholic Church, founded in 1539. This Society may be defined, in its original conception and well-avowed object, as a body of highly trained religious men of various degrees, bound by the three personal vows of poverty, chastity, and obedience, together with a special vow to the Pope's service, with the object of labouring for the spiritual good of themselves and their neighbors. They are governed and live by constitutions and rules, mostly drawn up by their founder, a Spaniard, St. Ignatius of Loyola, and approved by the Popes. They are a band of spiritual soldiers living under martial law and discipline. The ordinary term "Jesuit", given to the Society by its opponents is first found in the writings of Calvin and in the registers of the Parlement of Paris as early as 1552.

This order came into being at the time that Luther had begun his revolt against the Roman Church and it brought about a Counter-Reformation. It has two outstanding characteristics: a military system with a skilful union of strictness and freedom, of complex organization with a minimum of friction in working and an emphasis on teaching. It soon became recognized as having the best school masters in Europe and there developed the conviction that the Jesuits alone possessed the ability and the will to train the growing generation, which deserved a higher education, in accord with strict Catholic principles.

Nevertheless, power corrupts and absolute power corrupts absolutely. "There is plenty of evidence," says Boehmer,[1] "here to conclude that their primary concern was not to make men better and convert them, but to gain such a hold on them that they would submit to their direction permanently. They reached their goal through their practices in the confessional. The most dissolute and pronounced, artful and clever worldlings, who had never given as much as a thought to beginning a new life, willingly allowed the fathers to direct them 'spiritually', because they knew very well that they did not have to give up any of their evil habits or even have to avoid the much spoken of 'next opportunity to sin'. Just that easy and agreeable the good fathers had made religion for the worldlings in particular! This boasted Father Le Moyne in a book which he wrote in 1652." In their dealings with the Huguenots they stopped at nothing to achieve their end which in this case was complete annihilation of the Huguenots.

Maurois makes two statements that one should keep in mind if he is to understand many of the difficulties encountered by the French Huguenots: "Throughout the course of French history and even until our own times, without national unity ever being threatened thereby, deep political divergencies have been visible between north and south."[2] This perhaps gives one reason why Paris never favored Protestantism, whereas the southern provinces did. The second is: "The Renaissance was wrought in the palaces of princes and of bankers far more than in the universities. The shaping of powerful, distinctive individuals (compare the men and women of Italian birth who from time to time directed French policy) was furthered in Italy by the rivalry between States—Milan, Florence, Rome, Venice, Naples. There nothing was rigid in the feudal pattern, or even in the ecclesiastical hierarchy. . . . *The individual of the Renaissance did not cease to profess the Christian faith but he no longer practised it.*"[3] (Italics mine). He goes on to say, "when it came to religion, the age was so full of in-

consistency that Marguerite (d'Angoulême), a virtuous and believing princess, could write licentious stories in the Heptaméron,
and the King, as he left his mistress's arms, could proceed to a
chapel to pray." [4]

These were the days of great voyages of discovery. While
Columbus in 1492 and his Portuguese navigators were bringing
hitherto unknown regions of the earth to the knowledge of Europe,
Copernicus was reaching the conclusion that the ancient writers
had been misled in supposing that the earth was the centre of the
universe. He discovered that with other planets the earth revolved
about the sun and thereby brought down on his head theologians,
both Catholic and Protestant alike, who declared that his findings
were contrary to Scripture. By not publishing his great work until
just before his death, he escaped the persecution which would
inevitably have come his way. Some forms of progress other than
printing were the compass, spectacles, and a method of thoroughly
melting iron so that it could be cast.

The situation in France was unique as far as the Protestants
were concerned, not only because they quite generally had the
King, the Sorbonne, the Parlement, and the Jesuits against them,
but in each reign there was a woman who, to a great extent, determined what was to happen to them. In the end it was a woman
who brought Protestantism to an end in New France, and it was a
woman who was instrumental in destroying it in France. Perhaps
in no other country has the influence of women been so potent in
high places as in France, and in most instances it worked to the
disadvantage of the monarchy. Sometimes desire for power was
their driving force, but more often they were the tools of the
Church, particularly the Jesuits. Since their influence was such a
determining factor as far as the Huguenots were concerned, we
shall make them a focal point in telling the story of the rise and
fall of the Huguenots in France.

We shall commence with Louise of Savoy. She was the mother
of Francis I and Marguerite. The latter was married first to Duke
d'Alençon who died in 1525 and then to Henry d'Albret, King

of Navarre in 1527. Her daughter, Jeanne d'Albret, married Antoine de Bourbon; their son Henry became Henry IV, one of the most outstanding Kings of France.

Louise of Savoy and her daughter Marguerite moulded the character of Francis I and spoiled him. These three spoke of themselves as a Trinity, but how different they were. Louise was "proud, ambitious, audacious or pliant at need, and able and steadfast in mind, violent and dissolute in her habits, greedy of pleasure and of money as well as of power, so that she gave her son neither principles nor a moral example."[5] Marguerite, her daughter, was of another sort. Born in 1492 she was two years older than her brother Francis and possessed rare intellectual gifts and a keen relish for learning which showed itself in her interest in French Protestantism. After her marriage to Henry d'Albret she "gave effect to her religious convictions by receiving Calvin and similar refugees at her court. Her royal brother did not discourage her personal belief but she often found it necessary to conceal her faith and to conform to Popish worship, either through fear of persecution or through attachment to her brother and her political interests."[6]

Marguerite of Navarre has sometimes been condemned for her *Heptaméron*, a series of tales inspired by Boccaccio's *Decameron*, except that all the stories are real. "The riskiness of the *Heptaméron* is a little surprising, in one who was known to her contemporaries as a good and pious lady; but then we must not forget that they are only shocking according to the proprieties of our time, and that Margaret wrote in the sixteenth century, at a time when it was thought quite legitimate to laugh at the immoralities of monks and priests. In short, the grossness of some of the stories merely exemplifies the grossness of the language and manners of the time. The *Heptaméron* as is proved by the *Dialogues*, which separate the days, was written for the purpose of moral edification, strange as that may seem to us."[7]

Francis, who became King when twenty, had all the gifts from God that can adorn a man but his training had not built up a strong character. Religiously he was little inclined. At first he was quite sympathetic to the new religion until he came to believe that those who questioned the teaching of the Church and proposed to cast off its authority were guilty of the supreme crime of heresy not only against the church but against the King himself.

"A second reason of the estrangement of Francis from the 'new doctrines' has more frequently been overlooked. The rigid code of morals which the reformers established and which John Calvin attempted to make in Geneva the law of the State, repelled a prince...."[8]

Nevertheless, he responded to the spirit of the times by becoming interested in exploration and maintained a genuine navy. He equipped galleys upon the Mediterranean, on which the French flag was supreme, and larger vessels, propelled by both sails and oars, upon the ocean. The colonial movement which was to change the face of the world was then beginning. The Basques, Bretons, and Normans had established fishermen at Newfoundland as early as 1502. The navigator Verrazano explored in 1524, by order of Francis I, the coasts of North America; in 1534 Jacques Cartier discovered Canada and the next year entered the St. Lawrence River. Francis I was perhaps the founder of the French merchant marine and it is not unreasonable to assume that his interest in exploration grew out of his humanist mind which with his sister took the form of Protestantism.

Jacques Lefèvre, born at Étaples in Picardy, is credited with having been the one who initiated Protestantism in France where as a professor at the University of Paris he published a commentary on the Gospels and the Epistles of St. Paul. William Briçonnet, bishop of Meaux, a prelate who had been an ambassador at Rome opened his diocese to the preachers and writers recommended to him by his friend Lefèvre and supported them in the translation and propagation of the Bible. At the court was Princess Marguerite who did not hesitate to support the new religion. At this stage Francis I was sympathetic but when, in 1516, he signed the Concordat with Pope Leo X, he obtained the

right to choose the bishops and to apportion ecclesiastical benefices, he found that it was to his financial advantage to support
the Roman Church, particularly in view of the fact that his interest in religion was purely nominal. Here we find in this Concordat a reason why Protestantism never received the support of
the Ruler as it did in Germany and also in England where Henry
VIII became head of the church: The King in France always
needed finances and these he could obtain through the Roman
Church.

Probably the first persecution of those who became Protestants
in France was carried out by Louise of Savoy when she was
Regent at the time Francis I was a prisoner in Spain. Marguerite,
his sister, did her best to protect such brilliant men as Louis Berquin, but in the end he was executed along with many others.
Guizot gives a detailed account of how these Protestants were
tortured. It reminds one of what the French Jesuit priests under-
went at the hands of the Iroquois Indians in Canada a century or
so later. "The defeat at Pavia and the captivity of Francis I at
Madrid placed the governing power for 13 months in the hands
of the most powerful foes of the Reformation, the Regent Louise
of Savoy and the chancellor Duprat. They used it unsparingly,
with the harsh indifference of politicians who will have, at any
price, peace within their dominions. . . ."[9]

"It was under their regime that there took place the first
martyrdom decreed and executed in France upon a partisan of
the Reformation for an act of aggression and offence against the
Catholic Church. John Leclerc, a wool-carder at Meaux, seeing
a bull of indulgences affixed to the door of Meaux cathedral, had
torn it down and substituted for it a placard in which the Pope
was described as Antichrist. Having been arrested on the spot, he
was, by decree of the Parlement of Paris, whipped publicly, three
days consecutively, and branded on the forehead by the hangman
in the presence of his mother, who cried, 'Jesus Christ for ever'!
He was banished, and retired in July, 1525, to Metz; and there
he was working at his trade when he heard that a solemn pro-

cession was to take place the next day in the environs of the town. In his blind zeal he went and broke down the images at the feet of which the Catholics were to have burnt incense. Being arrested on his return to the town, he, far from disavowing the deed, acknowledged it and gloried in it. He was sentenced to a horrible punishment; his right hand was cut off; his nose was torn out; pincers were applied to his arm; his nipples were plucked out; his head was confined in two circlets of red-hot iron, and, whilst he was still chanting in a loud voice this versicle from the 115th Psalm,

'Their idols are silver and gold, the work of men's hands.' his bleeding and mutilated body was thrown upon the blazing faggots." [10]

The writer continues with another anecdote:

"A nobleman, A Picard by birth, born about 1490 at Passy, near Paris, where he generally lived, Louis de Berquin by name, was one of the most distinguished of them by his social position, his elevated ideas, his learning, the purity of his morals and dignity of his life. Possessed of a patrimonial estate, near Abbeville, which brought him in a modest income of six hundred crowns a year, and a bachelor, he devoted himself to study and to religious matters with independence of mind and with a pious heart. 'Most faithfully observant,' says Erasmus, 'of the ordinances and rites of the Church, to wit, prescribed fasts, holy days, forbidden meats, masses, sermons, and in a word all that tends to piety, he strongly reprobated the doctrines of Luther.' He was none the less, in 1523, denounced to the Parlement of Paris as being on the side of the reformers. He had books, it was said; he even composed them himself on questions of faith and he had been engaged in some sort of dispute with the theologian William de Coutance, Head of Harcourt College. The attorney-general of the Parliament ordered one of his officers to go and make an examination of Berquin's books as well as papers, and to seize what appeared to him to savor of heresy. The officer brought away divers works of Luther, Melancthon, and Carlstadt, and some original treatises of Berquin himself, which were deposited in the keeping of the court. The theological faculty claimed to examine them as being within their competence. On being summoned by the attorney-general, Berquin demanded to be present when an inventory was made of his books or manuscripts and to give such explanation as he should deem necessary; and his request was granted without question. On the 26th day of June, 1523, the commissioners of the Sorbonne made their report. On the 8th day of July, Peter Lizet, king's advocate, read it out to the court. The matter came on again for hearing on the 1st of August. Berquin was summoned and interrogated and, as the result of this interrogatory, was arrested and carried off to imprisonment at the Conciergerie in the square tower. On the 5th of August sentence was pronounced, and Louis de Berquin was remanded to appear before the Bishop of Paris, as being charged with heresy, 'in which case,' says the *Journal d'un Bourgeois de Paris*, 'He would have been in great danger of being put to death according to law, as he had well deserved.' The public were as ready as the accusers to believe in the crime and to impatiently await its punishment."[11]

He was released through the influence of Princess Marguerite and he lived quietly until eighteen months later when Louise of Savoy was in command his charge of heresy was again revived; however, the release of Francis I and the championship of Erasmus halted a decision but left Berquin in prison. Then pressure on Francis I by the Parlement prevented him from continuing his support with the result that Berquin was sentenced a second time to death. Because he would not recant the sentence was carried out and this is how Guizot described his execution:

"On the 22nd day of April, 1529, according to most of the documents, but on the 17th, according to the *Journal d'un Bourgeois de Paris*, which the details of the last days render highly improbable, the officers of Parliament entered Berquin's gloomy chamber. He rose quietly and went with them; the procession set out, and at about three arrived at the Place de Grève, where the stake was ready. 'Berquin had a gown of velvet, garments of satin and damask, and hosen of gold-thread,' says the *Bourgeois de Paris*: 'Alas,' said some as they saw him pass, 'he is of noble lineage, a mighty great scholar, expert in science and subtle withal, and nevertheless he hath gone out of his senses.' We borrow this account of his actual death from a letter of Erasmus, written on the evidence of an eye-witness: 'Not a symptom of agitation appeared either in his face or the attitude of his body; he had the bearing of a man who is meditating in his cabinet on the subject of his studies, or in a temple on the affairs of heaven. Even when the executioner, in a rough voice, proclaimed his crime and its penalty, the constant serenity of his features was not at all altered. When the order was given him to dismount from the tumbril, he obeyed cheerfully without hesitating; nevertheless he had not about him any of that audacity, that arrogance, which in the case of malefactors is sometimes bred of their natural savagery; everything about him bore evidence to the tranquility of a good conscience. Before he died he made a speech to the people; but none could hear him, so great was the noise which the soldiers made according, it is said, to the orders they had received. When the cord which bound him to the post suffocated his voice, not a soul in the crowd ejaculated the name of Jesus, whom it is customary to invoke even in favor of parricides and the sacrilegious, to such extent was the multitude excited against him by those folks who are to be found everywhere and who can do anything with the feelings of the simple and ignorant.' Théodore de Bèze adds that the grand penitentiary of Paris, Merlin, who was present at the execution, said, as he withdrew from the still smoking stake, 'I never saw anyone die more Christianly'. The impressions and expressions of the crowd, as they dispersed, were very diverse; but the majority cried, 'He was a heretic'. Others said, 'God is the only just Judge, and happy is the man whom He absolves'. Some said below their breath, 'It is only through the cross that Christ will triumph in the kingdom of the Gauls'. A man went up to the Franciscan monk who had placed himself at Berquin's side in the procession and had entreated him without getting from him anything but silence, and asked him, 'Did Berquin say that he had erred?' 'Yes, certainly,' answered the monk, 'and I doubt not but that his soul hath departed in peace.' This expression was reported to Erasmus; but 'I don't believe it,' said he: 'It is the story that these fellows are obliged to invent after their victim's death, to appease the wrath of the people.' " [12]

The story of the martyrdom of a wool-carder and a scholar of distinction has been given to point out that persecution was not restricted to any one class and that persecution was an end in itself. There was at this point no organized opposition such as later developed and actually brought about the downfall of French Protestantism.

Briçonnet, because he was a humanist rather than a Protestant, recanted in order to avoid death and Lefèvre, to save his life, fled to Switzerland. [13]

Francis I was really a humanist at heart for he had a sincere love for literature, science, and art. Maurois says, "In those days the King's court was France's well-spring of ideas, fashions, and arts. It followed the King wherever he went. It consisted of twelve thousand horses, of tents, of baggage, of tapestries, of gold and silver plate. . . . Everywhere he wanted to have near him not only his counsellors, but his 'Household', his 'company', his mistresses, and his sister Marguerite, his faithful confidants. 'A court without ladies is a springtime without roses,' he said: We must picture in our mind's eyes, at Chambord or at Fontainebleau, these unending revels, the beauty of the costumes, men clad in cloth-of-gold Doublets, silken tights, feathered caps; the King in silver cloth; music, games, schemes of love. Manners and minds were free. Gallantry which carried an overture of sport had taken the place of solemn courtesy. The court was hospitable to poets and artists." [14]

A basic characteristic of the Renaissance was that its culture belonged to the élite. Villon had written ballads understandable by every man; the sonnets of Ronsard and of Shakespeare were beyond the reach of simple folk. François Rabelais (1483–1553) in his life of *Gargantua and Pantagruel* presents a chaos of the most discordant elements in which the most boisterous laughter is but a terrible satire. Important as these poets were, it was Clément Marot who held sway at the court of Francis I with his elegies, epistles, roundelays, and epigrams. A groom-of-the-chamber to Marguerite and a favorite of the King, having fought with him at Pavia in 1525 when both were taken prisoners by Charles V, he later attached himself to Marguerite. His quick light style, his ease, his skill at turning an epigram began a whole lineage of French writers, among them La Fontaine and de Musset. Our particular interest in him stems from the fact that he translated the Psalms into French and was persecuted as a Protestant by the Sorbonne. Fearing for his life he fled to Geneva where he found intolerance in the other direction. Again he fled this time to Turin where he died in poverty and obscurity.

There remain three events in Francis I's reign which need to be mentioned because of their relationship with the Protestants. The King was in Paris on Monday, June 1, 1528, when he learned that some 'heretics' had destroyed some images by smashing them with hammers. To this act he reacted violently, went in a procession carrying a lighted waxen taper, bare-headed, and very reverent. Add to this the mad act of Antoine Marcourt, a pastor of Neuchâtel, who drew up some Articles, in which he attacked not only Catholic transubstantiation but also (not generally remarked on) Lutheran consubstantiation, had them printed in Basle and then fastened to the door of Francis I. The results were very far reaching. This second event seems to have been the turning point with Francis in regard to the Protestants because he then gave his approval for the martyrdom of many Protestants. "From 1524 to 1547, eighty-one death sentences for heresy were executed. At Paris only, from the 10th of November to the 2nd of May, a space of some six months, one hundred and two sentences to death by fire for heresy were pronounced; twenty-seven were executed; and seventy-three succeeded in escaping by flight." [15]

The third event had to do with the Vaudois. It will be recalled that these Vaudois or Waldensians were probably the first Protestants, at least they were the first group to successfully defy the Pope and continue their existence, not that they did not suffer persecution from time to time. This group finally came to the attention of Francis I and the episcopal prisons were soon filled with those who refused to abjure. The opposition continued and Francis vacillated until, urged on by the Church, the King gave a free hand to the Church officials. They acted without delay and two columns of soldiers ravaged with fire and sword three districts peopled by the Vaudians. In the end three small towns and twenty-two villages were completely sacked; three thousand persons massacred; six hundred to seven hundred sent to the galleys; many children sold as slaves; and the victors, on retiring, left behind them a double ordinance, from the Parliament of Aix and the vice-legate of Avignon, dated the 24th of April, 1545, forbidding that anyone, on pain of death, should dare to give asylum, aid, or succor, or furnish money or victuals to any Vaudian or 'heretic'.[16] It is said that Francis I, when near his end, bitterly repented his action in permitting this slaughter of his subjects.

Exactly at this juncture a young man, John Calvin, came into the situation and changed the history of the world. A Picard from Noyon, son of a hasty tempered ecclesiastical lawyer who died while his son was still a student, he had had his way smoothed by Church preferment and had studied at Paris, Orléans, and Bourges under some of the ablest professors that Renaissance France possessed. "A studious, asthmatic youth, life in childhood and early manhood had not been easy. The severities of the College de Montaigu, the endless disputations, the arid logic, the painful acquisition of a good Latin style and a more than ordinary knowledge of Greek and Hebrew, interwoven with the study of civil and canon law and a comprehensive understanding of the essentials of the Catholic faith had bred a keen mind, orderly, acute, and subtle. His hard legal studies taught him that enduring institutions must rest on clear, explicit written statutes while his classical knowledge opened to him the Greek text of the New

Testament and an independence of judgments in approaching the study of it. A youthful commentary on Seneca had brought him to the notice of the learned world, where he made many friends, and contact with some of the Lutheran thinkers who had gathered round Lefèvre d'Étaples and the Bishop of Meaux had set his active mind considering the issues raised by them. There was no profound psychological tumult such as sent Luther to a monastery and then out of it, no sudden revelation, no religious crisis. Calvin thought out for himself the implications of the revelation of Christian truth. He became convinced by cold reason that the teaching of the Church of Rome was wrong and he knowingly chose the path of heresy."[17]

After Francis I worked out his Concordat with the Pope, France was no place for a heretic like Calvin and to save his life he went to Basle. Here he wrote and published in 1536 his *Christian Institutes* which he prefaced by dedicating it to his monarch, Francis I, thereby showing his loyalty.[18] "The Church of Christ, as he saw it, one and undivided, was obliged, by the working of Satan, to act in many groups of true believers scattered over the face of the Christian world. It was their duty to spread the teaching of God's word, established for all time in the canon of the Scriptures. Like Zwingli, Calvin rejected tradition and would accept no doctrine that was not to be found in, or clearly and manifestly deducted from, the Bible. The sacrifice of the mass, the mediation of the Saints, or the Virgin Mary, the cult of images and relics, the monastic vows, auricular confession, and much else were as decisively rejected by the Frenchman as by the German. There was no need for bishop or priest; the minister of God's word was chosen by his hearers to lead them in prayer and to expound methodically, reverently, and regularly the duties and obligations of the Christian. Baptism was the necessary token of regeneration in Christ and of membership of his church and the commemoration of Christ's death in the Last Supper was indispensible. The 'outward and visible sign of an inward and spiritual grace' implied a Real Presence for believers, and Calvin's view of the communion, rejective, Catholic transubstantiation, Lutheran consubstantiation, and Zwinglian bare symbolism, came to be widely accepted later."[19]

Being a follower of St. Augustine he accepted what came to be known as predestination; that the elect could know by manifest signs that they were the chosen of God and could qualify for eternal salvation. The few chosen must fulfil the purposes of the Almighty; among the many there would be those who would not be saved but in this life none could know who they were.

Calvin accepted a strong pressure in 1536 to stay in Geneva where he became an organizing genius who was both realist and idealist—realist to assess the political situation of the times and idealist to scorn selfish ends or personal power. It is at this point that French Protestantism began to take shape. Up till then, humanism had played a major part but now "stark austerity, self-discipline, a life praising God with prayer and preaching, sin, vice, and self-indulgence publicly rebuked, the young instructed by a French catechism, the older by the consistory of pastor and elders, the externals of dress and behaviour made to conform to the new spirit. Calvin was very much in earnest and lacked a sense of humour; sixteenth century methods and earlier traditions account for the sumptuary and ethical regulations which were strictly enforced."[20] As Voltaire put it, "Every Huguenot with a Bible in his hand is a pope."

As might be expected there was a reaction and Calvin was forced to leave his pulpit and went to Strasbourg where he continued his writings and studies and made a happy marriage. Meantime in Geneva there was so much contention that Calvin was invited back. In 1541 he returned on his own terms and from then until he died in 1564 he ruled Geneva as an autocrat—a Protestant Pope, he has sometimes been called. Geneva under his direction became the chief school and seminary of the reformed doctrines, some of them were extreme negativism but good music, good cooking, and good wine were not prohibited. The sick and the poor were cared for and an admirable system of public education rivaled anything that the Jesuits could produce later. Missionaries were highly trained and many of them carried on active work in France and "the French wars of religion, the triumph of Henry IV, and even, in some measure, the failure of Louis XIV, were their doing." [21]

Geneva became the city of refuge for French refugees fleeing from the religious persecution by Catholics and because of her proximity to Savoy she had to take a strong stand for Protestantism when after Luther's death his followers were tempted to accept a compromise known as the *Interim* (1548). Servetus, a heterodox Protestant and Spaniard, whose views of the Trinity were unacceptable to Calvin, was publicly burnt to death on Calvin's order.

Maurois sums up Calvinism and its relation to France in this manner: "Calvin's tenets were harsh. Man was damned by the fall of Adam; the old Adam lives again in each of us and arouses within us our vices and our crimes. Jesus crucified has redeemed, not all men, but those who by their faith crucify within themselves the old Adam. To have this faith, grace is necessary. Every man is predestined either to salvation or to damnation, and he cannot redeem himself through works; on the contrary, good works are the proof that he already possesses grace. The worldly effect of this dogma is paradoxical: a Calvinist constantly tends to fall back on a life of action, for indeed why should he mediate on his own soul since he can do nothing to change God's judgment? But he can, by achieving success, prove to himself that he is one of the elect. This strangely practical aspect of Calvinism pleased a portion of the French middle class; and to Calvinism likewise were attracted men of cultivation: professors, doctors, and lawyers; the lower clergy and the friars; and a section of the nobility which, stripped of its benefices by the 1516 Concordat and full of resentment against Rome, constituted the 'assault troops' of the Huguenot movement. The new faith grew especially strong in Lyons, where there existed a traditional bond with Geneva; in Normandy, Languedoc, and the valley of the Rhone. Paris to a large extent remained Catholic. Since a military organization matched the religious, the Huguenot party soon became a State within a State, and we can understand why the Kings of France were worried." [22]

". . . What is Calvinism? It is a doctrine taken by Calvin from the Scriptures (or the Bible), that is to say, based on the sovereign authority substituted by the Reformers for the authority of the Church and the Pope; it is a reform of life and manners, then a discipline, equally taken from the sacred book. It is finally a religion, based on protestant simplicity." [23]

A rather detailed account of Calvin and his doctrines has been given because Calvinism provided the inspiration and philosophy for the Huguenot movement in France and later the Calvinistic doctrines in Scotland, England, and America. It was to Geneva that John Knox came in 1555 and it was at Dieppe where he preached for a couple of years. Later events in France can only be explained by a reference to these doctrines. And now let us return to these events.

When Francis I died at the age of fifty-two, he was succeeded by his son, Henry II, who was married to Catherine de Medici and who carried to excess his father's defects with none of his high qualities. During his reign he was dominated by Diane of Poitiers, a woman of forty-eight years but one of wit and beauty. He created her Duchess of Valentinois and allowed her to govern the court, in which the queen remained without influence. In our story she is important for it was she who introduced to the King the family of the Guises who eventually became the great protagonists for the Roman Catholics against the Huguenots. At this time on the Huguenot side we find Gaspard de Coligny and his brother Francis; Prince of Condé and his brother Antoine de Bourbon (King of Navarre having married Jeanne d'Albret, a staunch Huguenot).

By this time the Huguenots had become in numbers almost one quarter of the population of France and so powerful that Henry II feared them and rigorously persecuted them. Guizot states that "during the twelve years of Henry II's reign there were ninety-seven capital executions for heresy, and at one of these Henry II was present in person. . . . In 1551, 1557, and 1559, Henry II, by three royal edicts, kept up and added to all the prohibitions and penalties in force against the reformers."[24]

"But now, within a few months, the harvest seemed, as by a miracle, to be approaching simultaneously over the whole surface of the extended field . . . There was not a corner of the Kingdom where the incipient Protestant churches were not considerable. In large tracts of the country the Huguenots had become so numerous that they were no longer able or disposed to conceal their religious sentiments nor content to celebrate their rites in private or nocturnal assemblies. This was particularly the case in Normandy, in Languedoc, and on the banks of the Rhone."[25]

Henry II fell mortally wounded when taking part in a tournament in 1559 to be succeeded by his son, Francis II, sixteen years old, whose wife was Mary Stuart of Scotland. But because Francis was under tutelage the real power was placed in the hands of his mother, Catherine de Medici, a woman indifferent to religious matters, with a passion for authority denied her by her husband on account of the influence of Diane of Poitiers, his mistress; a characteristically Italian adroitness in intrigue; a fine political sense; and the feeling that the royal authority might be endangered both by Calvinistic passions and Catholic violence. For this reason throughout her control of her three sons it was her policy to play one religious group against the other.

It was about this time—1560—that French Protestants acquired the name of Huguenots. There are several explanations for the origin of the name, the most generally accepted being that it was derived from a French and a faulty pronunciation of the German word *Eidgenossen* or Confederates; the name given to those citizens of Geneva who entered into an alliance with the Swiss Cantons to resist the attempts of Charles III, Duke of Savoy, against their liberties. The Confederates were called *Eignots*, and hence, probably, the derivation of the word Huguenots. First used as a nickname, it soon was one borne with pride.

Another explanation of the term *Huguenots* states that the Protestants of Tours used to assemble by night near the gate of King Hugo, whom the people regarded as a spirit. A monk, therefore, in a sermon declared that the Lutherans (for this was the first term applied to them) ought to be called *Huguenots* as Kinsmen of King Hugo inasmuch as they would only go out at night the same as he did.

Although Calvin provided the philosophy for the Huguenots in France, his direction was one of remote control. Throughout Henry II's reign and the Religious Wars which began in 1562 and continued intermittently until 1595, Admiral Gaspard de Coligny and Prince de Condé gave leadership to the Huguenots. They were frequently caught between loyalty to the French King and his wars with the Spaniards, first with Charles V and then Philip II. At all times they remained loyal to the French King and he from time to time played on it. Nevertheless, the Sorbonne and the Jesuits were unrelenting in their opposition and Coligny urged the King to discover colonies in America where Protestants could worship as they wished and still remain loyal to the French Crown. To this end he organized an expedition in Brazil but was double-crossed by a nominal Protestant and the colony failed.

Gallicanism, a theory which maintained that the Church and King of France had ecclesiastical rights of their own, became during the Reformation period of great importance. Those who upheld this belief that the temporal sovereignty of kings was independent of the Pope and that the infallible teaching authority of the church belonged to Pope and bishops jointly, caused the Roman Church much trouble. It was because of this point of view that a strange alliance developed between the Calvinists and the Gallican *Parlements* and was directed against the Jesuits with their theory of the indirect power of the Pope over princes, as sustained by Cardinal Bellarmine and Franciscus Suarez.

An event that is still celebrated by French Protestants occurred in May of 1559 when the pastors of the reformed religion met in synod at Paris and felt themselves strong enough to set down their confession of faith founded upon the Scriptures and their ecclesiastical discipline founded upon the independence of the churches. From that time on Protestants adopted a new attitude and refused obedience to the orders of a persecuting monarchy when contrary to its faith and its interests, with the result that the Huguenot party became a State within a State which, in the end, brought about the defeat of the Huguenots, for the King "could not allow an aristocratic party, alleging religious reform, to attempt a political division of the Kingdom. For there soon sprang up a whole school of Huguenot publicists who denied the King's absolute power; staunch 'republicans' sought in Plutarch examples of holy uprisings against tyrants. Had it found popular support, this propaganda would have been dangerous indeed for the monarchy, but unlike his fellows in Germany, the French peasant remained loyal to his traditional Catholicism. In France Protestantism was—and to a certain extent still is—the religion of a liberal, semi-aristocratic elite." [26]

Francis II reigned only seventeen months but short as it was there are important events associated with it: one, that of the power of the Guises and the beginning of the wars of religion: the other, that of Mary Stuart, the wife of Francis II, who returned to Scotland to be known as Mary, Queen of Scots, and suffer the consequences.

The Guises were powerful enough, because backed by Catherine de Medici, to force the hand of Francis to wipe out the Huguenots. These in turn led by the Prince de Condé, Louis de Bourbon, offered resistance and Condé was arrested and condemned to death but his life was spared when Francis died. From now on, the power fell into the hands of the Queen-mother because Charles IX was only ten and a half years old. She tried to play the Guises and the Catholics off against Coligny, Condé, and the Protestants. She even tried to work out a compromise between them. By this time the Protestants appeared to have the upper hand but it was a see-saw battle until Condé was shot dead (1569). This was a great loss to the Huguenots but his place was

taken by Coligny, Prince Henry of Condé, and Henry, Prince of Béarn, later Henry IV, then fifteen years old, the son of Jeanne d'Albret, the staunch Protestant defender of La Rochelle.

In 1572 Catherine de Medici arranged a marriage between Henry, Prince of Béarn, and her daughter Margaret. Because she saw that Coligny was getting too much consideration from her son, Charles IX, she took advantage of the discords at the time of the wedding to urge Charles IX to take action against the Huguenots. He in desperation cried out that if they were going to kill Coligny he wished they would kill all the Huguenots in France "so that not one would be left to reproach him". This was done. Coligny was murdered in his room and then followed the massacre of St. Bartholomew, August 24th, 1572, when thousands were killed in Paris and many more in the provinces. While the streets of Paris were still besmeared with blood, the clergy celebrated an extraordinary jubilee. They appeared in general procession and determined to consecrate an annual feast to a triumph so glorious. A medal was struck in commemoration of the event, bearing the legend, "Piety has awakened justice"!

Catherine de Medici wrote in triumph to the Duke of Alva, to Philip II, and to the Pope, describing the three days' dreadful work in Paris. When Philip heard of the massacre he is said to have laughed for the first and only time in his life. Rome was thrown into a delirium of joy at the news. The cannon was fired at St. Angelo; Gregory XIII and his cardinals went in procession from sanctuary to sanctuary to give thanks to God for the massacre. The subject was ordered to be painted and a medal was struck to celebrate the event with the Pope's head on one side, and on the other an angel, with a cross in one hand a sword in the other, pursuing and slaying a band of flying heretics. Henry of Béarn and Henry of Condé escaped death by abjuring Protestantism. Charles IX died May, 1574, broken by grief and mortification; his last words were, "Let the memory of that accursed day be blotted out forever."

Henry III, the third son of Catherine de Medici, from 1574

to 1589 carried on a struggle now against the Huguenots, now with them and Les Politiques, a party of broadminded Catholics opposed to civil war; then against; and finally with the Holy League of Catholics under Henry of Guise. All the while his mother kept up her intrigues which usually complicated matters still further for him. In 1589 she died and he cried, "Now I am King." He opposed the League led by the Duke of Guise and finally had him killed, but he himself suffered the same fate when stabbed by a Dominican friar on August 2nd, 1589, yet declaring before his death that Henry of Navarre was to succeed him.

Henry IV (1589–1610) came to the throne and promised to give the Huguenots freedom of worship, but this did not please the Catholic League. Protestant King of a Catholic country, he had to play a difficult hand; however, his greatest asset was his attractive personality. A brave and good soldier he possessed the primary virtues of kindness and mercy. Always in love, nevertheless, Henry the King held Henry the lover in check. He became King at a time when the French had lost confidence in themselves and this he proceeded to establish with the help of his Protestant friend and companion, Maximilian de Béthune, Baron of Rosny, whom in 1606 he made duke de Sully. Maurois describes him thus: "Sully had more than genius; he had good sense, integrity, and a vast capacity for work . . . he was crusty and obstinate; even after the conversion of the King (which he recommended), he kept portraits of Calvin and Luther hanging on his walls . . . Had the King allowed him to do it (the lazy, idle, and pleasure-loving ways of life) Sully would have set up in each bailiwick an inspectorate of morals 'three censors and reformers', who would have had the right to look into 'the conduct and management of families'." [27] Here was Calvin turned artilleryman and financier.

Henry IV, since he was Protestant, was bitterly opposed by the League. Philip II of Spain also made claims but Spain was always unpopular in France. Henry IV in order to bring the civil war to an end, abjured Protestantism in 1592 in preparation for his crowning at Chartres in 1594. He said "Paris is well worth a mass." This marked the end of the League and it was dissolved.

The Protestants on the contrary bitterly resented their King's abjuration so to placate them and also, because he was really a Protestant at heart, he desired to protect them and came to terms with them by the Edict of Nantes, 1598, which gave them the right to hold synods, political assemblies, to open schools, and to occupy a hundred strong places, among them La Rochelle, for eight years at the expense of the King. This brought an end to the religious wars which had lasted off and on for forty years.

"Even for his brethren in creed his triumph was a benefit secured, for it was an end of persecution and a first step towards liberty. There is no measuring accurately how far ambition, personal interest, a King's egotism had to do with Henry IV's abjuration of his religion; none would deny that those human infirmities were present, but all this does not prevent the conviction that patriotism was uppermost in Henry's soul and that the idea of his duty as King towards France, a prey to all the evils of civil and foreign war, was the determining motive of his resolution."[28]

Henry IV was much interested in developing agriculture and industry but for our purpose we must remark on his colonization schemes. Much against the wishes of Sully, expeditions were sent to Canada under Marquis de la Roche, Chauvin, Pontgravé, de Monts, (the last three being Huguenots), Poutrincourt, and Champlain, men who co-operated willingly with the Huguenots. *Canada became French largely because of the interest of Henry IV and Huguenot merchants.*

Henry IV's first wife was Marguerite de Valois but their marriage was annulled in 1600 and he married Marie de'Medici at Lyons who bore him a son who was to be Louis XIII. Maurois states that when his mistresses had been added up they came to fifty-six,[29] however there was one woman who refused to submit to his attentions and one who played a determining part in regard to the Huguenots and their control of Canada. Her name was Madame de Guercheville, a lady of honor to the Queen. She became a very devout person who with other ladies of the court reacted "for the pious flame, fanned by the Jesuits, spread through hall and boudoir, and the fair votaries of the Loves and the Graces found it a more grateful task to win heaven for the heathen than to merit it for themselves."[30] She it was who became the tool of the Jesuits and who persuaded Henry IV to give the control of Canada to the Jesuits, and thus ended any connection the Huguenots had with Canada for from that time on they were not allowed even to land.

Henry IV was assassinated on May 14th, 1610, and Catholics and Protestants alike praised to the skies him they had so bitterly attacked and he remains together with Charlemagne, Joan of Arc, and Saint Louis, one of France's heroes.

Louis XIII (1610–1643) was only nine years old and that gave his mother Marie de Medici regency power. It was through her that Richelieu was brought into power for, recognizing him to have outstanding leadership qualities, she made him secretary of writs. When Louis XIII took control at sixteen he banished his mother but this did not diminish her power at court and the young King upon pressure from her made Richelieu his chief minister. Richelieu it was who brought to an end the political power of the Huguenots. He said, 'my first goal was the majesty of the King; the second was the greatness of the realm.' One of the chief obstacles was the continuance in France of Protestant fortified places such as La Rochelle and Huguenot armies. Richelieu was not opposed to them on religious grounds but on political. He said, "They must be reduced to that condition which befits all subjects in a State, which means that they must not be in a position to set up any separate body, and they must be dependent on the wishes of their master."

It was, however, basic to the Huguenot belief that they were not bound to a ruler who violated their moral principles and to this end they made overtures to England when Richelieu, after leading them to think he was sympathetic with them because he made alliances with Protestant countries, persuaded the King to attack La Rochelle as it was a true republic, the centre and capital of the Huguenots and with a navy larger than that of the King of France. The English made futile attempts to rescue the garrison but after fifteen months and in spite of the super-human courage of the Duchess of Rohan, the widow of the Duke of Rohan, one of the staunchest Huguenot leaders, the town was forced to yield and with it went the importance of the Huguenots as a political party. But to Richelieu's credit it must be stated that he allowed them liberty of worship and the enjoyment of civil liberty. During the whole of his ministry, he employed them equally with other citizens, in the army, the magistracy, and the offices of finance, and protected them always in their rights and in their persons.

In this connection Garneau, a Roman Catholic, says, "This conduct of France viewed in its political aspect merits not equal praise especially in regard to the pernicious sway she exercised over the moral regulations of her colonies. In Canada, for instance, from a fear of shocking the savages by a juxtaposition of men of diverse religious creeds the government was induced to permit none but Catholics to become settlers among them. Thus while Catholicism was obliged to permit Protestantism to subsist at its side in the mother country, it had force sufficient to exclude it totally in the plantations beyond the seas; a spirit of exclusion which, antecedent to the revocation of the Edict of Nantes, adumbrated the overturning of the system of compromise fallen upon by Henry IV and Sully. The liberal and somewhat republican tendencies of the Huguenot mind, made the Protestant party always appear menacing to the Crown; while the court viewed with a very different mind the submission of the Catholics and the higher clergy, as hostile at the least as the royal power to the liberty of the masses." [31]

Garneau is referring to the annullment of the rights of the Recollets in Canada in 1632 and the giving to the Jesuits the exclusive rights to missionary labour because the latter interpreted this authority to prevent the landing henceforth in Canada of any Huguenot.

Richelieu was highly thought of in his day. La Bruyère in *Les*

Caractères wrote thus: "Masters of the future will eagerly consider your portraits and your medals; they will speak of . . . that other (Richelieu) whose picture you see and in which people will see a strong face, together with an air, grave, austere, and majestic; his reputation will grow from year to year. His great plan has been to affirm the authority of the King and the safety of the people by debasing the great; neither parties, nor pressure, nor treasons, nor the period of death, nor his infirmities have been able to turn him from them. He has had time besides to undertake a work which was continued and completed by one of the greatest and best of rulers (Louis XIV), the extinction of heresy. (The Revocation of the Edict of Nantes.)"[32]

Louis XIII and Richelieu ended Huguenot emigration to Canada, an emigration which could have saved Canada for France a century later; Louis XIV brought about a migration of Huguenots from which France never completely recovered.

How much the tendency of French Kings to become despotic can be traced to compensation following their domination in early life by their mothers can never be fully appraised. It is evident, however, how eagerly they took over direction of affairs of State and in some cases banished their mothers. All through their lives they resented any form of opposition and this they frequently sensed to exist among the Huguenots. Their moral lives with the exception of Louis XIII were such that the Huguenots, although basically loyal to the King, refused to be coerced by him. Although granted freedom of worship by the Edict of Nantes in 1598 the results were nominal. Throughout the seventeenth century the Huguenots in France enjoyed little freedom of worship. On account of their political importance they were feared, hated, and persecuted. From time to time their numbers were almost wiped out but they always revived because of being such excellent artisans and so industrious.

And now let us turn directly to Louis XIV (1643–1715) who was but five years old when his father died. Consequently a regent was necessary. As in former like situations, the boy's mother was selected. Until Louis XIV grasped the reins of government in 1661 the first period of his reign was taken up with civil wars. The brilliant period, however, extended to 1683 when under Colbert agriculture and industry were organized at home; the army and navy were increased for successful campaigns with other nations. This was also the period when, because of the reforms of finances, there was great interest in Fine Arts, when such outstanding writers as Corneille, Racine, Boileau, and Molière received pensions. Versailles became the royal dwelling-place at a tremendous cost, where nothing is commemorative of France but everything suggests the King. Other architectural undertakings were the great Trianon and several chateaux, all built at great expense.

With the death of Colbert in 1683 the balance wheel was lost. Louis XIV, who was then advanced in years, became delicate in health and the last of the mistresses of this reign, Madame de Maintenon, ruled the monarch. Madame de Maintenon was the widow of Scarron, the deformed wit and scoffer. She belonged to the celebrated Huguenot family of d'Aubigny, her grandfather having been one of the most devoted followers of Henry IV. Her father led a profligate life, but she herself was brought up a Protestant. A Roman Catholic relative, however, acting on the authority conferred by a royal edict, of abducting Protestant children, had the girl forcibly conveyed to the convent of the Ursulines at Paris, where, after some resistance, she abjured her faith and became a Roman Catholic. She left the convent to marry Scarron and thereby enter the world of society and intrigue. When the witty cripple married her, he said, "His bride brought with her an annual income of four loves, two large and very mischievous eyes, a fine bust, an exquisite pair of hands, and a large amount of wit."

At Scarron's house she met the gayest and loosest of accomplished persons of his time and from them acquired a knowledge of the world which stood her in good stead after the death of her husband, Scarron, and when she obtained the post of governess to the children of Madame de Montespan, the King's then mistress, whom she soon superseded. She acquired so much influence over Louis XIV that even the priests could only obtain access to him through her and it was she who worked on the King's hatred of the Huguenots so that he issued edict after edict against them.

Never since the Reformation had Protestantism been in such danger as in the year 1685. James II, who had long since embraced Catholicism, now became King of England. The Elector of the Palatinate who died without heirs was succeeded by the Catholic House of Neuberg. Louis XIV had been brought up to consider himself a 'Vice-God' and when he took over the reins of government he determined to be just that. He hated the Huguenots not only because they opposed the Roman Church but because of their importance politically for he never tolerated any group or individual which threatened opposition in any way; consequently, after he had subdued the opposing nations of Europe—about 1678—he felt himself free to tackle the matter of Protestantism as represented by the Huguenots. He also wanted to show the Pope with whom he was not on such good terms that he was still 'The Eldest Son of the Church'. "At Louis' elbow there were many powerful elements which urged him to play the persecutor. Great courtiers, ladies of irregular morals but unblemished orthodoxy, and eloquent and eager bishops and leaders of the church, brought constant pressure upon Louis to undertake the conversion of his dissenting subjects. The first step was to cut off all privileges from the Protestants not carefully secured to them by the existing law; they were excluded from the teaching and medical professions and from all public offices. The next step was to send preachers into Huguenot communities to attempt by eloquence, cajoleries, and threats to sow the good seed. The next, and far more sinister, was to enact that at the age of seven a child could select its own religion. If a boy or girl could be tricked into making some statement indicating that he or she wished to be a Catholic, the child could be taken from the unbelieving parents and placed in some kind of non-heretical custody, although the parents had to pay a pension for its upkeep. The next state—beginning especially in 1681—was the deliberate process of 'dragooning'; billeting soldiers in the houses of peaceful Protestants who did not encourage 'instruction', and allowing and even inciting barrack topers to insult the women and to carouse like beasts all night. 'They entered an orderly and religious household and existence there became like life in a brothel or dram-shop.' "[33]

By this time Louis had allowed himself to believe that there were few Protestants left in France and it is just here where Madame de Maintenon determined policy towards the Huguenots. Like all proselytes she was most active in her new religion, one which would tolerate her machinations, and she persuaded the King that he would have a better chance of Heaven were he to exterminate the Huguenots. Reacting to her persuasion and other pressures he, on the 18th of October, 1685, signed the Revocation of the Edict of Nantes, and ordered all Protestant forms of worship forthwith to cease and all Protestant chapels and 'temples' to be immediately destroyed.

This was but an extension of the regulations which were then in existence : "Protestants could not practise as doctors, surgeons, lawyers, teachers, be employed by the government even as grocers. All Protestant books including Bibles and Testaments were collected and publicly burned. Artisans were forbidden to work without certificates that their religion was Catholic. Protestant washerwomen were excluded from their washing places on the river. In fact, there was scarcely a degradation that could be invented, even to dragging a dying man naked through the streets to be thrown on a dunghill, that was not practised on the Huguenots. Parents could neither be born, nor live, nor die, without State or priestly interference."[34]

Following the Revocation all Huguenot ministers were given a fortnight in which to leave the Kingdom but others were forbidden to follow them under pain of the galleys and the confiscation of their property. Terrible consequences ensued ; the Protestants had no longer civil rights, their marriages were regarded as null, their children as bastards. The property of all those who were proved heretics was confiscated and a great number of ministers were executed.

This action of Louis XIV should be regarded as a climax for the persecutions which had begun even in Henry IV's time. As a result "many of the nobility went to Geneva; tradesmen and artisans travelled to the Netherlands to settle either in Leiden or Amsterdam; vintners from Champagne and Burgundy crossed over into the German Palatinate, where they could worship as they pleased. In France or elsewhere the Huguenots were often prosperous citizens who were pietists and pacifists interested in setting up their churches, academies, and parish schools without interference and in directing the country's wealth into industry and agriculture rather than armaments." [35]

"The Calvinist mentality combined shrewd business sense with profound devotion wherever Calvinism established itself it soon attracted the circles engaged in productive work and money-making; most of its proselytes were artisans and merchants." [36]

"Inevitably, this philosophic revolution was also an enormous one. By laying stress on a man's daily labour, by denying the bishop precedence at the pearly gates over the clerk or the weaver, it permeated public life with the ideology of work. It declared that only he who works shall eat. . . . It drove the passivity out of the masses and replaced it with discipline. The century's achievements were put to use; the printer's art, which quickly spread, became a new weapon; industrial changes were followed by surprising industrial ones. Calvinist logic penetrated every phase of daily life, as when it instigated work on cattle breeding, which changed the structure of Holland by inducing the Dutch to eat more meat and cheese and catch less fish. Sailors took up farming; soldiers raised stock instead of hiring out for wars." [37]

These were the people to the number of some 400,000 whom Louis XIV literally drove out of France and thereby committed the greatest mistake of any French ruler. The Catholic population of France was overjoyed but it was soon realized that this was a suicidal policy, for France lost most of her skilled artisans who took the secrets of many French manufacturers to the Netherlands, England, and Germany. Furthermore, the departure of such skilled workmen meant a deathblow to several great branches of French industry. Then, too, an enormous amount of wealth went out of the country with the emigrants; French commerce was prostrated; eight to nine thousand of the King's best sailors, twelve thousand soldiers, and over five hundred trained officers left the country. Schomberg, one of William of Orange's best generals, was a Huguenot exile.

Marshal Schomberg was descended from the Duke of Cleves whose arms he bore. Several of his ancestors had held high rank in the French service. One of them was killed at the Battle of Ivry on the side of Henry IV and another commanded under Richelieu at the Siege of La Rochelle. The marshal, whose mother was an English woman of the noble house of Dudley, began his career in the Swedish army in the Thirty Years' War, after which he entered the service of the Netherlands, and subsequently that of France where he rose quickly to the rank of marshal. The great Condé thought highly of him and compared him to Turenne. He commanded armies in Flanders, Portugal, and Holland, but on the Revocation he felt he could no longer stay in France. Going first to Portugal he later joined with Frederick William of Brandenburg who made him many high offers if he would stay but he preferred to join up with William of Orange. When William became king he received many honours. At the Battle of the Boyne, he was killed and was buried in St. Patrick's Cathedral, Dublin.

"The flight of the French Protestants exercised a highly important influence on European politics. Among its other effects, it contributed to establish religious and political freedom in Switzerland, and to render it in a measure the Patmos of Europe; it strengthened the foundations of liberty in the then comparatively insignificant electorate of Brandenburg, which has since developed into the monarchy of Prussia; it fostered the strength and increased the power and commercial wealth of the States of Holland; and it materially contributed to the success of the English Revolution of 1688, and to the establishment of the British Constitution on its present basis."[38]

Even the persecution within France did not succeed. The Huguenots lost half their numbers but in the South of France a remnant revived "The Church in the Desert". This had a curious history. As the meetings were first held for the most part in Languedoc, and so much of that province specially in the district of Cervennes is really waste and desert land, the meetings were at first called "Assemblies in the Desert", and for nearly a hundred years retained that name. About 1700, steps were taken to revive the meetings of the Church in the Desert and to reconstitute the congregations and restore the system of governing them according to the methods of the Huguenot Church.

In their organization the French Churches approached nearer to Presbyterianism than to the Anglican ritual. Under the pastor *anciens* were appointed to deal with church matters and each congregation was disciplined by a Consistory which corresponded to the Scottish Kirk Session and was a local court for superintendence over the members of one congregation.

The years from 1683 to 1715 were spent by Louis in futile wars with neighboring nations, wars which strained the economy of France to the utmost. In the end he was forced to recognize William III—a Protestant—as King of England and later George I the Protestant Elector of Brunswick as heir presumptive of Queen Anne, another ardent Protestant. Louis XIV died in 1715 at the age of seventy-seven, having reigned seventy-two years, and leaving France in terrible poverty. History, however, remembers him for the incomparable splendor of the court of Versailles, with its marvels of letters and arts, which have given to the seventeenth century the name of the age of Louis XIV. France has paid a heavy price for this name; the loss of the Huguenots can never be appraised.

Louis XV, his great grandson, was five years of age when he became King but he took no authority until he was thirteen. As he grew older he gave little attention to government but much to his favorite mistresses, of whom he had many, Madame de Pompadour being the most powerful. It was during this period that France lost her colonies, Canada being one of them. It is said that never since the period of the Roman Empire had morality fallen so low. Liberty of conscience was forbidden and persecution of the Protestants went on apace; in 1746 two hundred of them were condemned to the galleys by the Parlement of Grenoble alone. Similar treatment was handed out in other provinces. Voltaire, although no Protestant, attacked the Church with stubborn animosity and he condemned the spiritual power which hindered thought much more than the civil power which hindered only action. Rousseau lived during this period and proclaimed his ideas about the social order which later played a great part in the Revolution of 1789.

Louis XV died in 1774 and was succeeded by his great-grandson Louis XVI, twenty years of age. Although a much better man than his grandfather, Louis XVI was without acute intelligence. Furthermore, he too, was at the mercy of a woman, this time, his wife, Marie Antoinette, ignorant, frivolous, and impatient of all restraint. At this time one-fifth of the whole soil of France belonged to the Roman Catholic Church and the income from 'tithes' and other sources has been set at $100,000,000 in modern money. It was against the coercion and persecution of the Roman Church as much as the taxation of the King that the Revolutionaries reacted in 1789 and this time the Roman clergy suffered as they had made the Huguenots suffer over the centuries. The wheel had made a complete revolution. By the Constitution of 1791 the Huguenots were given complete toleration; however, they were few in number because Louis XV and Louis XVI had continued the persecutions of their predecessors.

Louis XIV, when he revoked the Edict of Nantes in 1685, turned the first shovelfuls of the grave that a hundred years later was to engulf monarchy in France, for Louis XVI and his wife were both beheaded. Later France became a republic.

CHARACTERISTICS OF A HUGUENOT

Who and Why is a Huguenot?

The term Lutheran, which was applied to the followers of Luther, became fairly universal throughout Europe in those States which had a Germanic background. However, since the followers of John Calvin represented varied ethnic groups, a diversity came to apply to his followers. In England they were called Puritans; in Scotland, Presbyterians; in Holland, Walloons; and in France the term Huguenot came to apply.

It is worthwhile to give some estimate as to what special characteristics the French Huguenot possessed and the possible reasons for them.

In order to understand the many cross-currents that are to be found in France during succeeding centuries one must first appreciate the fact that racially there is little homogeneity in France. "The northeastern third of France and half of Belgium are today more Teutonic than the south of Germany. It should not occasion surprise when we remember the incessant downpour of Teutonic tribes during the whole historic period. It was a constant procession of Goths—from all parts of the compass—of Franks, Burgundians, and others. France, with the exception of Brittany, was entirely overrun by the Franks by the middle of the sixth century. All through the Middle Ages this part of Europe was not only ethnically Teutonic: it was German in language and customs as well. The very name of the country is Teutonic. It has the same origin as Franconia in Southern Germany. In 813 the Council of Tours (away down south), ordained that every bishop should preach both in the Romance and the Teutonic languages. The Franks preserved their German speech four hundred years after the conquest; even today after the cession of Alsace-Lorraine, a last vestige of Teutonic language, the Flemish, persists on French territory along the Belgian frontier. Mr. Abbé Sieyes uttered an ethnological truism when, in the course of the French Revolution, he cried out against the French aristocracy : 'Let us send them back to their German marshes from which they came.' "[1]

The south of France had long been separated from the north. It had another language and other customs and because of its interest in commerce and the outside world there was a diffused ease among the citizens with even luxury among the nobility. The cities of the South during the Middle Ages had brilliant courts that were enlivened by the songs of troubadours and religious doctrines were treated as lightly as manners and morals.

With such differences existing in France, is it any wonder that force would be the only means for getting any sort of unity? And another factor should be kept in mind : The constant striving for mastery on the part of the Pope, the ruler of Spain, and the rulers of France, with the rulers of England and The Netherlands in the offing hoping to keep a balance of power. As all these rulers were consistently jockeying for position, religion and religious leaders often became pawns in the game. In most cases the furthering of religion was but a camouflage; the end was the desire for control.

During the Middle Ages the Church was incomparably the most important institution of the time and its officers were the soul of every enterprise. The medieval Church had certain characteristics. Membership in it was compulsory; refusal to belong to it was punishable by death; there was a vast income from tithes from which none were exempt; it resembled a state, for it had an elaborate system of law with courts and prisons for offenders; it had the organization of a state, for there was one supreme head who made laws and controlled every church officer in any country with one official language, Latin. Therefore in its government it took on the form of a monarchy.

There is no gainsaying the fact that power politics played a determining part in the inception and development of Protestantism in France; however, it is possible that the type of mind possessed by the average Frenchman was quite as important. Francis

Parkman[2] describes the French Celt in this manner: "He sees the end distinctly, and reasons about it with an admirable clearness; but his own impulses and passions continually turn him away from it. Opposition excites him; he is impatient of delay; is impelled always to extremes, and does not readily sacrifice a present inclination to an ultimate good. He delights in abstractions and generalizations, cuts loose from unpleasing facts, and roams through an ocean of desires and theories."

How much of the foregoing is an accurate delineation of French character is a matter of opinion; nevertheless, it is a generally accepted fact that the French mind delights in 'abstractions and generalizations' and that is why humanism which grew out of the Renaissance made such a strong initial appeal to the upper classes in France. The middle classes also accepted it and related it to the Bible, but to the peasants and working classes it never made any appeal, for they preferred the rites of the Roman Catholic Church with its promise of salvation. The fact that Protestantism in France never reached the masses of the people is one good reason why it ultimately failed as a major religion in France. Professor Léonard says: "Let us not speak then of the French Reformation but the Reformation in France."[3]

Interest in Calvinistic doctrine was pretty much found in the south and southwest of France. It never made much headway in Paris. The Southern aristocracy were perhaps influenced in its favor because of social and political grievances.

During the sixteenth century there were at least two essentials if one were to become a Protestant: an enquiring type of mind and exceptional courage. The individual must be desirous of living by new ideas and also be brave enough to sacrifice friends, position, and even life itself in order to maintain them. In such a description there is the answer: Who is a Huguenot?

To a certain extent it partially gives the answer to: Why is a Huguenot? But not quite. More than an enquiring mind was necessary because there were Humanists who were not Protestants. Erasmus comes in that category, one might add. Briçonnet, one of the first Frenchmen to accept the new ideas of religion, never grasped the fundamentals of Protestantism and that was why he recanted when put to the test. Lefèvre remained half-way between the new religion and the traditional. Professor Léonard puts it this way : "The Christian demands salvation ; the humanists offer him knowledge and a powerless aspiration to reform the Church. Absolutely desperate and thirsting, he found in them only a weak optimism, compromises, a personal, indeed, very presentable and an evanescent God." [4]

Thus the individual with the enquiring mind who sought personal salvation found that humanism was not enough. Nor could he turn to the Roman Catholic Church because not only did it lack reality, it disgusted him with its practices. André Maurois states : [5] "The humanists who knew Greek and Hebrew were no longer satisfied with the Vulgate, read the Scriptures in the most authentic available texts and scorned the authority of ignorant clergymen. The French (Gallican) Church was becoming reformist, many of its bishops being cultivated and tolerant men. From their reading of the Bible there emerged a religion rather different from what the rest of Catholicism had become. In the Gospels they found Christ and His divine charity, but not rites and devotions, Purgatory, or the worship of the Saints. Salvation, the Christians' only personal concern, was not, in what they found there, dependent upon practices based upon custom."

To recapitulate : Who, then, was a Huguenot? He not only was a thinking type of person with courage ; he belonged to "The two classes among which, in the sixteenth century the Reformation took place in France. It had a double origin : morally and socially, one amongst the people and the other among the aristocratic and learned ; it was not national, nor was it embraced by the government of the country. Persecution was its first and its only destiny ..." [6]

Why was a Huguenot? Because he was responding to the

Zeitgeist : He wanted personal salvation which he could not obtain through humanism, though that sharpened his desire for it; nor could it be found in the Roman Catholic Church because of the evils which beset it. Driven then to the Bible, he found peace of mind through direct contact with God.

PART THREE

The Trail encircles Europe and extends to South Africa

HUGUENOTS IN THE BRITISH ISLES

Emigration of Protestants to England—
Walloons, Dutch, Huguenots

As early as Edward III a large number of Flemings came over and settled in London, Kent, Norfolk, Devon, Somerset, Yorkshire, Lancashire, and Westmorland. This continued through the reigns of successive English kings to that of Henry VIII, who encouraged armourers, cutlers, miners, brewers, and shipbuilders to settle in England; most of the principal craftsmen at the court were Flemings and Germans.

It was during Edward VI's reign that the influx began on account of the disturbed conditions on the continent. The Rhine River provided transportation to the Dutch and Flemish ports from which places they made for England. Because these were skilled mechanics and Protestants they were welcomed in England. Queen Elizabeth was particularly sympathetic to them when a large group of Flemings in 1561 settled at Sandwich, Harwich, Yarmouth, Dover, and other towns on the southeast coast. Others proceeded to London, Norwich, Maidstone, Canterbury, and other inland towns. The seaport of Rye on the coast of Sussex received from time to time groups of fugitives, among them many notable persons, as well as cloth-makers from Antwerp and Bruges, lace-makers from Valenciennes, cambric-makers from Cambray, glass-makers from Paris, stuff-makers from Meaux, merchants and tradesmen from Rouen, and shipwrights and mariners from Dieppe and Le Havre. The artisans set up their looms and began to produce many things for ready sale, but they were opposed by townspeople who feared competition and appealed to the Queen without result.

"Besides the cloth of Flanders, England was also supplied with most of its finer fabrics from abroad, the names of the articles to this day indicating the places where they were manufactured. Thus there was the Mechlin lace of Mechlin, the duffle of Duffle, the diaper of Ypres (d'Ypres), the cambric from Cambray, the arras from Arras, the tulle of Tulle, the damask of Damascus, and the dimity of Diametta. Besides these were imported delphware from Delft, venetian goods from Venice, cordovan leather from Cordova, and milanery from Milan. The Milaners of London were a special class of general dealers. They sold not only French and Flemish cloths but Spanish gloves and girdles, Milan caps, and cutlery, silk, lace, needles, pins for ladies' dresses (before which skewers were used), swords, knives, daggers, broaches, glass, porcelain, and various articles of foreign manufacture. The name 'Milliner' (from Milan) is now applied only to dealers in ladies' caps and bonnets."[1]

Besides cloth-making the Protestant exiles at Sandwich introduced the making of pottery; some were smiths, brewers, hatmakers, carpenters, or shipwrights. But probably most outstanding was the introduction of horticulture. Cabbage, carrots, and celery found a ready sale. It is even stated that it was the Protestant Walloons who introduced the cultivation of the hop in Kent.

London, as might be expected, received a large number of refugees, but they fitted in well because of their trades, an important one being the art of dyeing cloth. Dr. Kepler established the first dye-works in England, and cloth of the 'Bow-dye' became quite famous. Other industries were the manufacture of felt, pendulum or Dutch clocks, arras, printed paper hangings, and metal articles requiring skilled workmanship.

These developments caused considerable disturbance among the English working classes, but the influx continued until many industries were initiated which, with the later influx after the

Revocation of the Edict of Nantes, gave England tremendous industrial expansion.

Mention should be made of Norwich because of the attitude of the guilds toward the foreigners. There were riots, and many foreigners were forced to leave for Holland with the result that industry declined. Then a reaction set in, and there was a concerted effort to bring in Flemish workmen, with the result that prosperity returned to Norwich. All through the labour troubles Queen Elizabeth supported the refugees because she had the shrewdness of her father, Henry VIII, and realized how necessary prosperity was to a nation.

The manufacture of cloth spread into the north and west of England in Worcester, Evesham, Droitwich, Kidderminster, Stroud, and Glastonbury. In the east the trade flourished at Colchester, Hertford, and Stamford, Colchester in 1609 having as many as thirteen hundred Walloons. In the north we find establishments at Manchester, Bolton, and Halifax where they made 'coatings' and at Kendal where they made cloth caps and woollen stockings.

Thread and lace were made at Maidstone in 1567. Some lace-makers from Alençon and Valenciennes settled at Cranfield, in Bedfordshire, in 1568, while others went as far as the shires of Oxford, Northampton, and Cambridge. About the same time the manufacture of Bone lace, with thread from Antwerp, was introduced into Devonshire by the Flemish exiles who settled at Honiton, Colyton, and other places where we find descendants by the names of Stocker, Murch, Spiller, Genest, Maynard, Gerard, Raymunds, Rochett, Kettel, etc.

Other immigrants turned to working in metals, salt-making, and fish-curing, arts in which they were more skilled than the English then were. At Newcastle-on-Tyne they introduced the making of steel, and that district became noted for swords and edge-tools. Names such as Ole and Mohl became Oley and Mole. Here, too, glassworks were established and window glass began to be made in London in 1567. Up to this time window glass was a rarity in houses. In 1614 Barnard van Lingen, a Fleming, was the first to practise the art of glass painting in England. It was he who supplied the windows in Wadham College and for Lincoln's Inn Chapel.

Sheffield acquired its reputation for its fine iron and steel when Flemish workers located there under the protection of the Earl of Shrewsbury in order to instruct English apprentices in their trade. At Yarmouth the English learned the art of salt-making and herring-curing from the Flemings.

Cornelius Vermuyden, a Flemish merchant, organized a scheme to reclaim the drowned lands in Hatfield Chase and the great level of the Fens. Some two hundred Flemish families settled on land reclaimed in the Isle of Axholm and formed themselves into congregations and erected churches. Much of the reclaimed land became some of the richest and most fertile soil in England.

Huguenots fled to England at four different periods, although there was a continuous movement between those times. The first took place during the second half of the sixteenth century at the time when Catherine de Medici in France and the Duke of Alva in the Netherlands were persecuting them. The second was during Richelieu's regime, when he successfully ended the "State within a State" by the capture of La Rochelle; the third and perhaps the largest was following the Revocation of the Edict of Nantes in 1685; and the fourth when the Peace of Aix-la-Chapelle ended the War of the Austrian Succession in 1748 and set free the soldiery to help the Jesuits in hunting down the remaining communities who met in the "Church of the Desert". By this time only the peasantry, small farmer, and small manufacturing classes were left because they lacked wealth and opportunity to escape.

But it must not be forgotten that English kings who wished to encourage home industry had always been willing to give inducements to foreign artisans to come over and settle in England for the purpose of instructing their subjects in the industrial arts. This was desirable because the early industry of England was almost

T.O.H.—3*

entirely pastoral. It was a great grazing country and its principal staple was wool, which was sold in large quantities to Flemish and French buyers who had it manufactured into cloth on the Continent, and then partly returned in that form for sale in the English markets.[2]

Upwards of ten thousand artisans left Rouen. The whole Protestant population of Coutances emigrated, and five linen manufacturers of the place were at once extinguished. Cloth-makers, gauze-makers, and lace-makers, together with artisans of all kinds, went to England to carry on their activities. These were persons of comparatively small means, for the richest took refuge in Holland. The emigration from France did not come to an end until about the end of the eighteenth century. Every revival of persecution there was followed by a fresh influx of fugitives into England. They were well received, and given monetary assistance, and, because of being better economists than the English, managed with less. They brought with them the art of cooking. They formed societies for mutual assistance, and it is said that such fraternal organizations as Foresters, Oddfellows, and other benefit societies owe their origin to the French Societies.

London received most of them in such areas as Spitalfields, Bethnal Green, and Soho. Many settled in Aldgate, Bishopsgate, Shoreditch, and quarters adjoining Thames Street. 'Petty France' was the district leading from Broad Street to the Guildhall.

With the Revocation of the Edict of Nantes, eighty thousand French manufacturers and workmen fled into the British Isles— paper-makers of Angoumois; silk-makers of Touraine; tanners of Normandy; vine-dressers and farmers of Saintonge, Poitou, and La Rochelle. The principal early immigration into England was from Normandy and Brittany. Artisans came from Rouen, Caën, Coustances, Elbeuf, Alençon, Caudebec, Le Havre, Nantes, Rennes, Le Mans, Laval, Amiens, Abbeville, Doullens, Lille, and Valenciennes. England had imported many articles from France before the Revocation such as velvets, satins, silks, taffetas, silk ribands, galloons, laces, gloves, buttons, serge, beaver and felt hats, paper of all sorts, ironmongery and cutlery, linen cloth, salt, wines, feathers, fans, girdles, pins, needles, combs, soap, aqua-vitae, vinegar, and various kinds of household stuffs. Now that the artisans had come to England the foregoing articles were no longer imported; indeed, they soon were exported.

"The silk brocades which issued from the manufacturers of London, at the close of the seventeenth century, were due almost exclusively to the industry of three refugees, Lauson, Mariscot, and Monteaux. The artist who furnished the designs was likewise a refugee, named Beaudoin. A simple workman, named Montgeorge, brought them the secret, but recently discovered at Lyons, of glazing tapestry."[3]

Silk-stocking machines had been brought to England, and the stocking trade became a considerable business. "The first pair of silk stockings brought into England from Spain was presented to Henry VIII who highly praised them. In the third year of Elizabeth's reign, her tiring woman, Mrs. Montague, presented her with a pair of black silk stockings as a New Year's gift; whereupon Her Majesty asked if she had any more, in which case she would wear no more cloth stockings. Silk stockings were equally rare things in the royal court of Scotland, for it appears that before James VI received the ambassadors sent to congratulate him on his accession to the English throne, he requested one of the lords of his court to lend him his pair of silken hose so that he 'might not appear as a scrub before strangers'."[4]

James II, because of his championship of Roman Catholics and his high-handed methods, was forced to give up his throne to William of Orange and his wife Mary. William, Prince of Orange, had been able to hold back Louis XIV, and for this reason Holland and the Netherlands together with England became the refuge for the Huguenots fleeing from the ruthlessness of Louis XIV. Descartes went to Holland where he spent twenty years and published his principal philosophical works. Academies were set up at Leyden, Rotterdam, and Utrecht. Large numbers of the best sailors went to Holland and aided Prince William in gaining the

English throne. Many refugees joined his army when he settled in England. Schomberg, a refugee Marshal of France, was next in command while William's three aides-de-camp were French officers.

"Fine papers were first manufactured in England by these refugees. Lace manufacture originated by the Walloon refugees was greatly increased and improved by the influx of Huguenot lace-workers, principally from Burgundy and Normandy. Some of these exiles settled in Edinburgh where they began the manufacture of linen while some built a silk factory and laid out a mulberry plantation."[5]

Two articles of manufacture should be mentioned separately— glass and fine paper. The Parisian glass-makers were especially celebrated for the skill with which they cast large plates for mirrors and now these were made in England. English paper had been of an indifferent 'whitey-brown' sort—coarse and inelegant. Henry de Portal was a distinguished paper-manufacturer who was responsible for introducing the art of fine paper-making by starting a mill in Hampshire. At Canterbury they swelled the ranks of the silk-manufacturers; it is said there were one thousand looms employing three thousand workers, many of whom later removed to Spitalfields.

"One of the most distinguished of the refugee paper-manufacturers was Henry de Portal. The Portals were an ancient and noble family in the south of France of Albigeois descent, who stood by the Protestant faith when the reign of terror began in the south of France. During the reign of Louis XVI, Louis de Portal, the father of Henry, was residing at his chateau de la Portalerie, seven leagues from Bordeaux. To escape the horrors of the Dragonnades, he set out with his wife and five children to take refuge on his estate in the Cevennes. The Dragoons pursued the family to their retreat, overtook them, and cut down the father, mother, and one of the children. They also burned to the ground the house in which they had taken refuge. The remaining four children concealed themselves in an oven outside the building and were thus saved.

"The four orphans—three boys and a girl—immediately determined to make for the coast and escape from France by sea. After a long and perilous journey on foot—exhausted by fatigue and wanting food—they at length reached Montauban, where little Pierre, the youngest, fell down fainting with hunger at the door of a baker's shop. The humane baker took up the child and carried him into the house and fed and cherished him. The other three—Henry, William and Mary de Portal—though grieving to leave their brother behind them, again set out on foot and pressed onward to Bordeaux.

"They were so fortunate as to secure a passage by a merchant-vessel, on board of which they were shipped, concealed in barrels. They were among the last of the refugees who escaped, previous to the issue of the infamous order to fumigate all departing vessels; so as to stifle any Protestant refugees who might be concealed in the cargo. The youthful refugees reached Holland where they found friends and foster-parents and were shortly in a position to assert the dignity of their birth. Miss Portal succeeded in obtaining a situation as governess in the family of the Countess of Finkelstein. She afterwards married M. Lenormant, a refugee settled in Amsterdam, while Henry and William followed the fortunes of the Prince of Orange, accompanying him to England, and established the family of de Portal in that country.

". . . The youngest brother, Pierre de Portal, who had been left fainting at the door of the baker in Montauban, was brought up to manhood by the baker, held to his Protestantism, and eventually set up as a cloth-manufacturer in France. He prospered, married and his sons grew up around him, one of them eventually becoming lord of Penardieres . . ."[6]

Such is the story of this family which can be duplicated many times in the lives of the refugees.

In Norwich, England, the refugees made lustrings, brocades, paduasoys, cabinets and velvets; while others carried on the making of cutlery, clocks, and watches. Another body of refugees settled at Ipswich in 1681 where they began the manufacture of fine linen formerly imported from France. This group was initially supported by the French Church at Threadneedle Street. The manufacture of sailcloth was later added.

The manufacture of lace which had been first introduced by the Walloons was increased and improved by an influx of Huguenot lace-makers from Burgundy and Normandy. These artisans spread around first to London then in adjoining counties settling at Buckingham, Newport-Pagnell, and Stony Stratford and then extending to Oxford, Northampton, Cambridge and adjoining counties.

"In short there was scarcely a branch of trade in Great Britain but at once felt the beneficial effects of the large influx of experienced workmen from France. Besides improving those manufactures which had already been established, they introduced many entirely new branches of industry; and by their skill, their intelligence, and their laboriousness, they richly repaid England for the hospitality and the asylum which had been so generously extended to them in their time of need."[7]

Early Walloon and French Churches in England

Foreign Protestants came to England not so much to follow industry as to have freedom of worship. For this reason as soon as they had relocated they formed themselves into congregations for the purpose of worshipping together. When their numbers were small they worshipped in one another's houses, but as early as Edward VI churches were set apart for them in London, Norwich, Southampton, and Canterbury. In London, the church in Austin Friars called the Temple of Jesus was set up to be followed by the church of St. Anthony's Hospital in Threadneedle Street. In 1550 it was turned over to the French Huguenots; it was burnt down during the great fire of London, then rebuilt; only to be demolished to make way for the new General Post Office. It then moved to Soho Square where it now flourishes.

"The only refugee congregation outside London in King Edward's reign was established at Glastonbury in Somerset, unlikely as that western situation may now seem. The buildings and lands of the famous Abbey had lain vacant for ten years, since their expropriation by King Henry VIII and the legal murder of the last Abbot, when the Protector Duke of Somerset received them by exchange from King Edward, and founded there a colony of Flemish and French Protestant weavers . . . The settlers were a compact group of refugees, Flemish and French Protestants who had gathered at Strasbourg under John Calvin himself and now had to move again. There were forty-six families for whom thirty houses were allotted, and they were encouraged to pasture their cattle in the park of the Abbey, some of whose buildings were used for their weaving industry. It was a deliberate attempt by the Protector to found an industrial colony. They held their Calvinist services in the parish church and a special liturgy in Latin was printed for them in London in 1551. On Queen Mary's accession they migrated to Frankfurt." [8]

Flemish weavers found their first asylum in East Anglia at Colchester and at Ipswich there was a congregation as early as 1572. "At Norwich where the number of the settlers was greater in proportion to the population than in most other towns, the choir of Friars Preachers Church, on the east side of St. Andrew's Hall, was assigned for the use of the Dutch, and the Bishop's Chapel, afterward the church of St. Mary's Tombland, was appropriated for the use of the French and Walloons." [9]

Gradually the Norwich congregation merged into the general life of the community whereas at Ipswich the renewed immigration of French Protestants after the Revocation increased the community considerably.

At Thorpe-le-Soken a congregation was formed in the Harwich area, all of them being French Huguenots. Two unusual settlements were made in Lincolnshire by the Dutch engineer Vermuyden when he drained the fens and brought over Dutch and Flemish Protestants about 1626. Lincoln city turned down admission of a colony of weavers and thereby passed up much prosperity. At Sandcroft where the Isle of Axholm was one of Vermuyden's reclaiming land projects a church was built which eventually merged with the congregation at Thorney in Cambridgeshire.

The first French church at Southampton established in the reign of Edward VI was largely fed by arrivals from the Channel Islands and dates from 1567. The list of names started at that time includes numerous medical men, others being weavers, bakers, cutlers, and brewers. Their chapel was called "God's House" and in its register there were interesting references to fasts and thanksgivings having to do with events taking place abroad, one of them being the defeat of the Armada. Visitations of the plague reduced their numbers from time to time.

Other churches early set up in the south of England were the Dutch church at Dover which continued to thrive for a long time because of being continually fed by immigrants from the opposite coast and the parish church composed of French Protestant fishermen at Rye, a Cinque port which kept close contact with Dieppe. It also served as a listening-post for Elizabeth's government regarding the state of the Protestant cause in France during the Wars of Religion.

In the West Country there was a Huguenot colony at Bristol, also one at Plymouth ; most of these groups originated in the west of France. "At Plymouth and Exeter there were both conforming and non-conformist refugee churches and they flourished from the time of the Revocation until far into the eighteenth century."[9] The Huguenot community at Bristol received official support and built a church in 1727 which continued until 1814.

About 1700 there were thirty-five French churches in London and suburbs, eleven of these in Spitalfields. The French Church in Threadneedle Street was the oldest in London and the one to which the refugees reported for recognition. Many of those coming had escaped by abjuring their Protestant faith but before they were accepted again they had to receive a 'reconnaissance'.

Threadneedle Church received the Huguenot Calvinists while the French Episcopal Church in the Savoy was similarly resorted to by the foreign Protestants of the Lutheran persuasion. This was the fashionable French Church of the West-End and because of very prominent preachers attracted a large following. Other French churches in the West-End were le Marylebone, 1653, Castle Street Chapel, 1672, in Leicester Square, the little Savoy Chapel, 1675, in the Strand, and the Hungerford Chapel, 1687.

After the Revolution three new churches in the West-End were established in 1689 and one on Swallow Street in Piccadilly which became the "reconnaissance" church in the West-End. Six more churches were added about 1700, together with three chapels, but the principal increase was in the eastern parts of London. In Spitalfields, where eleven new churches came into being, one of them, l'Église Neuve, built in 1742, would accommodate fifteen hundred persons.

There were French churches in the suburbs, one of the oldest being at Wandsworth where a colony of Walloons had settled about 1570. Chelsea had two chapels; there was a French church at Hammersmith, at Hoxton, at Bow, and at Greenwich; the latter achieved considerable distinction.

The Walloon fugitives from the opposite sea-board had established a church at Southampton, but by 1685 they had dispersed and were replaced by French Huguenots from "Basse Normandie", "Haute Languedoc", and from the Province of Poitou. It was named "God's House". Many refugee military officers retired from active service settled in this area and connected with this church.

New settlements required new churches such as Bristol, Exeter, Plymouth, Stonehouse, Dartmouth, Barnstaple and Thorpe-le-Soken in Essex. In many of these congregations the refugees were seafaring people: captains, masters, and sailors from Nantes, Saumur, Saintonge, and La Rochelle.

By the middle of the eighteenth century the number of French Protestant churches in England had greatly diminished due to the assimilation of the French refugees into the body politic of England. This came about through the use of the English language, by intermarriage, and a lack of desire to remain an isolated group.

There are two churches and one institution which have survived to the present—the church which exists in the undercroft of Canterbury Cathedral and the Church in Soho Square and the French Hospital at Rochester. Four hundred years have passed since the first body of exiled Walloons met to worship in Canterbury. The visitor to the Cathedral in passing through the undercroft has usually pointed out to him the apartment still used as the "French Church". It is walled off from the crypt in the south side-aisle; and is plainly fitted up with pews, a pulpit, and a precentor's desk, the place has a long table at which the communicants sit when receiving the Sacrament of the Lord's Supper after the manner of the Geneva brethren. This French Church has existed largely because of an endowment of two hundred pounds per year.

"We should not forget that the Church of England during the early period of the Reformation became Calvinistic in doctrine and that it remained Calvinistic for many years afterwards. Indeed it was not until the Catholic revival of the last century that the bonds of Calvinism were broken and cast off. Thus at the time of the Huguenot emigration there was no vital antagonism between the Reformed Church of England and the Reformed Churches of the continent. The chief difference lay in the status of the clergy. The Anglican Church held that all ministers should be episcopally ordained; so many of the Reformed Church of France took English orders and this they did for two reasons. First, because of the hospitality they had received from the English people of high and low degree. Second, because of the pecuniary support they hoped to receive from the Society for the propagation of the gospel in foreign parts. The refugee Huguenot ministers were greatly in need of assistance." [10]

Perhaps the most active French Protestant Church in England

today is *L'Église Protestante Française de Londres* located in Soho Square. As stated previously, this was the old Threadneedle Church founded by Royal Chapter in 1550 by Edward VI and is really the cathedral church for French Protestantism in England.

The French Hospital now located at Rochester has played a long and highly creditable role with the French Protestants who fled to England. Granted a Charter of Incorporation by King George I in 1718 to be of assistance "for poor French Protestants and their Descendents residing in Great Britain", it has always been known as "The French Hospital" although it has never been a hospital but a "hospice". It was originally supported by private funds. A home was built near St. Luke's Church in Finsbury and at one time housed as many as two hundred and thirty people.

Throughout the rest of the eighteenth century and the first half of the nineteenth the French Hospital at St. Luke's was the centre to which all distressed Huguenots in England looked for help. As the demand for accommodation lessened, some parts were torn down until in 1868 new premises were built in the village of Hackney for forty women and twenty men and for over seventy years a place of relief was available for old people of Huguenot descent.

During the last war the hospital premises were bombed and then requisitioned, the residents being dispersed to private homes. This situation continued to exist until it was re-established at Compton's Lea, Horsham, but as the new quarters were found unsatisfactory it was decided to close the home as the Welfare Services of the country were better fitted to take care of the aged and infirm.

Nineteen houses in Theobold Square, Rochester, have now been converted into forty self-contained flats designed for the occupation by elderly people, either singly or by married couples or pairs of friends or relations. Tenants are descendants of French Protestant families and a small rent is charged. Thus the idea of mutual assistance so characteristic of the Huguenots when they were refugees for their religion will be maintained.[10]

Scotland

Martyrdom for Protestants in Scotland began as early as 1433 when Paul Crawar was accused of importing the doctrines of Wyclif and Huss, was convicted by the State and burned at the stake. In 1494 thirty "Lollards of Kyle" were summoned before the Bishop of Glasgow on charges of repudiating religious relics and images, auricular confession, priestly ordination and powers, transubstantiation, purgatory, indulgences, Masses for the dead, clerical celibacy and papal authority. All these sum up to the Reformation but took place twenty-three years before Luther's theses, thus showing that humanism with its concomitant protestantism had been extended to the British Isles.[11]

The basic fact in the history of the Scottish state is fear of England. English Kings, for England's safety from rear attack, time and time again tried to annex Scotland to the English crown. Scotland, to protect herself, accepted alliance whenever possible with France, England's perennial enemy.

Soon after 1523 the writings of Luther entered Scotland. A Scots translation of Wyclif's New Testament circulated in manuscript and a cry arose for a Christianity based exclusively on the Bible. Patrick Hamilton went to Paris, Louvain, and Wittenberg and returned to Scotland with the new dogmas and for doing this was burned. George Wishart, who about 1543 translated the First Helvetic Confession, was hanged. Calvinism replaced Zwinglianism and Lutheranism.

It has been said that the Huguenots had one foot in France and one in Scotland. If this be true it is difficult to understand why there have been so few studies of the Huguenot influence in Scotland. Of course John Knox's indebtedness to John Calvin has often been acknowledged but the interplay between Scotland and France of scholars and artisans deserves careful appraisal as well. Although France was large and opulent Scotland was small, poor and with a much sterner upbringing, yet a common love of liberty bound these two nations in a common cause against such foes as the Guises, Mary, Queen of Scots, and the power of the Pope. These were the people who hastened the Huguenot Movement and aroused such a passionate desire for complete freedom in matters of conscience that eventually it made Scotland a Protestant nation.

Scotland got into the picture when Margaret, Princess of Scotland, became the bride of Louis XI of France. James V of Scotland, son of James IV, was determined to marry a French woman and this he did twice : first, Madeleine, daughter of Frances I, who died after six months of marriage, and Mary of Guise, who became the mother of Mary, Queen of Scots. The latter, having married Francis II, of France, tried to unite her Scotland and France under her husband to please the Guises and some who hoped to make her Queen of England as well by deposing Elizabeth.

The story of Mary, Queen of Scots, is too well known to be repeated here but it must be pointed out that it was she who unwittingly brought the Huguenots and the Covenanters (an organized group who opposed the use of the Anglican prayer book in Scotland) together by the birth of her son, James, after her marriage to Darnley. At the christening of this heir to the Scottish throne, who was also heir-presumptive to the English throne, the Roman Catholic Princes were offering valuable presents, so Protestant Elizabeth very grudgingly had to follow suit. Thus Scotland came to play a key role in the Huguenot cause. Mary opposed Calvinism and chose the Roman Catholic faith, thereby bringing about her imprisonment and eventually her execution.

The resistance of the Huguenots in France greatly influenced the Covenanters in Scotland in formulating a thorough-going attitude towards the Church and State. In England the Church was treated as part of the laws and opponents to Divine Right. In this respect there is a resemblance to the Huguenots.

"Scotland, although possessing no accumulation of wealth like

France, had plenty of better riches of men of fine material. The Scots, moreover, had not, like the Huguenots, to continue with a Royal attack culminating in civil war. The growing sense of nationality enabled reform to be carried through with success. Intense indignation was a driving force. It has been declared that 'Calvinism put iron into the blood of the Scot' . . . Reform to the Scottish people meant not only freedom in Church matters but independence from the Monarchy. It was essentially a liberal movement. . . . In practice, the situation produced a feeling that any blend of confession and oppression, any uncertainty, meant the maximum of irritation, while it also gave an encouraging sporting chance that nothing serious might happen." [12]

Because of his physical environment in a land of shepherds the Scot was a mystic as in his loneliness he meditated on the Psalms and the Prophets. The barren nature of the soil bred a consciousness of something greater than himself and created a sense of the inadequacy of compromise making him choose the Calvinistic theology as best suited to his temperament.

Now let us turn to Flanders. United to Spain under Charles V it had prospered and had enjoyed certain liberties in matters of conscience and expression of thought. However, his son, Phillip II, a true Spaniard and ardent Roman Catholic, determined to purge Protestantism from the Low Countries. The Provinces formed a Confederacy to resist and were given assistance by Huguenots in France and the Presbyterians in Scotland. Admiral Coligny and the Prince de Condé gave what help they could. However, the treachery of the Spaniards following the murder of Counts Egmont and Horn brought William of Orange into the situation. He in turn was betrayed by Anjou, a brother of Henry III of France, who had undertaken to lead the Flemings against the Spaniards.

The repeal of the Edict of Nantes convulsed not only the Huguenots in France but the Scots and the Flemings. To all it was a sign of bitter days ahead but what was loss for France and Flanders was gain for the British Isles as well as other parts of

Europe. To the French democrats and French Huguenots faith was vital and it drove these diligent people to choose exile rather than submit to the evil dictation of France or Spain and caused them to seek refuge in other countries. It is worthy of note that such a migration starting from a religious basis soon took on economic importance, for the migrants came in contact with other races and conditions which gave them much stimulation. Carrying democracy and constitutional government with them they encouraged the Scots to develop from a remote nation on the edge of Europe to become important in the defence of political freedom. The inquisition of the Spaniards became a threat to the Scots but it was a reality to the Flemings.

John Knox, the protagonist of Protestantism, was born of peasant parents between 1505 and 1515, studied in Glasgow, was ordained and soon known for his learning in civil and canon law, became a follower of George Wishart and, following Wishart's death, he went into hiding and joined the band that killed the Cardinal of St. Andrews. Preaching against the Roman Catholics, he adopted Luther's doctrine of salvation : "Only by faith that the blood of Jesus Christ purges us from all sin." He was captured by the French fleet when it took St. Andrews and for nineteen months was a galley slave in France, being released at the request of Edward VI for whom he later acted as chaplain. Fleeing from Mary Tudor he went to Frankfurt where he was not well received ; he then went on to Geneva where he adopted Calvinism. After a few months he returned to England but went back to Geneva the following year at the request of the congregation which he had left there. He preached at Dieppe for two years in French, identifying himself with the Huguenots.

In 1559 Knox returned to Scotland, where, forming the Lords of the Congregation, he preached at Perth so effectively that his hearers destroyed Catholic churches and monasteries. He was appointed minister of Edinburgh and from that time until his death he took a leading part in the proceedings of the Protestants and had the principal share of the work in drawing up the confession of faith which was accepted in 1560 by Parliament. He became involved in the controversy with Mary, Queen of Scots, and was instrumental in turning Scotland away from France to England. He was twice married, first to Margaret Bowes and then to Margaret Stewart. He died in 1572.

There is sparse information regarding the part that John Knox played in the Huguenot migration to Scotland. Although Theodore Beza became the leader of reform in France after the death of Calvin in 1546, Knox was the one who carried the burden. His public career began in 1545 and ended in 1572. His convictions were real and compelling but bordering on the austere, he would have made the Scots Kirk as autocratic as the Roman Church. His writings as found in his Books of Discipline displayed a preponderance of French influence.

The Second Book of Discipline written by Andrew Melville in 1581 adopted the rules of the Synod of the Huguenots and became the guide of the Scottish Church. The sovereign was to be the guardian of the rights of the common people. Wholesome preaching was not to be smothered by ritualism and authority was no longer to be the guide.

By 1574 Scottish Schools and Universities were thrown open to French refugees and from time to time scholars from the Sorbonne when driven from France took positions in these places of learning. In like manner a number of Scottish professors held positions in France, some at the College of Saumur, a Huguenot institution, and some at the Sorbonne. There were others like John Cameron, who went to Geneva. Here, embracing Huguenot doctrine and taking a position at Saumur he was forced to flee to Scotland, whereupon James VI made him Principal of Glasgow University and Professor of Divinity. Later he returned to France because of the religious controversies in Scotland.

Some Protestant leaders who played their parts now in France, now in Scotland, were : John Boyd who first taught at Saumur but was recalled by James I in 1615 to be Principal of Glasgow University; his cousin Zachary Boyd who also went to Saumur but returned to be an outstanding preacher; Mark Boyd, who lectured at Bordeaux and published extensively; Gilbert Primrose, who went to University of Sedan, to be a strong protagonist for the Huguenots; William Carstares, persecuted by James II, escaped to Holland and attached himself to William of Orange and drew up plans for the downfall of James.

William of Orange was of Huguenot stock for his great-grandmother was a daughter of Admiral Coligny (who was a brother-in-law of Sir Walter Raleigh); his mother was the daughter of Charles I, and his wife the elder daughter of James II. These relationships to the Stuarts were of great importance to Scottish loyalty as well as to the political and religious position of the Scots on the Continent. France being an autocracy and allied to Rome and Scotland a democracy and non-conformist, the latter country profited by her independent character when Carstares commenced negotiations for the Act of Union in 1707. Scotland may have given up some of her nationhood, but she gained spiritually and economically with Carstares of St. Giles, Edinburgh, the leader of the Presbyterian Church, to remain the base of a sound Christian democracy and the guide of a nation's policy.

The Huguenots, who had quietly entered Scotland and soon became naturalized, were disturbed by false representation as late as 1745; however, there were no fanatical incidents recorded in connection with them. By 1707 there are records which state that more than 400 refugee Huguenots families had settled in Scotland; some of these were Brabant weavers of linen, silk, and worsted.

"A group of Flemish Huguenots settled in the Canongate in 1609 under the leadership of Joan van Hedan, spinning and weaving 'stuffs', and 'giving great light and knowledge of the calling of their native land which they taught to the country-folk around'. They enjoyed the protection of a special code of mercantile law and the good-will of their neighbors. Sir Patrick Drummond, resident-proprietor, and Conservator of Scottish trade at Campvere during 1625, performed a great service to the land of his birth by encouraging experts to immigrate and instruct the Scots in the cultivation and preparation of flax for linen yarn."[13]

But the migration was sometimes to France; some went and became artisans; others to hold high positions: Archibald, Earl of Douglas, became Duke of Touraine, and his son-in-law, Buchan, was made High Constable of France because of his military exploits, while Hamilton, Earl of Arran, a Stuart, was given the Dukedom of Chatelerault.

One of the problems of the immigrant Huguenots grew out of a very natural desire to bring their pastors with them and set up new churches. There was no special objection to this because in many instances on account of the similarity of creed with the Presbyterians there was an interchange of pastors and eventually a merging. For many years the Presbyterian Churches sent assistance to the persecuted Huguenots in France and in return the Huguenots provided much of the church government for the Scottish Church. The Scot inherited from Protestant France the General Assembly, Synod, Presbytery, and Session Courts, bicameral chambers both in doctrine and form. The system was introduced ready-made and the root of it is still to be found in "The Acts, Decisions, Decrees and Canons of the National Council of the Reformed Churches in France. The Moderator is essentially a Huguenot institution and the expression 'Overture' is another instance of that influence."[14]

Scotland like England was originally a pastoral country, but the coming of the Huguenots from France and Flanders was the beginning of many industries and the development of a high order of culture among the Scots, for the infiltration extended over a period of two hundred years.

Deschamps, a Huguenot, about 1650, came to Scotland, started his paper-making by gathering rags in the street, eventually being able to start a mill. In 1679 another immigrant, Nicholas Dupin, built a mill and initiated the use of strawboard for bookbinding. Next comes Henri Fourdrinier who fled from France to Scotland bringing machinery and being followed by expert craftsmen who along with him set up mills and produced printing and writing papers for which they took out patents. The Portals, a Huguenot family, still possess the secret of making the kind of paper required for Bank of England notes.

The development of different kinds of type deserves attention. What is called 'black letter' imitated the handwriting of the monk; italic is supposed to copy the style of Petrarch about 1492. Later arrived the 'Roman' letter with its capital and small letter, followed by the passing over from the thin Old Face to the heavy-stroked 'ionic' characters much more easy to read.

Various editions of the Bible appeared on the Continent, most of them in Latin. Huguenot printers from time to time put out in Scotland printings of religious books. Towards the end of the sixteenth century several editions of the Bible were attempted, the best being by Bassandyne (1579), one which pleased King James VI and inspired him to begin publishing an Authorized Version in 1601 and have it completed by 1611.

Henry Charteris, a Huguenot refugee, set up a printing press and published some interesting writings, among them a *Hebrew Grammar and Vocabulary*, in which Hebrew characters were carefully done. About this time Kirk censorship descended on Scottish literature as well as in France. But the Huguenots and Flemings fought back in the form of pamphlets, thereby developing the power of the 'Fourth Estate', in fact, this was its genesis.

In the field of drama there is quite a contrast between the Huguenots and the Scots as the former came from a country that enjoyed the finer things of life and for that reason they could never appreciate the Scottish notion that 'actors were the children of Satan'. Nevertheless from time to time in Scotland drama was very acceptable even if frowned upon or only allowed to take place by permission of the local Kirk Session.

No country has ever equalled the tapestries made in the Flemish-Huguenot city of Arras; in fact, this name came to mean a wall-hanging of any description and is thus used by Shakespeare in

Hamlet and *Merry Wives of Windsor*. Many weavers because of the enticement of royalty went to France and Spain only to be maltreated later as Huguenots. Many of these after 1685 returned to Scotland. Among them was Nicholas Dupin, the inventor of wallpaper in imitation of tapestry.

Blue and white Delft-ware was introduced into Scotland by Daniel Marot, a Huguenot refugee, who had been well-trained in France and Flanders. His 'delf' ware became very popular with the Scottish housewife and many of his designs bring high prices in auction rooms today.

On account of coal, sand, and kelp being readily available at Wemyss, in Fife, Scotland, Flemish Huguenots established glass houses for the making of stained and domestic glass. They possessed certain secrets in the making of glass which they guarded jealously.

The Goldsmiths' Company readily welcomed to their guild Huguenot silver workers who in turn affected the craftsmanship of the Scottish Silversmiths making it much more ornate and intricate. 'Dutch-clocks' were designed by Huyghens, a refugee, and introduced into Scotland by Fromantel and David Ramsay, the latter becoming clock-maker to James VI and establishing the Incorporation of clock-makers in 1631.

The fare of the Scottish people because of their pastoral nature was very plain. Such was not the case with the French and Flemish immigrants who were accustomed to vegetables, hence they introduced Brussels' sprouts, carrots, cauliflower, and beets. Although handicapped for some time in not being allowed to hold land, they made their influence felt by advocating fields laid out as now and divided by hawthorn hedges, walls, and fences; also the sowing of the best grain rather than the worst as was formerly the practice.

Modern botany was founded by a Huguenot refugee, Brunnier, who arrived in 1699; N. Cottereau, a horticulturist, introduced garden planning. The Flemings having brought the tulip and lilac from Turkey carried them to Scotland where they made the lilac bush their emblem. Other flowers introduced successfully were Roses-Damask, and Red of Provence; also the 'Cabbage' and 'Moss'. The Auricula was a favorite Flemish flower together with the Pink.

Likewise in the field of dress there was a wide disparity between the natural flair of the French for attire and the desire of the Scottish Calvinists for simplicity in clothing. The Flemings took after the French. One has only to view a Van Dyke or Rubens painting to appreciate their love of fine clothes. Nevertheless, woman's innate love for beauty and comfort brought about changes in household affairs. Flemish glass was placed in windows and chimneys came into being. Attractive woodwork and plaster were found in homes of the wealthy. Weavers' looms were improved so that finer fabrics were made available, some of them silk, satin, or velvet.

It has been said that the "breeding of sheep, the improved cultivation of pastureland and the weaving of fine textiles, laid the foundation of our (Scottish) wealth. The seat of our Lord Chancellor in the House of Lords is, for this very reason, a wool-sack." [15] (This statement can be questioned.)

Because of the scarcity of water-power in England, many 'walk-mills' (tread mill) for cloth makers were set up in Scotland for the purpose of producing textiles. After the Revocation the Huguenot immigrants greatly increased the production of all kinds of cloth. Flemish weavers brought and planted the plants which gave them the dyes they preferred. Efforts were made to plant mulberry trees and breed silk worms, but this effort was not successful in spite of the help of the Courtaulds. However, the making of gloves was much more profitable because they became very much in demand by the gentry. Lace-makers from Lille, Valenciennes, and Alençon migrated, bringing their pillows and numerous bobbins to establish an industry in Scotland. It was Huguenots who taught the peasants to spin 'fine' worsted by the 'rock and Spindle' for the making of stockings. Hitherto stockings had been cut out of a web, now they were made by women knitters during their spare time.

But it was in the realm of headgear that the Huguenot-Flemings made their greatest contributions because it had a bearing on the colonizing of Canada. "They invented the malleable but easily stiffened beaver-skin (from Canada), which was associated with the wide 'steeple' hats of the Puritan, and the soft felt of their Cavalier foes—though the Scot remained true to his woollen bonnet...

". . . Even Rome and her Cardinals had to obtain their proper headgear from Huguenot hatters. . . . It is a quaint anomaly for 'cardinal red' to be a Protestant secret, yet this brilliant crimson has been carefully handed down from father to son by a family at Burtscheid, near Aix-la-Chapelle, since the days before the Revocation of the Edict of Nantes. Although strict Lutherans, they enjoyed the monopoly of purveying cloth to the Sacred College for over two centuries. Pierre Jacques Papillon, an eminent dyer from Rouen, introduced the art when he came to this country."[16]

Straw plaiting from Lorraine, France, was brought to Scotland by persecuted Protestants at the invitation of James VI to settle in Luton in Bedfordshire, England. The bonnet as worn by women originated in Flanders and was made popular in Scotland by Mary, Queen of Scots.

Nor did styles in furniture escape. The 'Chair' formerly for the master's use only was comfortably upholstered and made available for other members of the family. The 'Bureau' and the 'Buffet' were of Flemish invention and design; also, the Chiffonier. The early importance of a 'Chair' is the origin of our expression, 'To take the chair', meaning the place of honour.

When we turn to music we find that Calvin so appreciated the value of congregational singing to a good musical accompaniment that he became eager to have a Psalter to satisfy this need. Clément Marot completed many Psalms while Calvin translated some together with the *Song of Solomon*. John Knox published in 1556 some fifty-one versions of the Psalms with tunes and from time to time more were added, until we find the 1635 edition of the Scottish Psalter considered the finest and most musical. These were not printed until 1662. Some of these were written according to Flemish modes; some in a Scottish minor key; but whether Huguenot or Scottish they expressed the emotions of a people deeply religious.

The Huguenots, whether French or Flemish, who came as refugees to Scotland became part of the warp and woof of the Scottish nation. They followed the tenets of John Calvin and made their contribution social, religious, and commercial.

Ireland

The English monarchs from time to time induced foreign artisans to settle in Ireland and establish new branches of trade. The Irish people had a rich land yet were poor because often idle. Elizabeth I encouraged such settlements though with indifferent results on account of the disturbed state of the country. There was one settlement of Flemish at Swords near Dublin.

During the early part of the reign of James I progress was made. In 1605 two men from Brabant and two men from Antwerp; in 1607 one from Antwerp; in 1608 one from Amsterdam and one from Dort; and in 1613 two from Holland settled at Dublin and Waterford as merchants. In the reign of Charles I, the Earl of Strafford established a new industry, that of linen manufacture by inviting French and Flemish workers to settle in Ireland. He invested much of his own private fortune and stimulated the new industry. The Duke of Ormond followed Strafford's example by establishing four hundred Flemish artisans at Chapel Izod, in Kilkenny, under Colonel Richard Lawrence, where houses were built for the weavers and a considerable trade grew up in cordage, sail-cloth, and linen. Walloon colonies were also set up at Clonmel, Kilkenny, and Carrick-on-Suir.

These industries were successful until the English Revolution of 1688 when civil war interfered. In 1691, William III took active steps to restore the industry by granting citizenship to Protestants who would settle there and guaranteeing religious freedom. Many of his officers took advantage of this offer and settled at Youghat, Waterford, and Portarlington while colonies of artisans located at Dublin, Cork, Lisburn, and other places.

Those who settled at Dublin began the manufacture of what came to be known as 'Irish Poplin' and for a time trade was very prosperous and attracted workmen from Spitalfields. Frequent strikes in the years following paralyzed the 'industry' and 'The Liberties' became one of the poorest parts of Dublin.

There were four congregations so long as the French colony lasted. Two were Episcopal and worshipped at St. Mary's Chapel in St. Patrick's Cathedral and also in the French Church of St. Mary's in St. Mary's Abbey which continued until 1816. The other two were Calvinistic; the first one had a chapel in Peter Street and the other in Lucas' Lane.

But it was in the northern counties of Down and Antrim where the refugees were most at home because here they found Scotch Calvinists who had been driven out of Scotland by the Stuart persecutions. Lisburn, about ten miles south of Belfast, was the chief settlement. William III invited Louis Crommelin, a Huguenot refugee, then temporarily in Holland, to come over to Ireland and supervise the new linen industry. Crommelin was the right man for the job as his family had been in the linen manufacture for some four hundred years. Louis was born at Armancourt, near St. Quentin in Picardy, and grew up there. Shortly before the Revocation he saw what was coming and sold his property and went to Holland. In 1698 he left Holland for Ireland at the invitation of William III and set up a linen industry at Lisburn by advancing much of his own money. The results were rewarding, both for the industry and for Crommelin until his death in 1727.

Another refugee was Peter Goyer from Picardy, who in France had been a large manufacturer of cambric and silk. When the Dragonnades began, he escaped to Holland and from there went first to England and then to Ireland. He began to manufacture silk and cambric at Lisburn. The silk manufacture was destroyed by the rebellion of 1798 but that of cambric survived at Lurgan.

William Crommelin, a brother of Louis, superintended a branch of the linen trade established at Kilkenny by the Marquis of Ormonde. At Limerick the refugees established the lace and glove trades. At Bandon they manufactured cloth, such names as Garretts, De Ruyters, and Minhears being Flemish, and Beaumonts and perhaps Willises and Baxters, being French from the banks of the Loire.

At 'The Mulberry Field', three miles below Bandon, an effort was made to rear silk worms but it failed and the colonists migrated to Spitalfields.

"The woollen manufacture at Cork was begun by James Fontaine, a member of the noble family of de la Fontaine in France, a branch of which embraced Protestantism in the sixteenth century, and continued to adhere to it down to the period of the Revocation . . . James Fontaine was the son of a Protestant pastor of the same name and was born at Royan in Saintonge, a famous Huguenot district. . . ."[17]

Because of his Protestant leanings he was in difficulties with the authorities, was arrested but acquitted ; however, following the Revocation, after many adventures, he managed to escape to England at Barnstaple. In England he became involved in several businesses and then became a pastor. In 1694 he went to Ireland where he established at Cork the manufacture of woollens. He also tried to form a fishing company but it was not too successful.

Because of his keeping down the 'Tories' and breaking up their connection with the French privateers who frequently came to the coast he carried their ill will and he was captured but released at the command of the British Government. He returned to Dublin where he spent the remainder of his life as a teacher of languages, mathematics, and fortification.

Nearly all Fontaine's near relatives took refuge in England. Fontaine's sons and daughters mostly emigrated to Virginia. His daughter Mary Ann married the Rev. James Maury, Fredericksville Parish, Louisa County, Virginia, from whom Matthew Fontain Maury, LL.D., lately Captain in the Confederate States Navy and author of the "Physical Geography of the Sea" is lineally descended.

The French refugee colony at Waterford was of considerable importance. About 1693 the city encouraged artisans to settle there and build up the manufacture of linen. The choir of the old Franciscan monastery was even assigned to them and a yearly stipend of forty pounds given to the support of the pastor. Such measures got excellent results, for Waterford became a centre of trade, the foreign wine trade operating almost exclusively from it. The linen and glass manufacture at Waterford became very important as well.

Portarlington was another important colony for refugees. The first settlers were retired French officers and men from the army of King William. Originally founded by the Earl of Galway he continued to take an interest in it and it soon became the model town of the province where persons of high culture, gentle birth, and manners formed a highly select society.

Among the early settlers were the Sieur de Hauteville, Louis de Blanc, Sieur de Pierre, Abel Pelissier, Reuben de la Rochefoucauld, Sieur de la Boissère, de Bonneval, de Villier, Vicomte de Laval, de Garedry, Abel de Ligonier, Anthonie de Ligonier.

Besides a church, the refugees also possessed a school. M. Le Fevre, founder of the Charter Schools, was the first schoolmaster in Portarlington. The professions were well represented. There were the Sourins, the Le Fanus, Espinasses, Favers, Corneilles, Le Bas, and many others. The social standards were perhaps higher in Ireland than in England as many were retired French officers belonging to the nobility. "It has been stated that the Barrys of Bandon and the Places of Kinsale were of Huguenot origin with the surnames of Du Barry and de la Place. A John Place had charge of the prison at Kinsale and his daughter Ann married the Rev. John Barry who was ordained in 1824 and sent as a missionary to Jamaica. Both families subsequently emigrated to America and now are extinct in the south of Ireland." [18]

"The name Martel is connected with Cork and Kinsale. (Although there were English as well as Huguenot Martels in Ireland.) The Fleurys were descended from the French nobility shortly before the Revocation. Louis Fleury, the Protestant pastor of Tours, fled with his wife Esther, his son born 1671, and his two daughters to England where they were naturalized in 1679. He came to Ireland as one of the private chaplains of William of Orange and was present at the battle of the Boyne." [19]

John and Robert Durant, the former from Canterbury, were appointed by Cromwell as chaplains to the French Garrisons. Both forms of the name Durand and Durant are found among English Huguenots. Smiles states that they originated in Dauphiny and were of noble rank. A François Durand at the Revocation fled to Geneva where he recruited a Dragoon Regiment of Colonel Blosset de Lache for King William.

There was Louis Aimee possibly a descendant of Cornet l'Amy who was pensioned in 1692. Henri David Petitpierre came in 1737 from Tournai to Dundalk.

"The Labatt's family came to Ireland from Claret, near Montpelier. One of them served under William of Orange, obtained his commission as Lt. in November, 1693, and was on the *Mountjoy* when it burst the boom across Lough Foyle and raised the siege of Derry. The name exists in the north and in Dublin. In 1740 Isaac and Joseph Labatt settled in Yougal as merchants in partnership where they were successful until 1755 when they failed." [20]

There is some question as to the Huguenot ancestry of the Trench family, however, it is thought that it originated in England from Frederick, Lord of Tranche in Pictou, when he took refuge in England about the year 1574, shortly after the massacre of St. Bartholomew. He settled first in Northumberland but later went to Ireland.

Mention should be made of the Huguenot goldsmiths in Dublin and Cork for they immensely enriched the craft there and

Huguenot names appear in the Journals of the Guild all through the eighteenth century.

"The foreigners certainly cost Ireland much in pensions and grants but that they earned the former by their valiant conduct in the armies of William and Anne and the latter by their assiduity in trade and commerce cannot be doubted." [21]

HUGUENOTS IN THE CHANNEL ISLANDS

"The Channel Islands are, thanks to their position, and to the language of their inhabitants, the recognized harbour of refuge, to which every one of the constantly recurring convulsions of France has, from time to time, driven a quota of outcasts quite out of proportion to the size of the islands or to the security which they afford. In the sixteenth century they found the Islands practically without any religious organization and introduced a Church disciple on the Genevan Calvinistic model." [1]

The first definite movement took place in 1548 and was due to the Lord Proctor who was then Governor of Jersey. Following the edicts of Henry II of France the Islands were soon overrun with religious enthusiasts. The death of Edward VI and the Restoration of Catholicism under Mary reversed the situation but Calvinism was too strongly rooted to die out and so upon the accession of Elizabeth the Protestants got the upper hand, the leaders of the refugees being Nicholas Baudouin, Guillaume Morice, and Adrian Saravia. These were the men who opposed the English Government in its demand to conform to the ritual of the Established Church. The striving for conformity was unsuccessful and by 1572 every person of influence in the Islands was enrolled in the cause of Calvinism.

The panic which followed St. Bartholomew's Day sent many refugees to the Islands but most of them proceeded to England. In 1576 the Synod of the Channel Islands took place in Guernsey in the presence of two Governors when the Calvinist form of Church discipline was agreed upon.

Sir George Carteret, a Huguenot of St. Ouen, supported the

royalist cause until his death when his nephew George Carteret became Lieutenant-Governor of Jersey. Later knighted because of his support of Charles II, he, along with John, Lord Berkeley, was given land in America in 1664 which they named New Jersey. The Island of Sark was also under the control of a Carteret—Hilary—who was given it by Elizabeth. Here where many Huguenots fled, a French Pastor, M. Cosme Brevin, a native of Angonville, took charge about 1570–71.

The Island of Alderney, or Aurigny (given to the Carteret family after the Reformation) as it was then known, came under the authority of Guernsey for ecclesiastical purposes but the control by the Anglican Clergy in England weakened and the Synod of the Channel Islands clergy in 1576 undertook to regiment the day-to-day life of the inhabitants of Jersey, Guernsey, Alderney, and Sark. "The adult population as well as the children must attend to the prescribed religious devotions on pain of disciplinary action. They must all learn the Catechism word for word, as failure to pass the tests would lead to exclusion from the Sacrement." An act of 1589 decreed : "All women and girls are forbidden to go sandeeling except in the company of their husbands or employers."

"Attendance twice on Sunday was rigidly demanded from all. At week day services (two in the town and one in the country) one member of the household at least 'able to hear and understand' was required to be present."

Such adherence to Calvin's maxim : 'Doctrine without discipline is a body without backbone'[2] was bound to bring about a reaction and again a great migration took place. This time to the British Isles and to America. Many engaged in the Newfoundland cod fishing trade or became master mariners.

The main industry in the islands in the sixteenth and seventeenth centuries was the manufacture of stockings following a grant of wool by James II. Woollen waistcoats or 'jerseys' along with stockings became a major industry.

It is difficult to say how many inhabitants of the Channel

Islands were Huguenots because there are few records of them. From the time of the Conquest these Islands have been French in population. Samuel Smiles, however, thinks there were many Huguenots who sought refuge in them: "It is stated in Falle's *History of Jersey*, that forty-two Protestant Ministers of religion, besides a large number of lay families, passed over from France into Jersey in the reign of Elizabeth, many of them before the Massacre of Saint Bartholomew. And although the refugees for the most part regarded the Channel Islands as merely temporary places of refuge—or as a stepping-stone to England—a sufficient number remained to determine the Protestant character of the Community, and to completely transform the islands by their industry; since which time, Jersey and Guernsey, from being among the most backward and miserable places on the face of the earth, have come to be recognized as among the most happy and industrious." [3]

HUGUENOTS IN CONTINENTAL EUROPE
Prussia

The migration to Brandenburg (Prussia) was deliberately encouraged. Because of the Thirty Years' War such cities as Magdeburg were in ruins. Frederick William, the Great Elector, in 1685 was interested for several reasons: His House had been Calvinist since 1614, his wife being a granddaughter of William the Silent and the great granddaughter of Coligny, the outstanding leader of the Huguenots in France. Always sympathetic to French teachers, soldiers and ideas, Frederick William realized the importance of these refugees for the rebuilding of his country.

"To this end he issued the Edict of Potsdam in which he offered them asylum and every assistance such as ships and provisions to allow them to travel to Hamburg and Frankfurt-on-the-Main. From these cities they would be taken to any areas in his territories, Stendal, Werbe, Rothenau, Brandenburg, Frankfurt, Magdeburg, Halle, Kolbe, and Konigsburg being recommended. Their property was to be free of taxation and houses were to be built for them. Industrial and agricultural workmen were particularly welcomed; also French nobles from the army." [4]

The French soldiers brought with them the system of fortification which Vauban had made so successful in France. Schomberg, who was a German, learned much of his army organization from them.

Two cities, Magdeburg and Berlin, profited most from French industry. For Berlin it was the beginning of her greatness. All the trades that the French brought with them were practised in Berlin by the ten thousand who settled there.

French culture and French scholarship came as well as French military and industrial science. Foreign doctors were eagerly welcomed. The French language became fashionable at Court and spread widely among the middle class.

Zoll states: "The Huguenots who stayed in Germany—their number has been estimated at some thirty thousand—created the entire German textile industry, besides developing the manufacture of ceramics and paper, and the printing trade. German writers and poets such as Fontane, La Motte-Fouqué, and Alexis, were among their descendants as was the great German military theoretician, Clausewitz. And Goethe as a boy, went to a kindergarten run by a Huguenot woman, and often wandered from Frankfurt to nearby Bockenheim to listen to a sermon at the French Reformed Church." [5]

One of the most important French Huguenot settlements in Germany is Friedrichsdorf, a town in the Province of Hesse-Nassau, three miles north-east from Homburg and twelve miles north of Frankfort-on-Main, which was founded by French Huguenots in 1687 at the invitation of Frederick II, the Second Landgrave of Hesse-Homburg. This prince who on his second marriage married the niece of Frederick William the Great and who had often suffered hardships himself, was very sympathetic to the refugees fleeing from France after the Revocation. "At the request of the Vaudois' minister, Daniel Martin, several Vaudois and French families came to Homburg in the year 1686,

. . . The refugees who settled there built half the new city. The following year Frederick took pleasure in opening up his estates to a large number of these unfortunates and decreed to that end patent or privileges under date of March 13, 1667; comprising eleven articles. . . ." [6]

These articles contain references to the privileges these settlers were to have such as, freedom from taxation for ten years, land without interest, meadows for their cattle, right to govern themselves, to establish industries, no taxes on imported silk.

This act so important was, thanks to the Christian Charity of Frederick II, the reason for the migration of about thirty families who after wandering hither and yon came to the village of Friedrichsdorf, originally known as *Das-Neue Dorf*. [7]

"The first inhabitants of Friedrichsdorf had come from several districts of France, principally from the north (Picardy, Ile de France, Champagne) and from the south (Dauphiné, Provence, Languedoc). Each of them had its own peculiar dialect, which, for quite a long time, was kept up in the different families. Little by little these dialects fused to form a special kind of French which lacked the purity and lightness of the language spoken on the banks of the Seine . . ." [8]

The French might be different but the language has continued to exist although surrounded by Germans. As elsewhere these Huguenots have put their skills to work and established textile manufactures. One particular industry originated there: the making of biscuits known as *Zwieback* which have been exported to all parts of the world.

Among the first families to locate in Friedrichsdorf were: Rossignol, Achard, Foucar, Garnier (Grenier), Dippel, Lotz, Rousselet, Privat. Germans did not settle in this town until 1741.

Dr. E. C. Privat, a direct descendant of one of the first settlers and President of the German Huguenot Society, published in 1950 a careful study of this settlement of French Huguenots in Friedrichsdorf. [9] His purpose was to consider this town representative of other Huguenot settlements in Germany and to note the contributions they have made. He states that those who settled in Germany retained their French characteristics such as their religion, language, dress, and even their general attitude to life. This is unique for one of the outstanding facts about Huguenots has been their tendency to assimilate almost completely. But this did not happen in Germany. To cite another example : In Berlin at the present time there is a Parish Church whose members are all persons with a Huguenot ancestry and who are exceedingly proud of it. Possibly the reason for this solidarity is to be found in the fact that these people's ancestors emigrated as a group, something not usual.

The Huguenots in Germany then are a rather different lot of people because of their ability to retain some of the original characteristics of their forefathers, particularly their language. But this has not prevented the Germans themselves from acknowledging the great services which the clear and cultivated intelligence of France has rendered to the thought and development of Germany. (For additional Huguenot German Settlements, see page 299.)

The Netherlands

On account of its proximity to France the Netherlands and Holland were the chief current in the Huguenot immigration from France. It is estimated that a hundred thousand of them reached Holland as compared with the eighty thousand that went to England and the same number to Germany.

"Since the war of 1672 the government of the Netherlands had regarded Louis XIV with great suspicion and hostility. The events of that year brought William of Orange to the head of the state and his whole career was inspired by a passion of hatred for France and her ruler . . . The emigration into the Netherlands had begun many years before the Revocation . . . Several states invited the Huguenots to settle in their midst in the most cordial terms. The city of Amsterdam gave to the Huguenots immigrants full rights of citizenship, the right of exercising any trade or profession without further formality, and freedom from city taxes for three years. The government of the State of Holland exempted them from taxes for twelve years. The Estates of Friesland welcomed them." [10]

The refugees, moreover, especially the first group, were not destitute men who needed to be supported for they were able to dispose of their property without any notice by the government. Thus they were able to bring much wealth into their adopted country and at one time there was such an influx of foreign capital into the Netherlands that the rate of interest dropped to more than half; furthermore, it was French money that helped William to embark for England. There were Huguenot sailors and soldiers with him when he landed at Torbay. Huguenot regiments served with him at the Battle of the Boyne and supported the allies in their struggle against Louis XIV, until the Treaty of Utrecht in 1713 marked the overthrow of his schemes and hopes. There can be no question that in military science and morale France had been half a century ahead of the rest of Europe and it was partly through the refugee soldiers that the methods of Turenne and Vauban, so successful in their day, passed to the enemies of France.

The Huguenots wherever they went took their trade secrets in the making of silk, cloth, and felt hats. Besides the French were good farmers and taught the Hollanders how to grow roses, carnations, and honeysuckle. (It was not long before the Dutch outstripped their teachers.)

Their thinking affected natural history, medicine, and mathematics. Jacques Bunard, the mathematician, and Lyonnet, a naturalist, were both Huguenots while Pierre Bayle was outstanding in the history of thought. Academies were expressly established at Leyden, Rotterdam, and Utrecht, in which the more distinguished of the banished ministers were appointed to professors' chairs, whilst others were distributed throughout the principal towns and placed in charge of Protestant churches.

"A French preacher, Jacques Saurin—who in Geneva had already stirred up such enthusiasm that people fought in the streets to force their way into the Cathedral, who later in London had transformed British phlegm into its opposite—this Saurin in 1705 called to The Hague for help, set the style not only for Dutch sermons ever since, but in many respects for Dutch literature as well." [11]

Another important feature of the immigration into Holland was the influx of a large number of the best sailors of France, from the coasts of Guienne, Saintonge, the town of La Rochelle, Poitou, and Normandy, together with a still larger number of veteran officers and soldiers of the French army. The accession of refugees had the effect of adding greatly to the strength of both the army and navy and later exercised an important influence on the political history both of Holland and England.

At one time the number of Huguenots became so great that the Dutch Government took some hundreds to the Cape of Good Hope and settled them on the Berg River at Paarl. Many years later their descendants fought with the Boers against Britain showing how well they had integrated.

Denmark, Sweden, Iceland, Russia, and Switzerland

Denmark and Sweden did not welcome Huguenots because they were Lutherans and opposed to Calvinism. Besides, Denmark was in the pay of France.

Huguenots went to Iceland and introduced the manufacture of flax and hemp.

A considerable number went even to Russia where their numbers were large enough to form a French Protestant church in St. Petersburg.

Because of being so close to France, also by being partly Protestant, it was inevitable that many refugees should go to Switzerland. During a period of five weeks following the Revocation some eight thousand passed through Geneva on their way to Eastern Switzerland or Germany. Many went to Berne in spite of the threats of Louis XIV, in fact the Government in Berne was in grave danger of calling down the wrath of the French King but it stood firm.

HUGUENOTS IN SOUTH AFRICA

"The story of the Huguenots at the Cape actually covers the last ten years of the seventeenth century and the first decade of the eighteenth. After that they merged into the racial stock which we today simply known as South Africa." [1]

The first European settlement was established at the Cape of Good Hope in 1652, when the Dutch East India Company, which was perhaps the most powerful association of its kind in all history, set up a revictualling station and a safe anchorage for its trading fleet operating on the Cape route to India. At first this was meant to be a half-way station, but settlement soon followed and suitable colonists were sought such as those who knew agriculture, vine culture, and fruit growing.

At that time part of the Netherlands—now part of Belgium —was settled by so many French-speaking Walloons that the authorities were embarrassed to accommodate them; hence, when this call came from the Cape for settlers, officials took steps to select potential colonists from them. The result was that the first Huguenots left Holland on the 31st of December, 1687, and seven months later arrived at the Cape.

"This settlement formed at the Cape of Good Hope was of considerable importance. It was led by a nephew of Admiral Duquesne, and included members of some of the most distinguished families of France—du Plessis de Mornay, Roubaix de la Fontaine, de Chavannes, de Villiers, Du Pré, Le Roux, Rousseau, d'Abling, de Cilliers, Le Sueur, Maudé, and many more. The names of some of these are to be found among the roll of governors of the colony under the Dutch. The refugees settled mostly in the Berg Valley, afterwards known as the Franch Valley and now as de Fransche Hoek." [2] Here they lived and multiplied and forgot the brilliant saloons of the Tuileries. It is said that Napoleon I in the early part of his reign wished to rally to his standard all the old families wherever scattered. He offered to de Plessis the restoration of his family title and estates but the now

Cape Boer turned down the offer preferring his own quiet vineyard.

These settlers were established among the Dutch and other farmers in order to fuse the different European elements. Since Huguenots as a rule made no effort to maintain themselves as an isolated group, in a quarter of a century they had become entirely one in thought and patriotism with the rest of the population. Religious observances, however, were a universal rule of daily life and had a profound influence on the thoughts of the people generally, although few in number themselves.

"The Huguenots were, however, a good and industrious people, and were settled in regions where they could adapt themselves to their environment and derive the greatest benefits from the soil. They became prosperous and played an ever-increasing part in the life of the community of which they had become a part. Their contribution to the development of their new fatherland was significant, and their descendants have continued to play an important part in the life of the South African people—of which they are members." [3]

Many outstanding figures in South African life have been descendants of these settlers. The de Villiers family provided two Chief Justices of South Africa. This family originated at La Rochelle in France. Pierre, the first to come, married twice, had twenty-five children, and lived to see his hundredth grandchild. General Smuts was a Huguenot on his mother's side; also President Malan.

In the Western Province town and district is a city named 'Franschhock' which means French Corner and plays an important part in the wine industry of the country. All in all, although the Huguenots who migrated to South Africa were comparatively few in numbers, their contribution as in other parts of the world where they settled was very great, largely because of their willingness to assimilate with the people among whom they settled.

In 1682 Benjamin Raulé made the first Prussian colonization in Africa (Guinea). He was a Dutch merchantman, director of Company Jacob Buriette from Aachen.

PART FOUR

The Trail crosses the Atlantic

HUGUENOTS IN AMERICAN COLONIES

Woodrow Wilson once wrote : "The Tudor monarchs had, it is true, established a political absoluteism; but, they had, nevertheless, somehow stirred individual initiative in their subjects in the process. In France, meanwhile, individual initiative had been stamped out, and the authority of the church and state consolidated to command and to control every undertaking. France sent official fleets to America and established government posts; while England licensed trading companies and left the colonists who went to America in their own interest, to serve that interest by succeeding in their own way. The French colonies expired under careful official nursing, the English colonies throve under a 'salutary neglect'. A churchly and official race could not win America. The task called for hard-headed business sense, patient, practical sagacity, and men free to follow their own interest by their own means."[1] Such were the Huguenots who came to America and who later in a number of cases took an active part in the Revolutionary War.

The French Protestant settlements in America divide themselves into two classes : those of choice and those of necessity. The former extend from the middle of the sixteenth century down to the capture of New York by the English in 1664; the latter comprise all those dating from the increasing severity of repression that heralded the Dragonnades after the Revocation of the Edict of Nantes to the end. The former were planned migrations but were complete failures due to being exterminated by foreign groups; the latter were desperate attempts of ruined exiles to find new homes and these were reasonably successful.

The first attempt at creating a New World asylum for Huguenots was made in 1555 when Nicholas Durand de Ville-gagnon pretended to undertake it for Coligny and settled a colony in Rio de Janeiro harbour, Brazil. But it was half-Catholic; Ville-gagnon was a scamp who persecuted and scattered the Protestants. He caused the death by drowning of Pierre Bourdon, Jean de Bordel, and Mathieu Verneiul who were the first martyrs to the Protestant cause in the New World. Then Villegagnon deserted the colony, and it was finally wiped out by the Portuguese in 1567.

South Carolina

A more honest attempt was made by Jean de Ribault in 1562 at Port Royal, South Carolina, on the St. John's River where Fort Charles was built. He was sent out by Coligny and Ribault took possession in the name of France. The civil war in France between Protestants and Roman Catholics caused Ribault to return home hurriedly to assist the Prince de Condé with the result that the small colony went to pieces.

In 1564 Coligny sent out Laudonnière who made a settlement on the St. John's River and called it La Carolina, but it did not prosper. Jean Ribault came out again, this time with seven vessels and a thousand men, many of whom were nobility. Ships under Ribault's command being wrecked at sea, the Spaniards captured La Carolina and massacred the inhabitants. Ribault returned to find the place in the hands of Spaniards, made a treaty with them, but he and his men were all killed.

The first permanent colony in South Carolina was established at Port Royal in 1670 by William Sayle. It was made up of English Cavaliers and Puritans and some Dutch from New Amsterdam who came and settled Charletown in 1679. French refugees came in, encouraged by Charles II. Many came after the Revocation of 1685 but were resented by the English until 1696 when the French were given the same rights as the English.

After the Revocation there was an influx to South Carolina, and three congregations were formed: Orange, St. John's,

Berkely, and one at Jamestown on the Santee. To the latter place came Pierre de St. Julien, his brother Louis, their brother-in-law, René Ravenal, and Samuel Bordieu, all wealthy nobility, from the town of Vitre in Bretagny.

South Carolina was once styled 'The Home of the Huguenots'. Its climate and soil suited them. Nearly a thousand came from the ports of Holland alone, beginning about 1686. During the reign of James II many Englishmen and Huguenots left England fearing persecution. Three colonies were established: Orange Quarter on the Cooper River where they planted olive, vine, and mulberry; Santee; and one at Charleston, the latter the richest and most populous. There were seven centres of Huguenots in South Carolina. Many of these eventually joined the Episcopal Church. In Charleston a Huguenot Church still exists. Later a colony was established at Perrysburg on the Savannah and New Bordeaux in Abbeville County.

Henry Laurens and John Huger were two leaders of the Colonials while Francis Marion was called the Garibaldi of America. Born in 1733 he went to the West Indies. In 1759 he was a volunteer and became a Lieutenant. In 1775 he was made Captain of a regiment and later led Marion's Brigade, all the officers of which being French. Due to Marion's bravery, they had remarkable victories and, because of establishing himself in a swamp, he became known as the 'Swamp Fox'.

By many historians John C. Calhoun is considered as having the keenest intellect ever brought into the service of the United States government, prior to Woodrow Wilson. He with Clay and Webster were the master minds of American political history during the early years of the nineteenth century. Calhoun was a powerful advocate of state's rights and an ardent advocate of slavery and the Southern cause. He died in 1850.

North Carolina

The first settlement in North Carolina was on the Trent River in 1707, and was made an offshoot of the colony at Mannakin

Town on the James in Virginia. It was founded by Philippe de Richebourg, one of the three ministers who came with the Huguenots to Virginia. He later joined the colony on the Santee River, South Carolina, where he became an Anglican and served until his death in 1718.

New England

Now let us turn to New England. One of the men who made the voyage on the *Mayflower* in 1620 was generally known by the Anglo-Saxon name of William Mullins. His daughter Priscilla later married John Alden after a courtship which Longfellow has romanticized. Mullins was a Huguenot refugee; his name originally was Molines. Some persons maintain that John Alden also was Huguenot. (A fourteenth generation descendant, Dana Wilson, lives at Delhi, Ontario.) This is not unlikely because the Pilgrim Fathers remained some time before setting out for America at Leyden, Holland, which was a Huguenot refugee centre.

"One year later, a nineteen-year-old French youth of noble birth arrived at Plymouth. Born in Holland, where his parents had fled because of their faith, he had sailed with the Pilgrims from Delfthaven to Southampton, but when the *Speedwell*—intended to accompany the *Mayflower*—proved unseaworthy, he had to wait in England for another ship to be fitted out. His family's name was de Lannoy; among the *Forticue's* passengers he was listed as Philip De-La-Noy, and his descendants shortened the name to Delano."[2] This name became better known when associated with the Roosevelt family.

In 1660 some families came to Salem from the Channel Islands, having fled there from France. In 1662 Dr. John Foutou of La Rochelle petitioned the governors of Massachusetts to bring some religious refugees. This was granted and many came. In 1680 permission was given to bring refugees to Boston and prior to 1690 hundreds more came.

The Huguenots organized a congregation in Boston as early

as 1685. In 1705 a site for a church was chosen, and the building erected in 1715. Rev. Laurent du Bois was the first pastor, followed by Rev. David de Bon Repos, a refugee minister from St. Christopher in the Antilles. In 1696 Bon Repos was succeeded by Rev. Pierre Daille who had ministered to a congregation in New York. In 1715 he died to be followed by André Le Mercier, a native of Caën in Normandy. In 1748 the church as such ceased to exist.

In 1687 fifteen families under Rev. Daniel Bondet made a settlement in the 'Nipmuck' country about 75 miles west of Boston where they with others founded New Oxford. Gabriel Bernon was a prime mover in this Oxford settlement. A refugee from La Rochelle, he came to London in 1687 and arranged the settlement under Du Tuffeau. Daniel Bondet was a member and it was quite successful until in 1694 when a band of Indians swept down on the colony and murdered several persons. In 1696 the Indians came again, struck again, and the colony abandoned the settlement. The following members retired to Boston : Sigourney, Germon, Johonnat, Boutineau, Dupeul, Cassaneau, Grignon, Barbut, Monther, Canton, Maillet, and Mousset.

In 1699 Bernon attempted a revival which was quite successful until the Jesuits again inflamed the Indians and, after the Deerfield Massacre, where over one hundred and fifty persons were slain or taken prisoner, the settlement was abandoned again in 1704 never to be rebuilt. Many of those who escaped took refuge in Milford, Connecticut. Many small groups settled in Rhode Island ; one of these had a miserable history, being defrauded by a New England company organized expressly to sell to innocent foreigners a tract of land to which it had no title. In Connecticut, Hartford and Milford received the greatest number.

Gabriel Bernon was born in 1644, the son of André, a Burgundian Count, who went to Canada and became the principal merchant in the Colony. But being a Protestant he became non persona grata and was given notice to quit. This he did and on his return to La Rochelle was thrown into prison from which he escaped to Holland in 1686, thence to London. In 1688 he went to Boston where he became a leading citizen and traded extensively with England, the West Indies, and Nova Scotia. He assisted the expedition to Port Royal. He removed to Rhode Island where his only son was lost at sea. He founded a number of churches—he became an Anglican—such as Trinity Church in Newport, St. Paul's Church in Kingston, and St. John's Church in Providence. He died in 1736 when 91 years of age.

The Narragansett Settlement (Rhode Island)

In 1686 a body of Huguenots in London made arrangements with the 'Atherton Company' which claimed the ownership of the 'Narragansett Country'. There were forty-eight families: ten of whom came from La Rochelle, ten from Saintonge, ten from Poitou. They built homes, planted grapes, mulberry trees, but in five years they found they did not own the land and they had to leave, some going to New York City, some to New Rochelle, some to Boston, Oxford, and South Carolina.

Pierre Baudoin was a physician who came from La Rochelle in 1685 to New England. His ancestry goes back to Balwin, Prince of Flanders in 862. Pierre married the daughter of Jean Bureau, mayor of La Rochelle. In 1687 Pierre Baudoin was granted land on Casco Bay, Maine, where he remained until 1690 when he and his family came to Boston where he lived until his death in 1706. His eldest son, James, was born in La Rochelle and, becoming head of the family, changed his name to Bowdoin. His younger son James born in 1726 graduated from Harvard, became an intimate friend of Benjamin Franklin, a Governor of the State, and the founder of Bowdoin College. His son, James, endowed the College.

Some Bostonians of Note

Rev. Peter Daille came to America in 1682 sent out by the Bishop of London to work among the Huguenots. He was at one time professor at the University of Saumur and has been called the founder of the French Reformed Church in America. He came to Boston after thirteen years in New York where preaching was in Dutch and French to congregations in Manhattan, Staten Island, Long Island, Wiltqyck (Kingston), Rondout, and New Rochelle. In 1659 a New York congregation was organized and in 1682 Daille came and reorganized the church, stressing laymen (anciens) elected by the congregation. They with the pastor and *lecteur* or *chantre* formed the church government. Daille founded French churches in Hackensack, Staten Island, and New Paltz; also in 1688 the Marketfield Street Church (Petticoat). In 1704 a stone building was erected on Pine Street—l'Eglise du St. Esprit, which became Episcopalian.

In Boston a church was built in 1715 with Van der Bosch (Du Bois) in charge but he was unpopular and David Bonrepos took over but he left after a year for New Rochelle, Staten Island, and New Paltz. Pastor Daille served for nineteen years as pastor of the Boston church. He was followed by André Le Mercier who held the pastorate for thirty-four years. The membership finally disintegrated going to English churches and the church ceased to exist in 1748.

Richard Dana came to Cambridge, Massachusetts, in 1640. His father was a Huguenot refugee in England about 1629; however, the name does not exist in England. Among descendants of Richard are Richard, a patriot, his son, Francis, a member of the Continental Congress, and his son Richard Henry, who was one of the founders of the *North American Review*, and his son, Richard Henry Jr., who wrote *Two Years Before the Mast*. Charles A. Dana was editor of the *New York Sun* and James Dwight Dana was a noted geologist.

The Faneuil ancestors were in France near La Rochelle 'rentiers', signifying that they lived on the income of their estates and probably dated back to the Crusaders. Three brothers, Benjamin, Jean, and André fled to Holland where André married and with his brothers emigrated to New England about the year 1686. Benjamin settled in New York while André came to

Boston. In 1791 they formed in Boston the firm of Faneuil & Company. Jean returned to New Rochelle and died there. In 1699 Benjamin left Boston and became associated with a band of French exiles at Narragansett where he married Anne Bureau. The couple moved to New Rochelle and had eleven children of whom Peter was the eldest. André's children never lived to maturity and he selected Benjamin's son, Benjamin, to be his heir on condition that he never marry. However, he did marry and Peter, the brother, was then selected as heir. Peter never married but lived on a very grand scale, became an Anglican, and joined Trinity Church. He was the donor of Faneuil Hall in Boston which was burned in 1761 but later rebuilt. Peter died in his 43rd year and his property reverted to his brother Benjamin. Some members of the Faneuil family remained loyal to England and fled there or to Nova Scotia. Probably no Huguenot name in America is more widely known than that of Paul Revere because of his famous midnight ride immortalized by Longfellow in the poem *The Ride of Paul Revere*. His ancestors came from Sainte-Forye, near Bordeaux, and the name was de Rivoire. Simon, the eldest son of Jean and Magdelaine Malaperge Rivoire, escaped to Holland after the Revocation. From there he went to the Island of Guernsey. Another son was Isaac, who married Serenne Lambert in 1694, one of their children being Apollos, Paul Revere's father, who was born in 1702 and baptized at Rioucaud, in France. He went to Guernsey thirteen years later. Soon after his uncle Simon sent him to Boston to learn the goldsmith's trade where he became a gold and silver smith and in 1729 married Deborah Hitchborne changing his name to Revere. Paul, the third of his twelve children was born in 1734 and he too became an engraver and printed the first paper currency of Massachusetts. In 1774 he became an active member of the Boston League. As an agent of the Committees of Correspondence he made his famous ride at midnight on April 18, 1775, to alert the militia of Massachusetts against the approach of British troops bent upon capturing continental stores in Lexington and Concord. He became Lieutenant-Colonel of the state artillery and accompanied the unsuccessful Penobscot expedition in 1779. He died in 1818.

New Netherlands (New York)

The city of Leyden in Holland early became the refuge of great numbers of Huguenots, the greater number of them being Walloons,* who established a strong congregation in 1584. Most intimate relations existed between these Walloons and the English Puritans who were then living there in voluntary exile. Walloons and Puritans both looked to America and Leyden became an emigration centre. The Puritans obtained a colonial patent from the Virginia Company and on August 5, 1620, left Delft Harbour, the seaport of Leyden, for America, several Huguenots in their number.

Meanwhile the Walloons followed their example and in July, 1621, the English ambassador to Holland was petitioned by them for a place of settlement by his government, their desire being to go to Virginia. The promoter of this movement was Jesse de Forrest, a very prominent Walloon of Leyden. However, the negotiations did not proceed very satisfactorily and as the government of Holland had chartered the Dutch West India Trading Company, the Walloons approached them and were given excellent terms of settlement. In March, 1623, thirty families set out in the 'New Netherlands' and arrived at the mouth of the Hudson River.

They settled on Manhattan Island, now New York City. Some went up the river to Orange and some to an island in the Dela-

* Walloons: (means 'foreign'—welch—a word used to characterize new products imported from the new World) a people akin to the French but forming a separate branch of the Romance race, inhabiting the Belgian provinces of Hainant, Namur, Liege, parts of Luxemburg, and southern Brabant. The Walloons are descended from the ancient Gallic Belgi with an admixture of Roman elements. They are, in general, characterized by greater vivacity and adaptiveness than their Flemish neighbors while they excel their French neighbors in endurance and industry. The Walloon dialect is a distant branch of the Romance languages with some admixture of Flemish and Low German. It was finally as a literary language superseded by French.

ware River. New Netherlands was all under the control of the Dutch.

The founding of New Amsterdam, usually supposed to be by the Dutch and Baltic peoples was largely by Huguenots under Dutch auspices. The River Hudson, 'The Great River of the North', had been discovered in 1609 by Henry Hudson, an Englishman, but Manhattan Island had become a trading post for Amsterdam firms and so when the first shipload of Huguenot emigrants came they did not come as strangers for French families had been there for years, in fact the first white child to be born (1614) on Manhattan Island—it is sometimes claimed for the American colonies—was Jean Vigne, of Huguenot parents. Virginia Dare is the other claimant for first. Sarah Rapelje was the second, born at Orange, in 1625, daughter of George Jansen de Rapelje, an expatriated Huguenot after the St. Bartholomew's Massacre, who emigrated first to Holland and then to New Netherlands. The Indians, it is stated, commemorated her birth by presenting to her father and his fellow-countrymen a liberal grant of lands around Wallabout, Long Island.

Peter Minuit was himself a Walloon and the leader of the first group. Minuit's family were Huguenots who had taken refuge in Wessel some fifty years before where Peter acted as a deacon. When New Netherlands had been erected (1623) into a province of the West India Company, that body chose the south end of Manhattan Island for a trans-Atlantic shipping station and for the seat of the government. In 1626 Peter Minuit became Director-General or Governor of not only New Netherlands but also the Dutch settlements on the Delaware River which included part of what is now Pennsylvania and bought the entire island of Manhattan from the Indians for goods valued at sixty guilders (about twenty-four dollars). At the southern extremity of the island he built Fort Amsterdam and at the close of the year the settlement, New Amsterdam, comprised thirty bark-covered dwellings. These settlers found the going hard because, being dyers, hatters, locksmiths, or weavers, they had no raw materials.

In that first group was de Rasieres who acted as secretary to Peter Minuit. Also there was Johannes La Montagne who came from Leyden in 1637. He became a member of the council, a schoolmaster, and finally gave all his time to civil and military service.

French and Dutch inter-married. Peter Stuyvesant, the famous Director-General, married a Huguenot wife, Judith Bayard. His sister was the widow of a Huguenot, Samuel Bayard, and it was her son who founded the Bayard family. Isaac Bethls or Bedloe of Picardy was another Huguenot who gave his name to the island on which stands the Statue of Liberty.

In 1656 some Waldensian refugees located on Staten Island among them the Le Contes-Guillaume and Pierre, who founded families that devoted themselves to natural history. Later members were geologists and entomologists.

Huguenots were the first families in Harlem and fourteen families went to Flushing and introduced fruit culture. In 1677 a French town was founded in Hackensack but the fast-breeding Dutch soon swamped it. Small French groups settled in various parts of New Jersey.

French Huguenots who were to be the founders of New Paltz in southeastern Ulster County of New York State first found refuge in Paltz on the Rhine River. Between 1660 and 1675 they left Germany to come to America settling at Wiltqyck, now Kingston, New York. By 1677 they had gathered in sufficient numbers to request a grant of land from the English governors and on May 26, 1677, they purchased land from the Indians.

The grant of land was given to twelve men in the name of James, Duke of York. Confirmation of the title to the Patentees was signed by Edmund Andros, Colonial Governor of New York, on September 29, 1677. It was due to the fact that Abraham Hasbrouck, one of the Patentees, having served in the English army before coming to America, that the twelve men were granted such a large and valuable area consisting of more than thirty-nine thousand acres.

The twelve men who were Walloons were Louis Du Bois and his sons Abraham and Isaac; Christian Deyo and his son Pierre; Louis Bevier; Hugo Freer; Abraham and Jean Hasbrouck, brothers; and Simon and Andries Lefevre. They held their land in common and the fruits of their labour were distributed by a committee of twelve known as 'The Dusine' until 1785 when the town was incorporated. They controlled it until 1826.

Upon reaching their land on the east bank of the Wallkill River (named after the River Wael, a branch of the Rhine flowing into Holland), they built log cabins which were replaced by stone dwellings between the period of 1690–1705. They named the place New Paltz after Paltz on the Rhine River where most of them had found refuge from persecution during the reign of Louis XIV in France. The street of these Huguenots where four of the original houses and the Fort still stand in their original state is said to be the oldest street in the United States with its original houses.

The following families are known in the Province of Ontario; doubtless, there is a relationship: Rutan (Rutemps), Deyo, Murdoch (Middagh), Davis, Krom (Crom), Rapelyea, Birdsall, Gerrards (Gerow), De Puy (Depew), Markel (Merkel), DeWitt, Constable, Lowe (Low, Louw), Helm, DuBois, Oosterhondt, Bush, Whittiker, Stillwell, DeVoe, Gillespie, Davenport, Mullenoux (Mulleneaux), Delamater, Freer, DeWald (DeWall), Lounsberry.

Westchester County, New York, was settled by emigrants seeking safety from religious persecution not only in France and England, but also in New England. As early as 1642 John Throckmorton, with thirty-five associates having been driven from New England by the violent Hugh Peters, commenced the first settlement in this region with the approval of the Dutch authorities. They called the place *Vredeland* or *Land of Peace*. Twelve years later this little Puritan colony was increased by the arrival of more emigrants from Connecticut.

New Rochelle, like New Paltz, has played an important part in Huguenot history in America and to this day is most conscious and appreciative of its French-Protestant background. Six thousand acres at New Rochelle, situated on the Hudson River near the shore of Long Island Sound, were deeded in 1689 by John Pell of Pelham Manor to Jacob Leister, a prominent Dutch merchant of New York who was hanged for high treason a couple of years later. This land had been bought for refugees from La Rochelle in France who left in 1681 and went to England, coming to America in 1689. On this land there were a few Huguenots and emigrants continued to come until 1700, one of them being Daniel Bonnet. The following story is typical of the escapes of these Huguenots from France :

"Daniel and his wife were attempting to reach the French Coast with two small children concealed in the paniers of a donkey, covered with fresh vegetables. The mother having warned the children to keep perfect silence no matter what might occur, they had scarcely commenced their journey when they were overtaken by a gendarme who demanded to know what the paniers contained. The mother replied, 'fresh vegetables for the market'. As if doubting her words, the rough soldier rode up to the side of the donkey and thrust his sword into the nearest panier; exclaiming as he rode away, 'Bon voyage, mes amis.' The agony of the parents may be imagined until the soldier was out of sight, when the panier was immediately opened and one child was found to have been pierced through the calf of his leg."

In 1692 a church was built with the Rev. D. Bonrepos as pastor, but in 1694 he went to New York City where he stayed until his death in 1734. Rev. Daniel Bondet was the next pastor at New Rochelle but in 1709 it conformed to the English Church as then established by law in the New York Colony. Then there was a secession by the 'French Protestant Congregation'.

Pastor Stouppe was in charge from 1722 to 1760 when he was followed by Rev. Michael Houdin who served until his death in 1766.

John Jay was the son of Peter Jay and Mary Van Cortlandt, a Huguenot and Dutch combination. Born in 1745, his father was a rich merchant; his great grandfather, Pierre Jay, was a Huguenot merchant at La Rochelle, who escaped in 1685, losing his property and going to England where he died. His son, Augustus, came to New York in 1686 and married Anna Maria Bayard, a descendant of a Protestant professor of theology at Paris who had left and gone to Holland.

John was taught by Rev. Stouppe until he entered King's College (Columbia University), when a little over fourteen. In 1764 he graduated, was called to the bar in 1768 and married Sarah Livingston in 1774. He became an ardent Patriot, member of the Congress in 1775 and a Constitution maker. Then he became Chief Justice of New York, President of Congress in 1778, and went to Spain in 1780. In 1781 along with Franklin, Adams, Jefferson, and Laurens, he arranged the peace with Great Britain. In 1784 he retired but soon was made First Justice of the Supreme Court. In 1795 he made the Jay Treaty with England and served as Governor of New York for six years; then retired. He died in 1829 and was known as a Christian philanthropist.

Alexander Hamilton, famed as a financier, was born in the West Indies, his father unknown and his mother a Huguenot refugee. In 1772 when fifteen he wrote an account of a hurricane which swept the island which so impressed the Governor that Alexander was sent to Elizabethtown, New Jersey, for education. Entering King's College, he soon graduated to become the spokesman for the colonists, then a soldier and aide-de-camp to Washington. At the end of the war he became a lawyer and in 1782 he was elected to Congress where he was made Secretary of the Treasury and restored the credit of the nation. In 1793 he used the dollar for the first time. Leaving public life he retired to practice law, but challenged to a duel by Aaron Burr, he was killed.

Etienne de Lancey born in Caën in 1663 came to New York in 1686. He brought money in the form of jewels and became a merchant: in 1770 he married Anne Van Cortland and acquired considerable wealth. He bought the first fire engine and brought it to America; he died in 1741.

James was born in 1703, educated in England at Cambridge University, returned to practise law and was made a judge. In 1753 he was made Crown Lieutenant-Governor and in 1754 granted a charter for King's College (Cambridge University).

James, son of Governor de Lancey, was born in New York and in 1732 became a soldier and went through the Niagara Campaign of 1755. In 1758 he was aide-de-camp to General Abercrombie and by 1760 was considered the richest man in America. Going into politics he tried to reconcile colonists to English government and remaining loyal to England, he lost all his property.

William Heathcote de Lancey, a nephew of James, was born in 1797, graduated from Yale in 1817, and took orders in the Episcopal Church. In 1827 he became Provost of the University of Pennsylvania, then Bishop. He organized Hobart College and Training School in Geneva.

Peter de Lancey, second son of Etienne, was born in 1705. His sons, James and Oliver, became royalists. Oliver raised three regiments of Loyalists known as de Lancey's Battalions. Oliver became a general and died in 1822 ; his two sons were Royalist soldiers.

Jesse de Forrest came from an old French family of Avernes but took refuge in Holland first at Leyden and in 1618 at The Hague. Having lost all his wealth, he yet planned a settlement in America. He himself went to Guiana but his two brothers, Henry and Isaac, came to what is now Harlem and built the first house in Upper Manhattan. Henry died in 1637 and Isaac married in 1641, went into the tobacco business, became a brewer, finally an inspector of tobacco and a member of the Council. Dying in 1674 he left a family of seven children who settled in various parts of the country. As previously noted, Jesse established the settlement at New Amsterdam.

General Richard Montgomery was descended from the Comte de Montgomerie who mortally wounded Henry II, in 1559 in a tournament. The Queen mother, Catherine de Medici, did not forgive him and finally hanged him in 1576. His family went to

Ireland where they won distinction. Richard, the third son, was born in 1738, was well educated, and entered the British army under General Wolfe in the French War but espoused the cause of the Colonists being made a Brigadier-General and marrying into the Livingstone family. He captured Montreal but in an attack on Quebec he was killed.

Philip Freneau, called the 'Laureate of the Revolution', was born in New York in 1752. He was the grandson of André Fresneau who came to Boston in 1705, thence to Connecticut and finally to New York where he took a position with the Royal West India Company. His son Pierre was a successful financier and his son Philip graduated from Princeton in 1771. He wrote many martial songs, edited *The National Gazette*, opposed Alexander Hamilton, and supported Jefferson and Madison. He later went into trade with the West Indies and died in 1832.

The Lefevre family can be traced back to Mengen le Fèvre, 1510, Strasbourg, Alsace. In 1552 the Lefèvres fled to the Province of Nivernois, southwest of Strasbourg, until 1685 when the parents of Isaac (the ancestor who came to America) his three brothers and three sisters were murdered by the Roman Catholics. Isaac, a lad of sixteen, was the only one to escape. He took with him his father's Bible, concealed by baking it in a loaf of bread.

And now we turn to another Huguenot family known variously as LeFerree, Ferree, Ferrie, Fuchre, Fierre, Firre, Ferie, who were nobility in France at Forchamps, in Lower Normandy, with Robert Ferree as founder in 1265.

A descendant, Daniel Ferree, was born in 1650 and in 1675 married Marie de la Warembur. Daniel was a Huguenot and a wealthy silk manufacturer and located at Landau, Bavaria, where Daniel, Catherine, Mary, Jane, Philip, and John were born. After the Revocation they all fled to Strasbourg where they were joined by Isaac Lefevre, a lad of sixteen. Later they went to Bavaria where Isaac married Catherine and where they all remained until 1708 when the father died.

Accepting Queen Anne of England's invitation they all went

to London and then in the Rev. Joshua Kocherthal's party proceeded to New York. From there they went to Esopus (Kingston, N.Y.) where they stayed several years and met up with two of Isaac Lefevre's uncles, Andrew and Simon, who had preceded them and who had been two of the twelve Huguenots to settle at New Paltz. In 1712 they left for Philadelphia where Madame Ferree was given two thousand acres by William Penn along the Pequea Creek some fifty-five miles west of Philadelphia. In 1716 Madame Ferree died and the two thousand acres were divided among the Ferree children, Isaac getting three hundred. When Isaac died in 1751 he owned fifteen hundred acres.

Other members of the Lefevre family settled in New Jersey, Delaware, New Rochelle, New York, and Virginia. The name is found frequently in Canada.

Henry David Thoreau was born in Concord, Massachusetts, in 1817, the great grandson of Philippe Thoreau and his wife Marie le Gallais, French refugees who settled at St. Helier in the Island of Jersey. Henry went to Harvard, taught school and devoted himself to the family occupation of pencil-making. He divided his energies among pencil-making, surveying, and writing, and spent much of his time in a hut at Walden Pond, beginning in 1845. After two years he returned to Concord where he died in 1862 at the age of 45. He emphasized the life of the soul and was a pioneer in nature study. He also stressed sincerity and might be called a Yankee Stoic. (E. C. Guillet, the Canadian historian, is a descendant.)

Matthew Vassar was born in England, the descendant of a Huguenot exile. His mother was led to brew ale to stop the common drinking of whiskey by the farm hands and her brew became so popular that it was the beginning of the Vassar brewery. Matthew was quite wealthy and endowed Vassar College for Women. His example was followed shortly after by Mr. Durrant who founded Wellesley College.

Thomas Hopkins Gallaudet came of a family that left La Rochelle shortly after the Revocation to settle in New Rochelle.

Thomas was born in Philadelphia in 1787 and graduated from Yale in 1805 and Andover Theological Seminary in 1814. Because of Alice Coggswell, daughter of a wealthy physician of Hartford, being a deaf-mute, Thomas was approached to make a study of teaching such persons. He accepted, went to France, and, returning, established the Hartford Institution for Deaf-Mutes where he remained until 1830. He died in 1851.

John Gano was a baptist clergyman born in New Jersey in 1727, graduated from Princeton and organized the first Baptist Church in New York City. During the war he became a chaplain and a friend of Washington. After the war he went to Kentucky. His son Stephen was a Baptist minister in Providence from 1793–1828.

Virginia

In 1610 Lord de la Warr arrived at the mouth of the James River and planted vines. In 1619 Sir Edward Sandys, treasurer of the Virginia Company, mentions vines and in 1621 the new governor, Sir Francis Wyatt, was instructed to plant mulberry trees and make silk. In the same year a request was made for Huguenot settlers under Jesse de Forrest to settle there but because of delay they went to New Amsterdam. After the fall of New Rochelle, the thirty-year-old Nicholas Martiau, the original patentee of Yorktown went to Virginia in 1620. In 1635 he led opposition to Governor Harvey who urged submission to all measures taken against the colonists by the Government of Charles I. His great-great-grandson was George Washington. Baron de Sauce took refuge in England and in 1629 begged to establish a Huguenot colony in Virginia. This request was granted but there is little record of what took place. It was to be in Norfolk County and some settlers did survive.

In 1690 under the patronage of the King of England there were several arrivals. In 1699 there was an expedition under Philip de Richebourg, a French nobleman, with six hundred members, who settled on the James River near Richmond. This was called Manikintown. As previously mentioned, a great number moved south to the River Trent in North Carolina in 1707.

In 1700 four fleets under Marquis de la Muce with Charles de Sailly as assistant came to Virginia, many being Waldensians. These were financed by England. In 1702 they began vine growing.

Because of opposition on the part of the English to the Huguenots, Philip de Richebourg, their pastor, felt compelled in 1707 to address a petition to the Honourable Council for redress in which the request was made that because of dissension in the parish the Huguenots be granted a parish of their own. This appeal was granted and they were exempted from public taxes for an additional year. (They had been exempt from levies for seven years.)

John Sevier, 'The Commonwealth Builder', came with his father, Valentine Sevier, from London in 1740 and settled in Rockingham County in 1745. John was a natural leader and became the first governor of Tennessee. He married Catherine Sherrill. He was governor for six terms and died in 1815.

These Huguenots had located in historic parts. "The suburbs of Richmond present many interesting recollections. Not far from it is the spot where Pocahontas, the Indian princess, resided. She may be called the heroine of her race, and the line is perpetuated through many distinguished families who boast of their Indian blood. The spot is still called after the name of her father, Powhatan, the great warrior. It is now (1843) in possession of a private family and is a well-cultivated farm, pleasantly situated on the banks of the James River. They show you the memorable stone on which the head of the captive Smith was laid. The savages stood round with their clubs ready to deal the fatal blow. Then was seen Pocahontas, in the bloom and grace of Indian beauty, rushing to the spot. She knelt beside the captive and, to use the words of an historian, 'clasped him in her arms, and laid her own head upon his, to save him from death . . .' Powhatan consented that Smith should live to make him and his daughter bells, beads, and copper jewelry."³

A hundred years later the Huguenots came to the James River but they found the Indians still hovering around with their minds inflamed by wrongs and considering the white man the enemy of their race.

In 1666 Maryland naturalized all French Protestants. In 1671 Virginia did likewise. About 1700, many came, some going to near Jamestown, others to Norfolk County, still others to Manikin. Eleven thousand came in four years; taxes were waived and they were encouraged to carry on vine culture, tailoring, shoe-making, or silk industry.

Pennsylvania

Pennsylvania is a state where it is difficult to discover those who have a Huguenot ancestry because many who fled from France before and after the Revocation went to Germany where they germanized their names and emigrated to Pennsylvania along with Germans considering themselves to be Germans. Furthermore, as Pennsylvania had a large number of settlers who were German, the French *émigrés* often changed their names to have a German form. Besides, they intermarried with the Germans and soon lost their French identity. In other words, the Huguenots who settled in Pennsylvania seldom located as a group, hence it is a difficult matter to say that any one county had a preponderance of French Huguenots; they have to be treated individually. It is stated on good authority that a "greater number of Huguenots settled in Pennsylvania than came to New York, to Virginia, to New England, or even to South Carolina, the only great notable Huguenot settlemen in America, great and noble because it influenced permanently the social character of the state by reason of its solidarity, a condition that Huguenots did not attain in any other of their American settlements".⁴

More than a thousand Huguenot families, who had preserved the original integrity of their surnames, came to Pennsylvania in the emigration previous to 1755 and many more after that date. Almost all those who came with the Palatines and the Swiss spoke German instead of French.

Probably the first Huguenots to locate in Pennsylvania were four Walloon couples whose names have been lost and who came from Holland in 1623 in the colony brought over by Jesse de Forrest who made the first permanent settlement in New York. Married on shipboard these couples went to the Delaware River to form a settlement. They did not stay but returned to New York. Fifteen years later in 1638 Peter Minuit, an ex-governor of New Netherlands but leader of a Swedish colony, and the first governor of Pennsylvania, sailed up the Delaware River into Bucks County and built Christiana, a fort and town.

Jean Paul Jacquet in 1655 was a governor until New Netherlands was captured by the English when he became a British subject and a justice under William Penn who was sympathetic to the Huguenots, since, when a young man, he had studied in France under Moses Amyrault, the celebrated Huguenot theologian.

As stated previously, the Huguenots did not settle in Pennsylvania in organized communities and the nearest approach was the one in Pequea Valley in Lancaster County. Here were located a number of Huguenot families of the name of Dubois, Boileau, Laroux, and Lefèvre. With them were also Charles de la Noue (now called Delano), a minister, and Andrew Doz and other Huguenots who were induced to settle on the Schuykill River by Penn, to cultivate the grape and lay the foundation of a wine industry but who later abandoned the project because of the unsuitability of the soil.

Other Huguenot families of prominence who settled in Lancaster County were those of De Haas; Pierre Laux; Abraham Le Roy, whose daughter became the wife of Rev. Philip William Otterbein, the founder of the United Brethren Church; David Marchard, Jean Matheot, Berks County at Oley had some outstanding Huguenots: The Bertholets, Berdos, de la Plaines, De-longs, Loras, Levans, and the Turcks. Also, George de Benneville. Huguenots came into Bucks County as early as 1738 and, on the banks of the Delaware, the Bessonet from Dauphiné, France, settled along with numerous other Huguenot families. Monroe County had Samuel Dupui prior to 1725 along with a relative Samuel who settled on two large islands in the Delaware River. To Northampton County went Peter, Charles, and Abraham Lebar; also the Lamars. In Lehigh located the Mickleys (originally Michelat) and Paul Balliet. Near Harrisburg in Dauphin County we find such names as Jury, Larue, Salladi, and Williard. Bedford County, Westmorland, and Somerset Counties became the home of numerous Huguenot families who came with the Germans from the Eastern countries. The Keffer family is interesting because of change of name. Originally Tonnelier, two brothers, Abraham and Casper escaped in 1685 from Paris and going to Zweibrücken changed the name to der Küfer which means Cooper. This was then spelled Kieffer (Keffer). Martin and Michael came to Baltimore in 1765. Daniel Kieffer of Oley, Berks County, gave ten thousand dollars to endow a Theological School of the Reformed Church. He arrived in Philadelphia in 1741. The first Kieffers arrived in 1732. In 1792, a descendant, John Jacob Keffer, migrated to Upper Canada (Ontario) and settled in Vaughan Township, York County.

Allegheny County received Colonel Stephen Bayard, born in Maryland in 1743, the descendant of Lazare Bayard, the Huguenot preacher of the Netherlands, whose daughter Judith became the wife of Peter Stuyvesant. In this County settled the Larges, Dravos, the Brunots through descent from Jacques Pons, a Huguenot of Offenbach, Germany. The Rutans (Rutemps) came originally from Lorraine; Abraham Ruttan came to New York in 1680 from the Rhine Palatinate. Fayette County claims Albert Gallatin and Alexander Hamilton. The Mestrezat family was also distinguished, particularly Judge Mestrezat of Uniontown.

Philadelphia attracted many who wished to follow a mercantile or professional career but strangely enough they never formed

a distinct community. Mention should be made of Antony Ben-
ezet, the philanthropist, born in St. Quentin, France, in 1713.
Fleeing from France he reached England by way of Holland and
after sixteen years in England he and his family in 1731 came to
Philadelphia.

Elias Boudinot born in Philadelphia in 1740 was a noted jurist,
statesman, patriot, and philanthropist. The name of Peter Delage
who gave liberally to the Pennsylvania Hospital should be noted.

Philadelphia was for many years a refuge for Huguenots fleeing from the West Indies. As early as 1625 the islands of St. Christopher, Guadaloupe, and Martinique had become an asylum until
the Revocation when persecution followed them. Daniel Roberdeau, patriot and soldier, was one who fled. He was the son of
Isaac Roberdeau, a Huguenot refugee and Mary Cunningham, a
descendant of the Scottish earls of Glencavin. He came to Philadelphia in 1740; became the first Brigadier-General of the
Pennsylvania troops in the Revolution and later was three times
a member of the Continental Congress.

The Bermudas furnished a number of Huguenot families to
Philadelphia; among them the Perot family whose ancestors
Jacques Perot and Marie Cousson who were natives of La
Rochelle, France.

The Antilles, French islands in the Caribbean Sea, were an
early landing place for Huguenots. In St. Christopher there was a
large number of them and they built a large church. Here they
remained unmolested until 1685 when Roman Catholic masters
made life unbearable with the result that many fled to the Colonies
locating at Charleston, Philadelphia, New York, Boston, and
other Huguenot centres.

Other Pennsylvania Huguenots :

Stephen Girard, 1750–1831, born at Bordeaux, France, established himself as a merchant in Philadelphia in 1777 where he
acquired great wealth with which he endowed Girard College.

John James Audubon, born in America in 1780, was the son of

Admiral Audubon. In 1798 he located near Philadelphia and became an outstanding naturalist. He died in 1851.

The Perine, Bartholomew, Durant, and Diamond families originated in Piedmont.

Abraham Dupont fled to England, thence to Santee, South Carolina, in 1794. His son, Gideon, invented a method of rice culture which made him wealthy. A grand-nephew, Pierre Samuel du Pont du Nemours, born in Paris in 1739, was an ardent supporter of Louis XVI. Condemned to death he escaped, coming to America in 1799 where he became an author and statesman.

André Souplis was a young officer in the French army, who in 1682 escaped to Germany where he married Gertrude Stressinger. In 1684 he came to Philadelphia and stood high in the estimation of William Penn. His one son, Andrew, changed his name to Supplee.

Dr. George de Benneville, son of George de Benneville, Sr., was the founder of the Universalist Church in America. He was born in 1703 in London, England, and died in 1793. His family came from Rouen in Normandy and his branch had a close relationship with the Protestant Court at Holland. From France at the invitation of William II the family went to England where they were well received. George Jr. was taken care of by Queen Anne and he was well educated in theology and medicine. In 1741 he came to America where he met Christopher Sauer; locating as a Physician in Oley Valley, he preached the doctrine of universal redemption and conducted a school. He married Esther Bertolet.

The Garrigues family descended from refugees of that name who fled from Montpelier to England during the Revocation period. The family under the name of 'Garrick' is still extant in England and has furnished in the person of David Garrick (1717-1779) one of the world's greatest actors.

The Levan family, fleeing to Holland after 1685, located at Amsterdam. In 1715 four sons went to Pennsylvania. They were Abraham, Isaac, Jacob, and Joseph; the latter died at sea. They were followed by their brother Daniel in 1727. They all settled in Berks County. There was also a sister Anna Elizabeth.

The Zeller (Zelaire) family came from Strasbourg to London in 1708–09. Clothilde de Valois Zeller came to America with her two sons settling at Livingstone Manor, New York, then Schoharie and later in Pennsylvania, at Newmanstown, and Womelsdorf in 1723.

The Depew family is of noble origin. Barthelmy Dupuy was born in 1650 and became a trusted lieutenant in the guard of Louis XIV. In 1682 he retired and married Countess Susannah Lavillon. In 1685 he escaped to Germany where he stayed fourteen years, then went to England in 1699 and from there to Virginia where he died in 1714. Chauncy Depew is a descendant.

Daniel Perrin came over in 1665 from the Island of Jersey, located at Elizabethtown Plantations and in 1666 married Maria Thorel a fellow passenger on the "Phillip". They settled on Staten Island where he died in 1719. The family is supposed to have fled first to England, or Ireland in the early sixteenth century.

Names of other families are: Boyer, Rettean (Rettie), Gobin (Goble), Markle (Merkle), DeLong, Girardin (Sheridin), Gerber, Moser, Beaver (Biever, Beeber), Hoch (High), DuCosson, Jourdan (Jordan), LaBar, LaVall, LaMar, Jessup, LeRoy (Konig, King), Dutay (Douty, Doute), Lacrone, Fleury, Coryell, Dusseaux, Espy, Laroux, Leconte.

The Raparlier family is descended from that of de Rapalje, which as early as the eleventh century possessed large estates in Bretagne, and ranked among the *arrière-ban* of the French nobility. Some of its members were distinguished as military leaders in the crusades, others were celebrated for political eminence and professional talent. But in the religious wars of the sixteenth century, being known as Protestants, they became the victims of Papal animosity and were scattered and expelled from France. The family subsequently gained prominence in Switzerland and Belgium, where they acquired large possessions and continue to the present time.

Joris Jansen de Rapalje, one of the proscribed Huguenot race, from La Rochelle in France, was the common ancestor of all the American families of the name. He came to this country with the Colonists in 1623, in the Unity, a ship of the West India Company, and settled at Fort Orange, now Albany, where he continued for three years.

George de Raparlier and his bride, Cataline Tricaud, or Joris Jansen Rapalje and Catalyne Trico, as their names were spelled phonetically by the Dutch people, came from Leyden in Holland, where he was born. The patronymic 'Jansen' indicated that George was 'fils de Jean de Raparlier'. His father, Jean Raparlier, a weaver, had settled there from one of the Belgian refugee colonies in the southern part of England, either from London, Canterbury, Sandwich, or Southampton, where he was born. Jean Raparlier's parents and his grandfather, Jean de la Raparlier, had fled to England after the Spanish capture and destruction of their ancestral city of Valenciennes in 1567, and they had landed in Southampton in September of that year. Valenciennes then a city in the French-speaking part of the Netherlands, was the first city which heroically opposed the tyranny of Philip, Lord of the Netherlands, and hereditary King of Spain. Those reverent martyrs, the well-known formulators of the Reformed Confession of the Faith, known as 'The Galic Confession', Peregrine de la Grange and Guido de Bray, preachers at Valenciennes, friends and probably relatives of the Raparlier family, had found their death and heavenly crown in 1567.

From family letters, in the possession of the New York Historical Society, based upon the statement of her great-grandson Gysbert Bogert, we know that Sarah Raparlier, daughter of George Raparlier and Cataline Tricaud, his wife, was born at Fort Orange (later Albany), on June 7, 1624, and not on the 9th of June as some have said. She was the first white girl born in New Netherland, the first-born white boy there being Jean de la Vigne, or an Finje, as named among the Dutch. A picture of the historical Raparlier Cradle, subsequently used for many children of that family, still exists. It is the first cradle of Huguenots in America and at the same time that of the white race in the Cosmopolitan Colonies of the Middle East.

A number of major poets in the United States trace their ancestry to Huguenots: Philip Freneau, often considered the first real poet; Whittier, the Quaker poet, was proud of his descent through his mother from Huguenot refugees who changed the name Feuillevert into Greenleaf. Longfellow counted Huguenots among his ancestors, as did Sidney Lanier.

Gilbert Chinard had the opinion that "in politics they (Huguenots) did not seem to have any clearly defined political doctrine. The fact that many of their descendants played an important role in the War of Independence and in the debates which preceded the Constitution has little significance in this matter. . . . Members of La Duzine of New Paltz never dreamed of giving opposition either to the governor or the royal government."[5] Possibly this is an explanation as to why many later migrated to Canada.

HUGUENOTS IN CANADA

Orientation to an Understanding of Huguenots in Canada

To understand the part that Huguenots have played in Canada two incontrovertible facts need to be realized. First, no study has ever been made of them in Canada although they have figured in her history since Jacques Cartier's time. Secondly, there has never been a Huguenot chronicler. What records we have of those early years have come from Cartier, Champlain, Lescarbot and the Jesuit Relations, all of them writing for a Roman Catholic public. This is particularly true of the Jesuit Relations for their purpose was definitely propaganda. They were meant to create in France an interest in missions among the Indians in Canada, and naturally anything detrimental for this purpose was omitted. This is even admitted by some Roman Catholic writers of that period. Mark what Le P. Camille Rochemonteux said: *It is necessary to admit, nevertheless, the Relations, as they were edited, do not give a complete picture of New France; they show only one side, the most attractive, the most consoling, concerning the progress of Christianity, its efforts, its heroic struggles, the inborn energy and brave undertakings of the colonists. The rest is deliberately kept in the background, or perhaps one should say, passed over in silence. One sees nothing or almost nothing of the other side of the picture.* (It is history but incomplete history.)

Probably the first and what is generally regarded as the best history of Canada *by Protestant and Catholic alike* was written in 1845 by Francis Xavier Garneau. Comparison of this edition with later ones shows that statements uncomplimentary to the Roman Catholic Church have been deleted in succeeding editions. Furthermore, Mason Wade states that "the Champlain Society translation edition (Toronto, 1904–7) omits friendly references to Champlain made by Lescarbot in his *Historie de la Nouvelle-France*, 1617 edition, Macmillan, Toronto, 1955."[1] These 'references' portray Champlain as an explorer and not as one interested in advancing the cause of the Roman Church. Thus we see that records of those early years must be accepted with discretion.

Mores and customs of those days in France were far different from those of today; hence, it is obviously unfair to judge Huguenot leaders by present-day standards. They must be appraised by comparison with their fellows and according to the code of the times. This appraisal can never be obtained from Roman Catholic historians (Garneau excepted) for it will be noticed as one reads them that Catholic explorers never do anything that is not commendable, whereas the opposite is the case when men of Huguenot faith or sympathy are portrayed. This should not be considered to the discredit of Catholic historians, for it is the Protestant historians who have never bothered to discover the Huguenot side of the story. With this orientation let us consider the facts about them in Canada as far as they are available.

It will be quite apparent that the point of view and conclusions in regard to the religious backgrounds of many of the early leaders

in Canadian life are not the generally accepted ones. In this connection the words of Parkman would seem to be appropriate:
"The conclusions drawn from the facts may be a matter of
opinion, but it will be remembered that the acts themselves can
be overthrown only by overthrowing the evidence on which they
rest, on bringing forward counter-evidence of equal or greater
strength; and neither task will be found an easy one."[2]

List of Governors of New France

1540—Jean François de la Rocque, Sieur de Roberval	(H)
1598—Le Marquis de la Roque	(RC)
1599—Chauvin of Rouen	(H)
1602—Commander de Chastes, Governor of Dieppe	(HC)
1604—Pierre de Gua, Sieur de Monts, Gov. of Pons	(H)
1611—Charles de Bourbon, Count de Soissons	(H)
1612—The Prince de Condé	(H)
1620—Prince de Condé sold control for 11,000 crowns to the Duke de Montmorency (RC) High Admiral of the Fleet, who delegated all the duties of the office to Samuel de Champlain	(HC)
1625—Henry de Levy, Duc de Ventedour	(RC)
1629—Louis Kirkt who installed himself as English Governor, treated the citizens with kindness and supplied the pressing wants of the people	(H)
1632—Quebec given back to French by Treaty of St. Germain	
1632—Samuel de Champlain	(HC)

H—Huguenot
HC—Huguenot Catholic
RC—Roman Catholic

Early Explorations in New France

Two facts about the discovery of Canada are worthy of note:
First, the discoverers—John Cabot originating in Genoa, Italy,
and Jacques Cartier in St. Malo, France—were both non-British;

secondly, desire for gold on the part of Henry VII of England, and prestige for Francis I of France were the motivating influences.

In this study French Protestants will be designated as Huguenots; Catholics who were either nominal or sincere yet willing to co-operate with Huguenots towards a common end are called Huguenot-Catholics. Catholics determined to oust and exterminate Huguenots are called Roman Catholics.

John Cabot (1450–1498), whose real name was Giovanni Caboto, was born in Genoa but in 1461 went to live in Venice, becoming a naturalized citizen in 1476. During his trading voyages to the eastern Mediterranean, Cabot paid a visit to Mecca, then the greatest mart in the world for the exchange of goods of the East for those of the West. On enquiring whence came the spices, perfumes, silks, and precious stones bartered there in great quantities, Cabot learned that they were brought by caravan from the north-eastern parts of farther Asia. Having knowledge of the sphere, it occurred to him that it would be shorter and quicker to bring these goods to Europe straight across the western ocean. Herein we find the reason for later persistent voyages to find a short way to the East.

In order to find this short way across the ocean from Europe to Asia, Cabot moved his family to London about 1484. His desire for exploration was doubtless a response to the Humanist movement much to the fore in Italy about that time. He probably went to Bristol, England, because this was a leading port in an extensive trade with Ireland. When word came that Columbus, another Genoese, had reached the Indies by sailing west, Cabot and his friends decided to push on to Asia in the same direction and Henry VII giving his niggardly support, demanded one-fifth of the net gains.

In 1497 Cabot set sail in a small ship manned by eighteen men and, because of depending on a compass which was inaccurate, after 52 days reached the northern extremity of Cape Breton Island where he unfurled the royal banner and formally took possession of the country in the name of Henry VII. Because the soil was fertile and the climate temperate Cabot was convinced that he had reached the north-eastern coast of Asia. Later he discovered the islands of St. Pierre and St. Miquelon. Although he found no silk and spices he returned home to receive the King's munificent (?) gift of ten pounds for having "found the new isle".

In 1498 Henry VII issued new letters patent and Cabot with three hundred men set sail, this time because of having met a man in Lisbon called Fernandes Llavador, who about the year 1492 had made his way from Iceland to Greenland; Cabot headed for Greenland, and called it terra dos lavradores. (This name was later transferred to the mainland now known by that name.) In hopes of finding a passage he proceeded northward along the coast but encountered nothing but icebergs, and with the increasing cold his crews refused to continue with the result that he was forced to go southward. He continued along the coast of Nova Scotia and New England as far as the 38th parallel. Returning to England late in the autumn of 1498, Cabot shortly after died.

Sebastian Cabot (1476–1557) a son, accompanied his father on his expedition to Newfoundland and is remembered by his report of it. Later he alternated his activities between the English rulers and the King of Spain and is remembered best for the contact he made with Russia out of which developed considerable trade.

England, because there were no immediate financial returns for her Kings, made no attempt to colonize the lands which Cabot had found, although the fisheries of Newfoundland were developed by enterprising captains from Bristol, St. Malo, and the Basque and Portuguese ports. Had Henry VII and Henry VIII not been so niggardly as to advance only ten pounds and five pounds respectively, private enterprise might have been encouraged to follow up the exploits of Cabot and the new land might have belonged to England.

All this time Spain was achieving world leadership through the wealth which followed her vigorous conquest of the continent Columbus had discovered, and Charles V was astute enough to support claims already made of America. Into this situation came Francis I of France and Henry VIII of England. Francis, the darling of the gods, felt that he must challenge the other two rulers and so determined to get into the race for gold in America. To this end he sent Verrazzano from Dieppe in 1524 who reached the coast of the Carolinas and made his way north to Belle Isle between Newfoundland and Labrador. On his return he reported how rich that part of America was and if Francis had not become involved in a struggle with Charles V and been taken prisoner this report might have been followed up with other expeditions.

Nevertheless, fishing boats crossed the Atlantic continuously although they never penetrated the gulfs and rivers. This situation continued until 1534. Francis I, upon regaining his liberty from Spain, decided he must bolster his reputation and decided once more to get into the field of exploration. This was not out of character for him because of his humanistic type of mind : he was fond of doing things differently. And so when Philippe de Chabot, Governor of Burgundy and Normandy, grand admiral and chief companion in land war for Francis I, reminded the King of the possibilities in discovery of land, he became interested.[1]

In the commission of Philippe de Chabot, a Huguenot, October 31, 1534, there is no mention of religion : "We charge and command all the said pilots, masters, and seamen, and others who shall be in the said ships, to obey and follow you for the service of the King in this as above...."[2]

In Francis' I letters patent January 15, 1540, there were instructions "there to construct and build towns and forts, temples and churches for the communication of our Holy Catholic Faith and Christian doctrine . . . and to the increase of our Christian Faith, and the Growth of our Mother the Holy Catholic Church, of the which we are said to be entitled the first son . . ."[3] And to accomplish this aim the King appointed a Protestant and the mention of 'temples' suggests that he had Protestants in mind as well as 'churches' for Catholics.

This is repeated in another document : "As we have constituted, ordered, and established, do constitute, order and establish, our lieutenant-governor, chief and leader, our beloved and trusty Jehan François de la Rocque, Knight, lord y Roberval, in a certain army which we are presently to send into divers countries, transmarine and maritime, for the enlargement and increase of our holy Christian faith, and Holy Mother Catholic Church, be it known that we have given or do give to our lieutenant full authority, charge, commission, and special mandate to provide and furnish for himself all things necessary to said army. . . ."[4]

Charles de Moury, Sieur de Mailleraie, Vice-Admiral of France recommended Jacques Cartier to Chabot, and it is now time to mention certain facts relative to French Protestantism and its relationship to Canada. As has been pointed out elsewhere, Francis I was brought up to be sympathetic to Protestantism ; also, that many persons of French nobility had become interested in humanism, some to a great degree like Marguerite d'Angoulême the sister of Francis I, who was an ardent Protestant, and some, of course, to a lesser degree. This latter group remained nominal Catholics but worked amicably with those who became Protestants. Philippe de Chabot came of a Protestant family, was supported by the influence of Duchesse d'Etampes, long time mistress of Francis I, who saved Admiral Chabot against the Constable of Montmorency and Diane de Poitiers, both of them Roman Catholics. The Duchesse was a friend of the new ideas and a close friend of Marguerite d'Angoulême. Burgundy had a considerable number of Protestants, and since Chabot being Governor of it was a Protestant, it is natural to assume that he would select someone who was sympathetic to Protestants. It was through these two that Jacques Cartier got his appointment and this we do know : that the Cartier family was Protestant,* although Jacques himself observed the Catholic rites.

In this same listing is Guillaume Chartier, living in Geneva, who was associated with Calvin in 1556 in attempting to establish a colony in Brazil. Possibly he got his inspiration for colonization from Jacques Cartier.

Garneau, Canada's first and a very reliable historian and a Roman Catholic relates, "Cartier, conforming to the laudable custom of the day, before setting out on his second voyage repaired with his men, in procession, to the Cathedral of St. Malo, to crave the blessing of Heaven upon the enterprise he undertook to carry out. There, after having assisted in a solemn mass and communion very devoutly, the adventuring sailors received from the Bishop, clothed in his priestly habits and surrounded by his clergy, a pastoral blessing." This historian makes no reference to what was done at the time of the first voyage. It should not be forgotten that the years during which Cartier made his voyages were the years in France when Protestants were bitterly persecuted, and that if one were to receive any recognition by Francis, it would be the better part of wisdom to conform to the Roman Catholic religion. It is also significant that in the oath he and his men took there was no reference to religion; each man had to stand before the Admiral in turn and swear an oath to "serve faithfully and truly the King and your commander".[5]

But let us return to the voyages. Two ships sailed on April 20, 1534, carrying four cannon each and a crew of sixty-one. In twenty days they came within sight of Newfoundland and found

---

* "Cartier, nom très répandu en France, non seulement avec le sens de conducteur de char, mais avec un sens géographique dont on trouve une trentaine d'exemples dans le dictionn: des postes. Aussi s'est-il écrit, indifférement jusqu' au XVIIe siecle: *Quartier, Chartier, Charettier*, ou en latin *Carterius, soit Quarterius, Quadriguarius, et de Carterio*. Le plus célèbre Français de ce nom, après le poète normand Alain Chartier (1386–1458) fut Jacques Cartier, de S. Malo (1494–v. 1551) le hardi navigateur qui découvrit le Canada. *La France Protestante* par MM. Eugène et Émile Haag Deuxième edition, Tome Troisième, pp. 794–795, Paris, Librairie Sandos et Fischbacher, 1881."

shelter in a harbor Cartier called St. Catherine, named after his wife, the daughter of M. Honoré des Grauches, the constable of St. Malo. Going through the Strait of Belle Isle he came into a bay on St. Lawrence Day and so he named the river and gulf after that Saint. He continued westward until he came to a bay which he named Chaleur and here he saw Indians for the first time. On the shore in this vicinity he raised a cross, *Vive le roy de France,* and met and traded with the Indians. Going north he came to an island later to be known as Anticosti, and because he noticed that the passage was narrowing, he realized that he was at the mouth of a large river. As conditions made it impossible to progress farther that year, he decided to return to France.

A year later, on behalf of the King, Philippe Chabot, Admiral of France, gave Cartier a commission to return, this time at the King's expense. Two sons of an old Indian chief had returned with Cartier on his first voyage and, as they talked about gold being readily obtainable, doubtless this was one reason Francis was so generous.

This time three ships set out from St. Malo with crews totalling one hundred and twelve men. Arriving at Newfoundland after some delays, they sailed past Anticosti and came in sight of the Saguenay River. This was where the two Indians had stated gold was to be found, but Cartier decided to press on to the country called Canada (Indian word meaning a village). Coming finally to a beautiful island, he called it Bacchus, because of the wild grapes, a name later changed to Island of Orleans. Here he met the tribe of Indians from which the two had come who had gone with him to France and whose father was called Donnacona and here they found a village of wigwams called Stadacona, later to be known as Quebec.

Against the wishes of the Indians, Cartier proceeded up the river until he reached the island of Montreal where he found a settlement of a thousand natives. Hochelaga was its name and it was well fortified. There is some doubt, however, as to Cartier's veracity when he mentions this village for, whether it ever existed or not, it soon disappeared, since Champlain found no trace of either Stadacona or Hochelaga.

Returning to Stadacona Cartier decided to remain the winter and this he did, but found the excessive cold and scurvy from lack of fresh food were great dangers, in fact, fifty of his men died. From one of the Indians he learned that the use of the bark and the leaves of the white spruce when ground up and boiled would restore to health those afflicted with scurvy, and so using this medicine his crews were soon active again. Fearing attack by Indians Cartier decided to get away secretly and this he did leaving a tall cross with the words: *Franciscus Primus Dei Gratia Francorum Rex Regnat*; no mention was made of having acquired the land for the Pope. Cartier returned to France taking as hostages Donnacona and a dozen Indians.

This omission of reference to the Pope can be explained by the fact that Francis I and the Pope were not on too friendly terms because any expedition to America by Francis was contravening the preposterous bull of Pope Alexander VI which had given all America to the Spaniards.[6]

And now Jean-François de la Rocque de Roberval, very definitely a Huguenot, takes over. Possibly none of the early explorers has suffered as much at the hands of historians as he. Historians of this period have usually been Roman Catholics, and when a Roman Catholic and Protestant comes into association such as Cartier and Roberval or de Monts and Champlain, it is quite understandable that the Catholics would be given the preference. For instance, de la Roncière wrote, "Roberval did not have the least title to take command of the fleet. But the Admiral of France, Philippe de Chabot, had he any more? A rich landed proprietor in an age when flattery gave quick advantage, Roberval had met as master of the horse at court and ensign bearer in the army opportunities to make his fortune. And what a fortune! The seigneories of Roberval, Noe-Saint-Remy, Noe-Saint-Martin, Bacouel and Mauru, and duche de Valois; celles de Seuil, Poix et Acy, dans le Rethelois; d'Arzains et d'Armenys, dans le Languedoc, which made him a great seigneur. And the royal patents, which gave him on the 4th of April, 1537, the right to exploit gold and silver mines and precious metals for the royalty, gave him another great source of fortune where he would have for his associate the German captain Rene de Guelff, one of the hundred gentlemen of the King."[7]

The foregoing titles do not coincide with those mentioned in Charlesvoix[8] for he gives them as "Lord of Norumbega, Viceroy and Lieutenant-General of Canada, Hochelaga, Saguenay, New-foundland, Belle-Isle, Carpunt, Labrador, and Great Bay and Baccalavs". Now, neither of these lists is found in the Letters Patent of January 15, 1540.[9] A good deal has been made of the statement that Roberval was far from being as qualified as Cartier because he was not trained for the sea, but here are the facts about his appointment: "And what touches navigation and the discovery of land, Roberval and all others will obey Jacques Cartier. And as for the land that will be conquered the said Roberval resident general for the King, will arrange for the buildings, fortifications, provisions, and other necessary things."[10] This means that the arrangement was for Cartier to be in command at sea but Roberval on land, and, as for Roberval being given recognition, we have this statement from J. B. Baxter, possibly the best biographer of Jacques Cartier that at this time Jean François de la Rocque, Lord of Roberval, whom Francis playfully denominated "the petty King of Vimeux", was high in his esteem, and, being a man of energy and influence, was available for the undertaking. Quite aware of the honors he might achieve thereby, Roberval entered warmly into the scheme of planting a colony, and was rewarded. Francis I might have thought that Cartier was excellent as an explorer, but did not have the necessary experience to take over the organizing of a large colony, hence he turned to Roberval.

It must always be kept in mind that exploration in France was basically a matter of private effort, at least up to the time of Richelieu. If sufficient pressure were put on the King and sufficiently imposing visions of financial return offered, the King might give his consent and contribute a small amount of money. The war with Charles V ended in 1538 and during the next three years Garneau says: "The party of progress won out. In this group distinguished above all others, François de la Rocque, seigneur de Roberval, whom Francis called the Little King of Vimeau. This noble who was known to have acquired the esteem of his King for his bravery and fidelity, asked and obtained the control of the newly discovered country."[11]

Such a man would find it impossible to be responsible for the act related about him by Thevet[12] and repeated by historians not too friendly disposed to him. A niece or cousin of Roberval was supposed to have been left with her sweetheart and nurse on the Isle of Demons. The lover died, also the newborn child, also the nurse, but the girl survived to be rescued two years and five months later by the crew of a small fishing craft. She returned to France where she told her story to Thevet. The story is very colorful but in all probability apochryphal.

Dr. H. B. Biggar has vindicated Roberval on a number of points: "Through a report by a Spanish spy on the third voyage which was found in Imperial Archives of Vienna in 1910, it has been learned that the third voyage was a much larger enterprise than was thought of by such writers as Parkman. There were ten ships in all varying in size from seventy to one hundred and ten tons' burden, each provided with a chaplain, two pilots, and an average of forty sailors and a barber. Roberval had command of three hundred soldiers, sixty masons and carpenters, twenty workmen, twenty horses, and a number of live cattle. The provisions included fifteen hundred swine and eight hundred beef in pickle, one hundred tons of grain, part of it seed corn; two hundred tons of wine and one hundred of cider, and other stores in proportion. There were between eight hundred and nine hundred persons altogether."[13]

This was no small expedition which probably explains why a man of Roberval's prestige and experience took charge other than Cartier. Much has been written about the delay in setting out, but the document just quoted from gives an explanation. While waiting for ammunition and other supplies, the crews became mutinous. This is not to be wondered at—since to quote the King : "Therefore, be it resolved to cause to be delivered to our aforesaid (Roberval) such and so many criminals and malefactors detained in our prisons as may seem to him useful and necessary to be carried to the aforesaid countries."[14] In order to control the situation, in the summer of 1542, Roberval put to sea and, in conjunction with a notorious pirate Bidoux captured a number of British ships in the chops of the Channel. Henry VIII, who was at peace with Francis I, complained, and Roberval's departure was further delayed.

Meanwhile Cartier had sailed for New France on the 23rd of May, 1541, and landed at Quebec. Here he had to account for the non-return of the Indians. Parkman says that with respect to Donnacona and his tribesmen, basely kidnapped at Stadacona, their souls had been better cared for than their bodies; for having been duly baptized, they all died within a year or two, to the great detriment, as it proved, of the expedition. Cartier stated that Donnacona was dead but that many others had married and were living in state in France.

Cartier went up the St. Lawrence River and anchored off the mouth of the River of Cap Rouge. Here he found some quartz crystals and took them for diamonds; later gathering some scales which looked like gold, he returned to his boats. During the summer some clearings were made and some seed planted, also some forts erected. Cartier went with two boats to explore the rapids about Hochelaga but as the autumn was coming on he returned to Charlesbourg-Royal, as they called the fort.

As Roberval did not put in an appearance, Cartier became impatient and decided to return. Roberval in the meantime had arrived and to his amazement saw Cartier headed for France. He commanded him to stay in New France, but Cartier escaped under cover of night and returned to France carrying with him his quartz diamonds and grains of sham gold. In France he was given a title and spent his last years in St. Malo.

There seems to be some dispute as to how much gold Cartier took back with him. On September 23, 1542, there was an examination of Newfoundland sailors regarding Cartier near San Sebastian on the French border. When asked what gold Cartier had "when he was with his ship bound for Terra Nova, and after wards when he was with his ship in a harbour of Terra Nova, known as the island of Spear (St. John's), they said Jacques came there and he had eleven barrels of gold ore and close on a fanege (bushel) of precious stones, rubies, and diamonds." [15]

Another sailor states that "in that district they had discovered gold, silver, and precious stones, and found pearls, and that they carried ten barrels of gold ore and seven of silver and seven quintals (about seven hundred pounds) of pearls and precious stones; and the gold mine was of good quality and they returned very rich." [16]

No very adequate explanation has been given for Cartier's refusal to return when Roberval commanded him so to do. Possibly he objected to taking a secondary position but there might be another reason: Thevet assures us that the gold Cartier brought back was sham, also the diamonds. Yet we know that Roberval was to have charge of the mines, and it is possible that Cartier thought he had secured his fortune as mentioned by the sailors and felt that he could be independent. Two things we do know about him: one, that he never made another extended trip to New France; and two, that his latter days were lived in comfort. How much 'sham' gold he acquired will never be known.

Roberval pursued his course as far as Cap Rouge where he set up a number of buildings and called the place France-Roy, which, although unsuccessful, must be rated as the first settlement in Canada. Unfortunately, supplies ran out and sickness killed one-third of the colony. On June 6, 1543, Roberval started up the St. Lawrence with seventy men in eight boats to discover the 'Kingdom of the Saguenay' leaving thirty men in charge at Fort

France-Roy. The gold and silver he hoped to find were not there, and he returned to the fort. During the summer the King sent out a ship to bring back Roberval and his companions. He is said to have organized a second expedition in 1549 which perished at sea. Roberval was assassinated in 1560 after having assisted at a reunion of Protestants in Paris, and so passed out the first French-man to establish a colony in Canada.

It was left to another Huguenot to keep alive an interest in America. "This catastrophe (the sinking of Roberval's second expedition in 1549) would have caused the abandonment of Canada," says Garneau, "had it not been for Admiral Coligny. In 1555 as chief of the Huguenots, one of the most outstanding geniuses, said abbé Raynal, the stoutest, the most active, that ever belonged to that powerful empire; a great politician and citizen even during the horrors of the civil wars; proposed to Henry II to form a colony in some part of the new world where his subjects of the reformed religions might go and exercise their religion in peace. The King approved at first this effort but unfortunately abandoned it later. In fact, what sources of riches and power it would have assured France! What internal strife and disaster it would have spared its children! And for result what a magnificent empire attached to the French empire in America! But in this period of hate and passion, the best interests of the country were sacrificed to the fury of fanaticism and fears of an egotistical and suspicious tyrant."[17]

Another Frenchman, Eng. Réveillaud, agrees, for he says, "What a pity that this idea of genius hadn't been carried out! What might have happened if, in the example of the Puritans of England, the French Huguenots had a free exodus to the land of promise for liberty, of conscience and of faith? Suppose at the time of the Revocation of the Edict of Nantes instead of spreading over the beaches of England, Holland, and Prussia, in all these countries they contributed wealth and defence, supposing they had been left to freely betake themselves—with the certainty of finding their brothers who spoke the same language and had the same faith—in that Protestant New France that Coligny proposed to found, what a harvest there would have been from such a seed in that virgin land of America! . . . Thus Coligny had dreamed it and we can never assert enough of what a great misfortune it was from the French point of view that his patriotic dreams did not become a reality." [18]

Coligny's interest in the New World may have been fostered by the fact that he was a brother-in-law of Sir Walter Raleigh who was a half-brother of Sir Humphrey Gilbert, also a great navigator. Raleigh in 1560 followed his cousin Henry Clampernoun to France when he took over a body of English volunteers to serve with the French Huguenots. It is supposed that Raleigh was at the Battle of Jarnac and in Paris during the Massacre of St. Bartholomew in 1572. Be this as it may, we do know that Coligny had an abiding interest in colonizing America and passed on this interest to Henry IV; thus we see that Coligny was the link between Roberval, Chauvin, and de Monts.

Gaspard de Coligny (1519–1572) was one of three sons of Gaspard de Coligny and Louise de Montmorency, sister of Anne de Montmorency, both Roman Catholics. One brother, Odet de Chatillon, was Cardinal of Chatillon, and the other, Francis, Seigneur d'Andelot. Gaspard was made Admiral in 1552 and by 1558 he had become a Huguenot through the influence of his brother d'Andelot. The first letter Calvin wrote Gaspard was in September of that year.

Coligny provides still another link in the Protestant chain. The first William the Silent's parents were Lutherans, but he was brought up a Roman Catholic to inherit estates, at the request of Charles V. His son, Henry, married Anne of Egmont and their son was the better known William the Silent, who married Anne of Saxony by Lutheran rites. In 1573 he accepted Calvinism and for his fourth wife he married Louise de Coligny, daughter of Gaspard de Coligny, and their grandson, William III, became King of England. Thus we see that Gaspard de Coligny becomes associated with Protestantism not only in Holland but in England

and later in Canada, for Van Egmont, another descendant, was an important surveyor in Upper Canada.

In 1555 under King Henry II, Coligny had tried to found a Protestant colony in Brazil. Durand de Villegagnon, a former Knight of Malta, caught with the ideas of reform, had been put at the head of the enterprise. "But when Villegagnon returned to Catholicism he lost the confidence of his companions, and the French, deprived of their leader and too few in number, were not able to maintain themselves in that country."[19]

Coligny then sent out Jean de Rebault, a Huguenot, in February, 1562, who located at Port Royal in South Carolina; however, failure to get support from France together with sickness and hunger decimating his numbers, he was forced to return to France, and but for an English ship, they would have all perished.

Undaunted, Coligny in 1564 sent out Laudonnière, a Protestant gentleman from Poitou along with Jean de Ribault, also a Protestant, to the River May in South Carolina. This colony flourished until destroyed by Spaniards. Garneau considered that Catherine de Medici had connived at this massacre.[20] He continues: "In forming establishments of Protestantism in the New World, Coligny executed patriotic projects, which England came afterwards to profit by, and of which we daily see the immense results. The admiral desired to open up an asylum in America for all his co-separatists from the established religion of the country; whereby, inhabiting a dependency of the Kingdom and forming an integral, if distant part of one extending empire, they might therein enjoy the same advantages as the orthodox people of their common country. That project was one of the most beautiful conceptions of modern times; and since it did not succeed, although at the outset supported by government aid, it was because the Catholic party, which had always predominating influence over French royalty, constantly opposed the realization of Coligny's views, sometimes covertly, sometimes openly. This is especially true of the state of things at the epoch the annals of which are now passing under our review. The long period of time which elapsed from the expedition of Roberval until that of the Marquis de la Roche in Acadia, 1598, was entirely taken up by the struggle France had to maintain against the powers of the German empire and Spain, or by the prolonged and sanguinary wars of religion rendered so sadly memorable through the massacre of St. Bartholomew; and which wars were terminated by the Treaty of Vervins. During all this space of time the attention of the chiefs of the state was absorbed by a series of memorable events, the effect of which was to shake the French empire to its very foundations and the New World was almost forgotten".[21]

Coligny was the leader of the Huguenots up to his assassination on St. Bartholomew's Day in 1572. But he had had a very apt pupil in the person of Henry of Navarre who was just married at the time of Coligny's death. When Henry became King he did not forget the vision of his teacher; furthermore, fearing the Edict of Nantes would not last, he established colonization to Canada as an insurance scheme for the people whose religion he had abjured. Although Henry IV could never be accused of being a religious man, what religious leanings he had were definitely Huguenot. Evidence of this is to be found in the persons with whom he surrounded himself. Sully, his first minister, remained a Calvinist to the end. There was Duplessis-Mornay and "in his sickness," states Viénot, "Henry IV seemed to have recourse to Protestant doctors. Let us recall the names of d'Héroard, or Jean d'Alibourg, d'Abel Brunier whom Henry IV, taken by his reputation, named physician to the sons of France, of Turquet de Mayerne. (The latter, however, was not retained as his first physician because he was a Protestant. That is why in 1611 Turquet went to England where he became Physician to James I who treated him as a favourite.)"[22] Henry IV kept his old nurse, a Protestant, in his household to the very end.

We are now coming into the period that Mason Wade describes as follows: "To this golden age of French Canada its own historians have devoted disproportionate attention; every aspect of the French period has been fondly discussed and re-discussed, while many important phases of the English period (1760–1867) and the Canadian period (1867 to the present) have been left untouched and unconsidered. The French-Canadian tends to console himself for an uncomfortable position in the present by dwelling upon the glories of the past. This very undesirable psychological reaction also explains the tendency of his historians to romanticize the history of New France which in itself is so romantic as to need no added coloring. Many English-speaking writers have been moved by the same subject to romantic excesses. This general tendency has had the affect of spreading a golden haze of glorious legend which clouds the facts."[23]

What Wade says is particularly true of what historians have suggested about the explorers such as Cartier and Champlain being activated by strong religious motives. It cannot be denied that they were present but to under-estimate the pioneering instincts of these early colonists is to miss the point entirely. It would be just as far from the truth to say that the Huguenots were interested in New France solely because they wished a land where they might have freedom of worship. This doubtless was present to a large degree but the commercial motivation was probably just as strong if not stronger.

With this orientation let us look at the next and last phase of colonization in New France as far as the Huguenots are involved. Champlain is considered to be the father of New France but what of the men who preceded him, who selected him to go along with them and who fought the battles to secure money and rights to undertake the voyages? It is something like solving the problem of which is the more important, the hen or the egg. At least it can be agreed that one person alone could have accomplished little and that perhaps they all should be considered on an equal footing. If this is granted, Pontgravé, Chauvin, Poutrincourt, and particularly de Monts should be given equal credit with Champlain.

"It is necessary to be satisfied with Henry IV for his colonial policy; the King took up again the idea of a New France abroad.

This idea came naturally to Huguenots persecuted in France for so many years. They had early asked if it would not be possible to create in new lands a new homeland where there would be toleration of religions that would permit living and working in peace. We know that Coligny had tried to create this kind of France abroad and would have succeeded but for the opposition at court. The honor of bringing back this project belongs to Henry IV. It was his chancellor from Navarre, Michel Hurant, who, about 1583, revived a public and marked interest in this matter." [24]

In 1598 a Roman Catholic nobleman of Brittany, the Marquis de la Roche bargained with Henry IV to colonize New France. He was granted a monopoly of the trade and made Lieutenant-General of Canada, Hochelaga, Newfoundland, Labrador, and adjacent lands and given sovereign power over this vast region. Frenchmen do not migrate readily and leaders of expeditions to Canada usually had to get their complement of people by ransacking the prisons from which they got thieves and desperadoes. La Roche set out in a small vessel and when he arrived at Sable Island off the coast of Nova Scotia he landed forty convicts on the desolate sandbar. He, with his more trusty crew, sailed to select a more satisfactory site, but a storm coming up blew them back to France leaving the forty convicts stranded. On his return to France La Roche was seized by his creditors and thrown into prison, and it was not for five years that any attempt was made to rescue the stranded convicts. These in the meantime had subsisted on wild cattle, products of the sea, and native fruits; however, true to their background they quarrelled and fought until when they were rescued and taken back to France, there were only eleven. They were pardoned by the King and went into trade on their own account. La Roche following his imprisonment died miserably, and thus ended the only expedition organized *completely* by Catholics until 1633 when the Jesuits took over.

"It is not strange that the Huguenots under the protection of Henry of Navarre should have had a special interest in developing the fur trade with the American Indians for to them belonged exclusively the trade secret of making beaver hats which were made chiefly of hare and rabbit skins until beaver became more plentiful, as a result of the Transatlantic adventurers. Their secret consisted of a formula for the liquid with which the furs were treated in converting them into material for hats. England, Italy, Holland, and other countries were all under the necessity of buying their hats from the Huguenots and France continued to profit by this remarkable trade until the Revocation of the Edict of Nantes when the hat makers were among those who fled from France to England. For the next half century, the hat trade was conducted to the profit of their adopted land and even princes of the Roman Catholic Church on the continent had to buy their hats from the exiled Huguenots. The trade did not filter back to France until a Frenchman succeeded in stealing the secret of the formula from one of the English factories."[25]

Two Huguenots were the next persons to respond to the call of 'New France' with her potential wealth. They were Pontgravé and Chauvin who were followed by de Chastes, Champlain, and de Monts, a Huguenot who measures up with Coligny. We shall let Garneau tell the story as he understood it because historians differ as to who did the initiating of the various voyages:

"The Sieur de Pontgravé, a rich merchant of St. Malo, formed a plan to obtain, for his own exclusive benefit, a monopoly of the fur trade both in Canada and Acadia; and in order to gain this end, he took into his confidence a master-mariner named Chauvin, who besides having influential friends at court, had obtained some personal favor with the Government, from services in late wars. He obtained a royal grant in his own favor of all powers and privileges conceded to La Roche, armed with which he set sail for Canada, and landed a dozen men at Tadousac, in such forlorn plight, that they would have died of hunger during the winter, had they not been succoured by the natives of that country. Chauvin himself dying shortly thereafter, Pontgravé would have found himself no further advanced than before had not that reckless officer's mantle fallen on the shoulders of the Commander de Chastes, Governor of Dieppe, who was now invested with all privileges granted to Chauvin. Trading interests, however, were but secondary objects with de Chastes, but Pontgravé, whose sole aim had been to enrich himself, showed to him how needful the profits attending a monopolizing traffic would be found to defray the unpaid cost attending the work of colonization, and persuaded the Commander to join with him in forming a trading society, having for its chief partners several men of rank and the leading merchants of Rouen. All other preliminaries being arranged, Captain Samuel Champlain, a distinguished naval officer, who had voyaged in the West Indies, and enjoyed favor at court, was invited to command an expedition, and otherwise to carry out the views of Pontgravé and the other associated adventurers. With three barks of the pettiest dimensions, each but of twelve to fifteen tons burden, Champlain set sail in 1603. Arrived in Canadian waters, he, accompanied by Pontgravé, ascended the river St. Lawrence as far as the Sault St. Louis. Upon his return to France, he showed a chart and relation of his voyage to his royal patron. King Henry was so well pleased therewith that he promised to countenance the objects in view with all his power; and, M. de Chastes having died meanwhile, his functions devolved on Pierre de Gua, Sieur de Monts, Governor of Pons, and a placeman at court. To him was accorded the monopoly of the fur trade in all parts of North America lying between Cape de Raze in Newfoundland, up to the fiftieth degree of North latitude, inclusive. All Huguenot (French Protestant) adventurers, it was ordained, were to enjoy in America, as in France at that time, full freedom for thir public worship; conditioned always, however, that they should take no part in native proselytizing; the charge of converting the aborigines being exclusively reserved for professors of the Catholic faith.

"Much good was expected to result from the enterprise, if only through the merits of its chief, M. de Monts being a man of superior talents and much experience. He was distinguished, also, as one ever zealous for the glory of his country. The association, formed by his predecessor and still subsisting, was increased in number; several of the chief merchants of La Rochelle and other cities and towns joining it. Four ships were manned and victualled; two of which were destined to commence the traffic for the company in peltry at Tadousac; thence proceeding to range the whole seaboard of New France, and seize all vessels found trafficking with the natives, in violation of the royal prohibition. The two other vessels were destined to bear the colonists embarked to such landing places as should be agreed upon, and to aid in suitably locating them afterwards. Several gentlemen volunteers, some soldiers, and a number of skilled artisans, were embarked in these vessels." [26]

Now let us get a close-up at the men Garneau has just mentioned, and we shall start with Chauvin. A Huguenot from Dieppe he lived in Honfleur where he became a skilful navigator and a captain in the French Navy. In 1583 with Aymar de Chastes he took part in the naval engagement in the Azores and later commanded an infantry regiment, after which he was appointed to a post in the King's household. As a Huguenot Chauvin was highly regarded at the court of Henry IV and was appointed Governor of Honfleur. He became an associate of Pontgravé who for some time had enjoyed activity in the Canadian fur trade in the vicinity of Trois Rivieres. In 1599 he was made Lieutenant-Governor of Canada with a ten-year monopoly of the fur trade on condition that he built a habitation and established colonists in New France. He went to Tadoussac in 1600 with four ships and left sixteen men to winter there. He made a second voyage in 1602 and was planning a third at the time of his death in 1603.

Francis Parkman speaks highly of Aymar de Chastes whom we would designate a Huguenot-Catholic because of his willingness to work with the Huguenots. A gray-haired veteran of many civil wars, he was Governor of Dieppe and wished to leave his mark by what he did for his country and his Church—for he put his country before his Church. He had chosen to give refuge to Henry IV when the Catholic League was trying to drive him from his throne. He was "one of those men who, amid the strife of factions and rage of rival fanaticisms, make reason and patriotism their watchwords, and stand on the firm ground of a strong and resolute moderation . . ." [27]

De Chastes knew Champlain well and urged him to accept a post in his new company and this he did after clearing with the King about his pension. Armed with a letter from de Chastes, he set out for Honfleur where he became the companion of Pontgravé. The second voyage took them to St. Louis Rapids where they met Indians who drew plans of the river above. With this information they returned to France to find de Chastes had died.

In 1604 Pierre du Guast, Sieur de Monts, gentleman-in-waiting to the King, and Governor of Pons, was appointed Lieutenant-Governor in Acadia with vice-regal powers. He was no stranger to Canada because he had accompanied Chauvin in 1600 to Tadoussac and had not been favourably impressed by that part of the country. De Monts, who had been named the first colonizer of Canada—if we do not count Roberval—has never received his due recognition, possibly owing to his Huguenot beliefs. All the credit has gone to Champlain whereas, if Chauvin, Pontgravé, and de Monts had not paved the way and even got the financial backing for Champlain, it is very doubtful if he could have continued, let alone begin his explorations. De Monts played a larger part than Champlain at the start, and at one critical stage he displayed such firmness and courage that victory was achieved in the face of what seemed sure defeat. Morris Bishop writes : "The constancy of de Monts, a necessary fortitude of Champlain, has been too little recognized." [28]

Born about 1560 in the Province of Saintonge, France, de Monts served under Henry IV against the Catholic League and was appointed Governor of the town of Pons. He was a member of the lesser nobility and like most Huguenots was keen on trade and a silent partner of sea-captains who sailed from St. Malo and La Rochelle. In appearance he was strikingly handsome and in character completely honest.

And now we come to Champlain. To quote Bishop : "In fact we know little of Champlain's origins. We do not even know the religion in which he was baptized. His Christian name Samuel hints strongly of Protestantism, for French Protestants commonly gave their children Old Testament names, while the Catholics chose the names of Saints, thus affording their offspring a personal advocate in heaven. Also Brouage, where he was born, was in the heart of the Huguenot country. But these are mere indications, not proofs. We know only that Champlain was at thirty, a nominal Catholic, and that in his later years he was ardent and devout in the faith."[29] Dr. Earl A. Bates of Ithaca, New York, Indianist and student of Masonic history, has reason to believe that Champlain and Lescarbot were members of the Grand Lodge of Freemasons in 1604.[30] Catholics seldom become Freemasons.

"Historians," Duclos states, "are not in agreement on the religious convictions of Champlain. The majority of Catholic historians declare that without doubt he was a Catholic.

"Kingsford affirms that he was a Protestant and gives the following reasons :

1. He was born at Brouage, seaport near La Rochelle, a Protestant city.

2. We do not find his name in the register of a Catholic church where he was baptized.

3. The name Samuel was given at that time only to Protestant babies and never to a Catholic.

4. He married a Huguenot girl.

5. De Monts, who had obtained from the King the renewal of his privileges for one year in order to indemnify himself for his expenses, names Champlain as his Lieutenant. Would he not choose a person of his own faith?

"These reasons are not sufficient to give a complete judgment, but throw doubt in the matter. But let us not forget that Champlain was a diplomat; it is very possible that he sought favors from the Jesuits. He was not the only one who sought interest in the cause of those of different religious persuasion." [31]

Whether he was brought up a Protestant can never be proved, but one thing we do know : he fits into our category of Huguenot-Catholic since he worked agreeably with Protestants and was under great obligation to them until 1633. Moreover, as Bishop puts it : "Certainly he was a competent businessman, scrupulously serving his employers, the French fur-merchants. The interests of the fur trade came first, for without the fur trade, there would be no settlement and no exploration. But the fur trade was but a means to greater ends : the extension of the French dominion to all the barbarous continent, and the extension of God's dominion to bring all these pitiable souls out of the darkness to salvation.

"Champlain reflected that to bring the Hurons to the knowledge of God it was not sufficient to send friars ; French settlers also were necessary to set an example of an upright and godly life. Inhabitants and families are needed to keep them to their duty and by gentle treatment to constrain them to do better and by good example to incite them to correct living. Father Joseph and I have many times conversed with them on their beliefs, laws, and customs ; they listened attentively in their councils, saying to us sometimes, 'You say things that pass our understanding and that we cannot comprehend by words ; as something beyond our intelligence ; but if you would do well by us, you should dwell in our country and bring women and children, and when they come to these regions we shall see you serve God whom you worship, and your mode of life with your wives and children, your way of tilling the ground and sowing, and how you obey your laws and your manner of feeding your animals, and how you manufacture all that we see proceeding from your invention. Seeing this we shall learn more in one year than hearing your discourses in twenty, and if we cannot understand, you shall take our children who will be like your own ; and thus judging our life wretched by comparison with yours, it is easy to believe that we shall adopt yours and abandon our own!' Their speech seemed to me natural good sense, showing their desire to know God."[32]

Parkman expresses the same point of view: "The Christianity that was made to serve this useful end did not strike a deep root. While humanity is in the savage state, it can only be Christianized on the surface, and the convert of the Jesuit remained a savage still. They taught him to repeat a catechism which he could not understand, and practise rites of which the spiritual significance was incomprehensible to him. He saw the symbols of his new faith in much the same light as the superstitions that had once enchained him. To his eyes the crucifix was a fetish of surpassing power, and the Mass a beneficial 'medicine' or occult influence, of supreme efficacy. Yet he would not forget his old rooted beliefs, and it needed the constant presence of the missionary to prevent him from returning to them."[33]

Champlain being of a practical turn of mind understood the mind of the Indian and that was why he preferred the approach of the Récollets to the Jesuits. Garneau appreciated the difference for he wrote, "He (Champlain) had a religious turn of mind but like many of his compatriots he distrusted the influence of the Jesuits. He preferred the Franciscan order to that of St. Ignatius, the former having as he says, 'less political ambition'."[34]

The foregoing authorities have been given to suggest that Champlain as a Catholic until 1633 had a Huguenot point of view, that is, his main purpose was colonization with missionary effort a secondary matter and one that was not to be done by priests alone but by colonists who would exemplify the qualities of Christianity.

Explorations without someone to chronicle them are seldom remembered. Had Jacques Cartier or Champlain not written down their adventures, it is doubtful if their discoveries would have redounded to their credit. The explorers de Monts, Pontgravé, Poutrincourt, and Champlain were fortunate in that there was one of their number who could not only take his share of responsibility, but as well could write a history of their experiences and could gather information of the voyages of Verrazano, Cartier, Villejardin, and Laudonnière from books in the King's Library and publish it. That person was Marc Lescarbot.

Born in Vervino in 1570, Lescarbot took up the study of law and in addition translated works from the Latin by Cardinal Baronius. His work at the bar in Paris evidently did not hold his interest, except that one of his clients was de Poutrincourt who accompanied de Monts in 1604 on the expedition to the Bay of Fundy where, at Port Royal, de Poutrincourt was given possession of that settlement. While Poutrincourt was absent, Lescarbot was placed in charge. When in 1605 de Monts moved back from St. Croix to Port Royal he asked Poutrincourt to take charge and Lescarbot, who had returned to France in the meantime, accompanied him back to Canada where he remained until 1607.

In 1609 he published a *Historie de la Nouvelle-France* and for the same he was thrown into prison on the charge of having written a work against the Jesuits. He was released shortly and spent from 1612 to 1614 in Switzerland. In 1612 he continued his history of Poutrincourt in Canada and in 1619, after being appointed a Naval Commissioner, he married Françoise de Valpergue which gave him possession of the seigneuries of Wiencourt and St. Audeubert, near Amiens. In 1615 Poutrincourt was killed, but we do not know the date of Lescarbot's death although we know he published a work in 1629.

Lescarbot has been variously described as a Catholic and as a Huguenot. Le P. Camille de Rochemonteux, a Catholic writer, accepts him as a Huguenot for he quotes from N. E. Dionne's *Samuel Champlain*. "Although Huguenot, Lescarbot was not a bad influence for colonization . . . He did not like the Jesuits, like all those who ha ' embraced Gallicanism or Protestantism." [35] Parkman considered that he professed himself a Catholic, but his Catholicity sat lightly on him; and he might have passed for one of those amphibious religionists who in the civil wars were called 'Les Politiques'. Certainly his writings suggest that if he did not become a Huguenot he could qualify for our terminology of Huguenot-Catholic and for the following reasons: He was closely associated with Poutrincourt who, we consider, belongs in that category; secondly, he was imprisoned by the Jesuits for having written his history; thirdly, he went to live in Switzerland which was the usual asylum for persecuted Protestants; and lastly, his familiarity with quotations from the Bible is not characteristic of a Roman Catholic but it is of a Huguenot. The following taken from his *Muses de la Nouvelle France* is significant for both Poutrincourt and Lescarbot. "I am not ashamed to confess that at the request of our chief, M. de Poutrincourt, I devoted some hours each Sunday to the religious instruction of our men, both in order to improve their minds and to offer an example to the Indians of our manner of living. And these efforts did not prove fruitless: for several admitted they had never heard matters pertaining to the Deity so well set forth, having previously been ignorant of the doctrines of Christianity, which is indeed the state of the greater portion of Christendom." [36]

Dr. Biggar gave the following as an explanation for his importance as an historian: "Lescarbot had an inquisitive mind and an original manner of looking at life. The result is that, thanks to an agreeable style, he gives us a most entertaining account of the foundation of the first French colony in Acadia and of his own journey across the Atlantic in 1606. He tells us that during the long winter evenings in Canada he used to retire to his room, which contained the few volumes he had brought with him from Paris. Here, far from the company, he read and wrote as at home...

"It was this independent outlook, with a faculty for clear thinking, which gave to this work its special value. No work on the early history of America has been written with anything like the same vivacity and alertness of mind. To read Lescarbot is to enter again into the outlook of an intelligent Frenchman of the sixteenth century." [37]

In 1603 when Pontgravé commanded one small ship and Captain Prevert, a Huguenot from St. Malo, in charge of another, with Champlain acting as official observer and historian, they proceeded from Tadoussac by canoe as far as the Lachine Rapids. But they found no Hochelaga village as mentioned by Cartier. They did hear great tales of large rivers and gigantic lakes from the wandering bands of Algonquin Indians. Returning in the fall, Champlain wrote a book, *Des Sauvages*, which attracted much attention.

Sieur de Monts, having taken over from de Chastes in 1603, was granted a charter by Henry IV to have a monopoly of the fur trade and to "represent our person in the countries, territories, coasts, and confines of La Cadie from the fortieth to the forty-sixth degree". He had persuaded the King that farther east there was a country of La Cadie, a name which is from the Indian word *Aquoddie*, meaning Pollock fish. Sections later known as Nova Scotia, Cape Breton, New Brunswick, and parts of Maine and Gaspe, were included under that name.

Merchants of Rouen, St. Malo, La Rochelle, and St. Jean de Luz were included by de Monts who, however, held about one-tenth of the stock. Stiff opposition for this enterprise came from several sources. Sully, although a strong Huguenot and Henry IV's first minister, was opposed because he had no use for colonies. Independent traders in furs and fish who had been carrying on business for a quarter of a century or more fought the monopoly idea; and lastly, de Monts was opposed for being a 'Calvinist'.

But de Monts was equal to his opposition and sailed in March, 1604, with two ships, one priest, and an equal number of Protestant and Catholics. "Eleven years after, four Récollets came from France who found only one priest in the colony." [38]

Along with de Monts went de Poutrincourt for the purpose of finding "some fit place to retire himself into with his family, wife, and children". Pontgravé was in charge of one of the ships on which were the stores. Champlain, a man in his middle thirties, was official recorder and geographer. The latter relates colorful stories about the dissension between Catholic priests and Protestant pastors but Lescarbot makes no mention. It is not impossible that

Champlain could be mistaken. Bishop states: "Too often the painstaking reader of his works finds patent errors and indications that the more uncertain he was, the more specific he became." [39]

Proceeding to the Bay of Fundy, passing through the narrow channel into the beautiful basin now known as Annapolis Harbour, de Monts named the basin Port Royal and here de Poutrincourt, "having found this place to be his liking, demanded it, with the lands thereunto adjoining of Monsieur de Monts, to whom the King had by commission, before inserted, granted the distribution of the lands of New France from the fortieth degree to the forty-sixth. Which place was granted to the said Monsieur de Poutrincourt. . . ." [40] De Monts proceeded to explore the Bay of Fundy which he named Le Baye Françoise and sailed round the head of the Bay, coasted its northern shore, visited and named the River St. John, and anchored at last in Passamaquoddy Bay. He continued until he found an islet fenced round with rocks and shoals which he called St. Croix and where he set up camp because of its excellent defensive nature.

One day, when a fishing party was exploring, they located Aubrey, the priest of the expedition who had become lost some sixteen days previously and whom they thought to have perished. He had subsisted on berries and wild fruits.

At St. Croix a number of buildings were put up, but it was soon found that the place might be excellent for defensive purposes but it was very exposed to the elements. The winter saw many die of cold and scurvy, but spring came at last and de Monts and Champlain sailed down the New England coast as far as Nauset Harbor. Returning to St. Croix without finding a spot to his liking, de Monts, leaving Poutrincourt in charge at Port Royal, returned to France to find his enemies active against him. According to Garneau "Poutrincourt may be regarded as the real founder of Port Royal and even of Acadia itself, as a French colony: for the destruction of Port Royal (by the English) did not cause the abandonment of the province, which ceased not to be occupied at some point or other by the remaining colonists; whose number was augmented from time to time by other immigrants."[41]

Because of the opposition to de Monts on the part of the independent traders in furs, de Poutrincourt arranged to take over de Monts responsibilities. This was done and Lescarbot joins the expedition in May, 1606, and here is the story in his own words: "Being come to La Rochelle, we found there Monsieur de Monts and Monsieur de Poutrincourt, that were come in port, and our ship called the *Jonas*, of the burden of one hundred and fifty tons, ready to pass out of the chains of the town, to tarry for wind and tide. . . . But the workmen, through their good cheer (for they had everyone two shillings' a day hire) did play marvellous pranks in Saint Nicholas quarter, where they were lodged, which was found strange in a town so reformed as La Rochelle is, in the which no notorious riots nor dissolutions be made; and indeed one must behave himself orderly there, unless he will incur the danger either of the censure of the mayor or of the ministers of the crown. . . .

"And, seeing I take a hand to relate an history of things according to the true manner of them, I say that it is a shameful thing for as that the Ministers of La Rochelle pray to God every day in their congregations for the conversion of the poor savage people, and also for our safe conducting, and that our churchmen do not the like."[42]

Réveillaud comments as follows: "In following this history we shall soon find these same Jesuit Fathers very much occupied with New France, but very much less it seems for the conversion of the souls of the savage to the Christian Faith than in frustrating de Monts and de Poutrincourt from getting the concessions of land which had been given them and having them made over to them in the name of the Marquese de Guercheville, the devoted and approved person of the court of Marie de Medicis."[43]

The *Jonas* arrived at Port Royal on July 28th very welcome to a colony that thought itself deserted. Poutrincourt began agriculture in a serious effort, the first on the American continent; for he realized the dangers of putting all emphasis on minerals, fish, and furs. To this end he wished to establish a feudal estate where men could live and work with nature and enjoy the finer things of life. Lescarbot worked his garden and wrote his books; Champlain established the 'Order of Good Cheer' made possible by the "liberality of Huguenot de Monts and the Huguenot merchants of La Rochelle who had freighted the ship *Jonas*. Of wine in particular the supply was so generous that every man in Port Royal was served with three pints daily. . . ."[44] This was a sort of culinary school where each took his turn as maître d'hôtel and undertook the preparation of food and thus gave proof of his gastronomical knowledge. "Our people," says Réveillaud, "joined the agreeable with the useful; in turn they were farmers, seamen, carpenters, hunters, or cooks. Lescarbot was no less successful in his garden and in mechanical things, than he was in things of the spirit. 'Every day,' wrote Charlesvoix of him, 'he invented something new for the use of everyone. . . . He was just as capable in establishing a colony as in writing history.' "[45]

Everything was flourishing at Port Royal but jealousy gained control in France and de Monts learned that Poutrincourt and he had lost the monopoly. Bitterly disappointed they left everything in the hands of the Indians until thirty months later, February 25, 1610, they returned. This time Poutrincourt brought with him his son Charles, then fourteen years of age, and Claude de la Tour, both of whom were later to play an active part in the new colony. Everything seemed to suggest prosperity when in the same year catastrophe overtook them in the assassination of Henry IV. Garneau remarks, "This calamity had no less catastrophic reactions in the distant and weak colony on the French bay than for the rest of the Kingdom. The intrigue and violence which replaced it under Marie de Medici and her minister Concini, the tolerant politics of the late King, reached even to disturb the humble cabins of Port Royal and bring about for the second time their ruin."[46]

Probably the year 1610 with the death of Henry IV is the turning point in Huguenot-Catholic relations in New France. Up to this point the Huguenots had only to reckon with the independent traders and in supporting them the King ran few risks. But at this point the Jesuits become involved. "The control of the fortunes of the trading stations was naturally distasteful to the Jesuits, and they succeeded in getting support for their missionary plans in the person of the Duchesse de Guercheville, who obtained from the King a concession of all the known lands in America from the St. Lawrence to Florida. Under her patronage three Jesuits were appointed as missionaries in her territory."[47]

This interest on the part of the Jesuits in Canada had shown itself in Poutrincourt's expedition of 1610. Great pressure was placed on him to take Jesuits with him; in fact, "Pierre Briard, Professor of Theology at Lyons, was named for the mission, and repaired in haste to Bordeaux, the port of embarkation, where he found no vessel, and no sign of preparation; and here in wrath and discomfiture, he remained for a whole year. . . . But, like other good citizens, he (Poutrincourt) belonged to the national party in the Church—those liberal Catholics, who, side by side with the Huguenots, had made head against the League, with its Spanish allies, and placed Henry IV on the throne. The Jesuits . . . were to him, as to others of his party, objects of deep dislike and distrust. He feared them in his colony, evaded what he dare not refuse, left Briard waiting in solitude at Bordeaux and sought to postpone the sail day. . . ."[48]

Parkman tells of Poutrincourt's efforts to head off the Jesuits by doing through his own priest a mass conversion of the Indians; however, his efforts availed him nothing for on his return to France his rights on Acadia were bought out by the Marquise de Guercheville who from then on had control of the situation. A short time after, Biencourt, the son of Poutrincourt, was obliged to conclude an arrangement with her by which the priests were to get a certain percentage of the fishing and fur returns and thus discouraged those who might have been willing to participate. Réveillaud quotes Lescarbot as saying, "If it was necessary to give something, it should have gone to Poutrincourt rather than the

T.O.H.—6*

Jesuits who could not exist without him. I wish to say that first of all it was necessary to establish the colony, without which the Church could not exist in the same way as once an old bishop said, the Church is in the State, not the State in the Church."[49]

Garneau carries on the story: "Matters soon came to a head. They were carried to the point where the Jesuits, acting in the name of their powerful patron, had the ships of Poutrincourt seized, imprisoned some and by law suits ruined him and reduced the inhabitants of Port Royal, to whom he was unable to send supplies, to live on acorns and roots all winter. After having thus ruined him, Mdme. de Guercheville withdrew from the Society and sought to establish the Jesuits elsewhere, leaving Port Royal to get out of the hole as best it could. Champlain did everything he could to let him associate himself with M. de Monts—who was then turning his sights on the St. Lawrence side—but she would have nothing to do with a Calvinist. Besides, the Jesuits hoped to form in Acadia an establishment similar to that which they already had in Paraguay and which was entirely dependent on them, as we are going to see, had the most unfortunate consequences."[50]

Garneau adds this reflection: "Protestants, like the Catholic partisans of Sully, composed the most industrious class in France and therefore provided the most favourable backing for progress in commerce and colonization. Their enemies, who undertook to dominate forcefully political matters as well as religious, wished from the day that they were masters in America as elsewhere, that commerce should support all the expenses, ecclesiastical as well as civil, a load far too heavy for it, and they sacrificed, as much by false zeal as by ignorance, the dearest interests of a country in the sublime but blind devotion of the seventeenth century."[51]

Now that the Jesuits were in control, young Biencourt was obliged to take Briard and several priests because the Jesuits had entered into a commercial bargain with two Huguenot merchants of Dieppe by buying out their shares. Thus the first contract of French Jesuits in America relates to a partnership to carry on the fur trade. They left on the 26th of January, 1611, and went first to Port Royal where they found a band of half-famished men expecting succor. Here Bienvourt came into conflict with Briard who continually interfered with the transacting of the fur trade with the Indians. However, Biencourt won out, but the gain was only temporary because the Jesuits in France started litigation to get rid of Poutrincourt.

On the 12th of March, 1613, La Saussage took an expedition to the island of Mount Desert where all went well for a time until a storm came from another direction, this time from another nation, England. Captain Argall, from Virginia, acting on a charger of James I which was supposed to give all the land below the forty-fifth degree of latitude to the English, attacked this colony although France and England were at peace. He took the inhabitants as prisoners to Virginia and destroyed the colony. At the end of October, 1613, another expedition was sent against Port Royal where again, the colony being unguarded, the English moved in and burned and destroyed much of the fort and buildings. Biencourt was away at the time among the Indians, but when he learned of the attack, hurried to put himself at the head of the men to fight; but the English escaped. However, much of the stores, arms, and animals were left and the inhabitants were able to carry on, until the spring of the following year (27th March, 1614), Poutrincourt arrived with a ship that some merchants of La Rochelle had permitted him to charter. This gave new hope and new buildings were put up. Biencourt gave to his father enough furs to cover expenses. "Poutrincourt, after having looked after the establishing of everything, in this dear colony in which he had spent eleven years already of his life, left for France, leaving his son at the head of the domain that his energy had created and maintained. He promised himself indeed that after selling his cargo he would return the following year (1615) to Port Royal, but Heaven decided otherwise for that noble career came to a glorious end on the field of honour. On his return to France he was in effect required for service by the King to hold in Champagne the royal authority against Prince Conti. It is in this campaign that he died (December, 1615) in the attack on the small town of Méry-sur-Seine. He was then fifty-eight years of age."[52]

His son Biencourt carried on but he lacked the credit and the connections of his father; nevertheless, he did his best to carry on his father's traditions and united his fate with his father's domain counting on nature and the opportunity to do business with the fishing vessels that from time to time came to his shores. Thus we bring to a close the story of Poutrincourt, father and son, who played a large part in colonizing New France, men who worked at all times with Huguenots, who put commerce and colonists ahead of religion and priests and thus fit into our category of being called Huguenot-Catholic.

As we return to discuss Champlain in Canada, 1608–1635, we enter the last chapter of Huguenot influence in Canada. From the persons discussed their predominating influence must be very apparent. Even those like Poutrincourt and Lescarbot who considered themselves Catholics resembled much more their Huguenot confreres than they did their Catholic brethren. Then again one must admire the persistence of the Huguenots who time after time had success within their grasp only to be frustrated by Roman Catholic jealousy. "But their rigid discipline also made the Protestants a prime factor in the public life of the nation. It was chiefly thanks to them that trade and industry prospered in France during the seventeenth century—the very period in which Spain became impoverished.

"It was the Protestants who promoted colonization and supported the East and West India Companies. Protestants founded the great merchant firms of La Rochelle, Bordeaux, Dieppe, Nantes, Calais, and Rouen. They established the big textile mill at Abbeville, the biggest in France, employing 1,200 workers. . . . They developed the silk industry at Lyon, the paper factories at Auvergue, the tanneries of Tournise, the iron foundries of Sedan, the weaving mills of Gevaudan, the lact-making plants of Paris. Their strong and capable Huguenot spirit made France into an active, bourgeois state. It prevented the degeneration then advancing irresistibly in Italy and Spain."[53]

The foregoing may be an exaggerated statement, but, if Protestants could by their initiative, industry and skill accomplish so much in France, what could they not have done in New France had they not been frustrated at every turn by the Jesuits who pursued their strangulation policy after there were in Canada no Huguenots to annihilate. Champlain in all his efforts to colonize and explore struggled with them even after he had to capitulate and take them into his colony in order to get financial support to carry on his explorations.

Without detracting in any way from the great achievements of Samuel de Champlain, it must be admitted in fairness to de Monts that if it hadn't been for de Monts it is problematical if Champlain would have been able to get back to New France in 1608. It was de Monts who was the personal friend of King Henry IV, who was always a Huguenot at heart, and it was he who got the King to agree to a new monopoly of trade in furs. On the 13th of April, 1608, two ships left Honfleur, one, commanded by Pontgravé which was to operate from Tadoussac to gather furs; the other, in charge of Champlain was to go farther up the St. Lawrence and locate a place for the eleven artisans he had with him; there were no colonists in the group. This place turned out to be Quebec, an Algonquin word meaning strait, and here trees were cut down, a barracks built, seeds and fruit trees planted.

In the spring of 1609 the Montagnais, Algonquin, and Huron tribes of Indians persuaded Champlain to take their side against the Iroquois. Two things he did not know about these tribes: that the former were undependable and that the latter were the better fighters. Champlain has been criticized for taking sides and forever making the Iroquois the enemies of the French, but Bishop considers that "by joining the Hurons Champlain merely recognized that the French could not be neutral and remain in the fur trade. In the circumstances and according to the code of the times, and of most times, Champlain's policy was fully justified. It was, in fact, the only reasonable policy."[54]

Champlain and his tribes of Indians met the Iroquois a second time, and, because of his firearms, the Indians fled when his first shot killed two of the Iroquois chiefs and wounded the third. Champlain was not deceived because he knew that sooner or later the Iroquois would get guns and ammunition from the Dutch in New York with whom they were on friendly terms. Returning to France in 1609 he reported to Henry IV and being able to get some assistance from de Monts and his associates, he went back to Canada. This time he fought once more against the Iroquois, but was slightly wounded in the neck and ear. On his return to Quebec, he learned of the tragic death of Henry IV who had supported him; then, fearing for his colony, he hurried back to France to find that he could expect no more help from de Monts as the latter felt "that his religion would be an insurmountable obstacle to the success of the colonization and preferring the general welfare of their particular interests, he counselled Champlain to place the establishment of Quebec under the protection of some powerful personage who professed the Roman religion."[55] Thus de Monts passes from the active scene although despite heavy losses he continued to maintain interests in Canada until 1617 when he gave over, though holding shares in succeeding trading companies; he retired to his estates in Pons, in Saintonge. Had he not organized the early expeditions in which Pontgravé, Poutrincourt, and Champlain took part, it is highly probable that France through lack of explorers might never have got a foothold in Canada and England would have moved in because, as Parkman says, "The New England colonists were far less fugitives from oppression than voluntary exiles seeking the realization of an idea. They were neither peasants nor soldiers, but a substantial Puritan yeomanry, led by Puritan gentlemen and divines in thorough sympathy with them. They were neither sent out by the King, governed by him, nor helped by him. They grew up in utter neglect and continued neglect was the only boon they asked. . . .

They chose their Governor and all the rulers from among themselves, made their own government and paid for it, supported their own clergy, defended themselves and educated themselves. Under the hard and repellent surface of New England society lay the true foundations of a stable freedom—conscience, reflection, faith, patience, and public spirit. The cement of common interests, hopes, and duties compacted the whole people like a rock of conglomerate; *while the people of New France remained in a state of political segregation, like a basket of pebbles held together by the enclosure that surrounds them.*[56] (Italics mine.)

What Parkman has stated refers to a situation to be found later than the period we are now discussing; however, it graphically pictures by contrast, the problems that the French explorers were up against. There is no argument that French people did not migrate willingly; moreover, time and time again authority was given by the King for the explorer to get his colonists from the prisons and workhouses. And this was not the end of the difficulties because the Roman Catholic Church insisted on determining policy. The party which sought to destroy the Edict of Nantes in France aspired to submit in like manner the New World to its narrow religious formula. This policy frightened away from the service of France a large number of men like de Monts. "This man," said the traveller Charlesvoix, "was a very honest man, whose views were right; who had a zeal for the state and the necessary capacity to succeed in carrying out the enterprise with which he was charged but he was unfortunate and almost always badly served"; and P. de Lanux adds that a "Frenchman cannot think of it without a bitter sadness; not so much because of the loss of those vast territories . . . but it is a tragedy that so much intelligence and united effort for a plan so fine has almost fallen into oblivion."[57]

In 1610 at the age of forty-three Champlain was alone in the world and beginning to feel his loneliness, he decided to marry. Bishop says, "He made a surprising choice. He found a girl twelve years of age, Hélène Boullé, daughter of a Paris functionary,

Nicholas Boullé, *secrétaire de la chambre du roi*; the well-to-do family is said to have been Huguenot, but it must have turned Roman Catholic, or at least have permitted the daughter's conversion, for the marriage was celebrated in one of the most important Paris churches.

"The contract was signed on December 10, 1610. The witnesses on Champlain's side were de Monts, himself, his secretary, Jean Ralluau, who had made at least two trips to Acadie, and Lucas Legendre, one of de Monts' Rouen partners.

"The contract contained the usual provision for marriage portions. M. Boullé agreed to provide six thousand livres, Champlain only eighteen hundred. Since usually the two parties matched their sums, there is a suggestion here that Champlain made up for the difference by his prestige and prospects. He was a desirable *parti*.

"The contract contains an unusual provision. In consideration of the tender age of the said Hélène Boullé, the marriage should not be consummated until two years should elapse."[58]

One cannot help remarking on two things : the age of the partner of his choice and the fact that if he was such a strong Roman Catholic why his witnesses should all be Huguenot Protestants. Moreover, it points out the regard he had for de Monts. This marriage as might be expected never gave him much assistance and happiness. His wife did not go to Canada until 1624 and then stayed only four years. Returning to France she became very religious, eventually becoming a nun and endowing a nunnery with Champlain's money. Considering the difference in ages between her and her husband, the primitive conditions under which she was expected to live in Quebec, the interest that Champlain had in exploration, and the fact that they had no children, it is not to be wondered at that she did not remain longer in Canada and that she eventually turned to a life as a religeuse by way of compensation.

When de Monts gave over as Governor of New France the choice was Charles de Bourbon, Count de Soissons, another Huguenot, who received the title of Lieutenant-General. Upon his death in 1612 Prince de Condé was named vice-roi by the queen-regent with Champlain as his lieutenant. At this time Condé was Protestant and plotted against the queen-regent. (After his imprisonment, 1616–19, he became an ardent Roman Catholic.)

In May, 1613, Champlain returned to Quebec, went to Montreal and from there up the Ottawa River as far as the Allumette Island. In 1615 he made a new expedition, this time going west by way of Lake Nipissing and the French River. He proceeded as far as Lake Huron and spent the winter with the Huron Indians. The following summer he returned to Quebec where he found a warm welcome since he had been reported dead.

Back in 1614 when Champlain spent some months in France with the help of Prince de Condé, a new society for exploration in Canada was formed with merchants from St. Malo, Dieppe, and La Rochelle. Those from La Rochelle dropped out doubtless because they saw what was going to happen : "that in the future Huguenots would be excluded. This was an attempt at the Revocation of the Edict of Nantes in America."[59] In 1615 Champlain took four Récollet priests with him in order to placate the Catholic opposition.

When Champlain returned from his voyage of 1616–17 he found everything in confusion. Prince de Condé was in prison ; de Monts had tried to hold the company of merchants together but the Estates-General in 1618 had taken into consideration opposition from Brittany against Champlain's monopoly of the fur trade. Champlain won out and the expedition was set up on a grand scale, but nothing happened until 1620 when Prince de Condé sold his rights to the duc de Montmorency and Champlain was made Governor of New France and it was made very clear that he was to promote the Roman Catholic religion.

This time he took his wife with him for the first time to a place —Quebec—which after four years was composed of some fifty inhabitants counting women and children, but among them one worthy of note, Louis Hébert. He was an apothecary from Paris who had come out to Acadia with de Monts and de Poutrincourt and who, having returned to France, decided in 1617 to follow Champlain to Canada and, locating at Quebec, he cleared a portion of the ground on which upper Quebec now stands. Not till 1628 was the arable land tilled otherwise than by hand; at that time bullocks began to be used; in fact, the attention of the French colonists was almost entirely taken up by peltry traffic.

As we have seen, four Récollet priests came in 1615 followed by others who raised the cry that the Huguenots made the Catholics assist in their songs of Marot and demanded their exclusion from the colony. This demand backfired on the Récollets for the Jesuits came in in 1625 with the approval of the Duc de Ventadour, a bigoted Roman Catholic. He made the Huguenot members of the Company to understand that they could accept them willy-nilly.

The Company composed mainly of Huguenots had been willing to accept the Récollets and pay them money but when the Jesuits arrived they rebelled. William de Caën, one of the Huguenot merchants who brought five priests and the duke's command to Quebec, offered to take them back since there was no accommodation for them, when the Récollets offered them hospitality in their convent at Saint-Charles. This generous act was their undoing for "by 1633 the Récollets had disappeared from Canada, driven out by the good friends the Jesuits." [60] We shall have more reference to make to the antipathy between the Récollets and the Jesuits a little later on.

In 1626 de Caën was compelled to have a Roman Catholic as commander of his ships and the following year a Jesuit leader, P. Noyrot, chartered a vessel himself to bring more support for the missions. De Caën attempted to prevent him from landing but the Jesuits raised such a hue and cry at court that the Protestants were defeated. Richelieu then took a hand and Garneau sums the matter up in these words: "Richelieu committed them a great mistake when he consented to excluding the Protestants from 'New France'; if it was necessary to expel one

of the two religions, it would have been better, in the interests of
the colony, to let the expulsion fall on the Catholics who emigrated
in small numbers. He gave a mortal blow to Canada by shutting
out the entry of the Huguenots in a formal way by the act of
establishing the Company of One Hundred Associates (an association of merchants to whom the Government gave the fur trade
monopoly in Canada) this joined to the religious persecutions of
which a condition of entry was the object, caused to diminish
their regrets in leaving a country where the present and past
presented such dark images. Up to this time, it is true, they had
been kept remote in a heavy-handed manner and systematic." [61]

This Company which Richelieu established was the first purely
Roman Catholic undertaking and one financed by the Government, that is, if we except the expedition of M. la Roque, which
accomplished nothing. Actually, Champlain was demoted in organizing this Company since Richelieu put himself at its head with
several Government and Church personages next to him while
Champlain is listed with several merchants from Paris, Rouen,
Dieppe, and Bordeaux. The Duc de Ventadour was indemnified
and relieved of being vice-roi and Champlain took over his duties.

And now it was the Roman Catholics who were to have
enemies, for France and England were at war. The first ships that
Richelieu sent out were captured by the English, and an English
cruiser in 1628 commanded by a Huguenot refugee, David Kirke,
entered the St. Lawrence and at Tadoussac commanded Champlain to surrender but he refused. Kirke, thinking that Champlain
was stronger than he was, withdrew to return the following year
with his two brothers and attack Quebec. Champlain no longer
young and with only fifty men and little food surrendered on
July 19, 1629.

"The Kirke family played an important part in the struggle
between English and French in Canada. Gervase Kirke appears
to have been a London merchant and was interested in the expedition. He was born at Norton, Derbyshire, and afterwards went to
Dieppe where he married in 1596 Elizabeth Goudon and had five

sons and two daughters. He died in 1629 in London and was buried in the Church of All Hallows. He and his associates fitted out three small vessels commanded by Louis, David, and Thomas Kirke with letters of marque to drive out the French in Canada from Acadia. As might be expected a large number of Huguenot sailors shipped for the expedition, among them a certain Captain Michel who had been in the service of Caën, 'a furious Calvinist' who is said to have been the instigator of the attempt acting under the advice of his former employers—so says a French Romanist historian. It is probable that the French Protestant sailors formed a majority in the expedition; and Graneur, a modern historian, calls David Kirke 'a Calviniste française de Dieppe'. At all events the three ships commanded by Louis, David and Thomas Kirke seemed to have formed only part of the squadron which consisted of eighteen vessels in all."[62]

Because of persecutions on account of their religion the Kirkes were forced to leave France and take their talents and services to England. However, they still remained Frenchmen at heart and, having captured Champlain, they treated him courteously and allowed the French colonists to remain where they had settled. About the same time Emery de Caën, a nephew of William, was coming back to Canada escorted by a Captain Daniel. In a storm they became separated and de Caën was captured by Thomas Kirke while Captain Daniel, having learned that a Scottish Lord had settled on Cape Breton Island, steered in that direction, attacked the fort, took the Scottish Lord prisoner, and raised the flag of France. Leaving a guard there, he tried to reach Quebec but storms prevented him.

"While Kirke was taking Quebec and his Lieutenant losing Cape Breton, the French located in the southern part of Acadia were engaged in repelling the attacks made by two vessels of war commanded by Claude de la Tour, a French Protestant, who lately had taken service in the Royal Navy of England. This enterprising man, owning a larger fortune, had been taken prisoner in one of Roqueont's vessels and carried to London where he was well received at court. While in England he married one of the maids of honour to the Queen (Henrietta-Maria, younger daughter of Henry IV and Marie de Medici) and was created a baronet of Nova Scotia. Having thereby obtained a concession of territory as a species of fief, in that province, situated near St. John's River, he made an arrangement with Sir William Alexander to found a settlement there with emigrants from Scotland. The ungrateful duty also devolved upon him, meanwhile, of attempting to bring his own son (Charles) under submission; the latter true to his country's cause, being in command of a French fort at Cape de Sable." [63]

This story about Charles de la Tour and his father Claude is one that resembles the one told of Roberval leaving his niece on a lonely island. It must be remembered that the historians of this early period have been of the Roman Catholic faith and with the exception of Garneau have never hesitated to give credence to colorful stories of the defections and shortcomings of Huguenots. Seldom if ever do we read anything detrimental to those who were considered true Roman Catholics. As regards the La Tours, we can quote Viénot : "In reality, the only facts that are known to us (about the La Tours) of a serious nature are : The letter Charles de la Tour wrote to the King of France, the capture of Charles by Kirke, and the inscription of their names on the role of baronets of William Alexander." [64]

Canada remained in the possession of England until 1632 when by the treaty of St. Germain it was returned to the French but it is interesting to note that it was a Huguenot (this is questioned by some), Emery de Caën, who was asked to take possession, in the name of France, of Quebec and Canada. For a year the Company of One Hundred Associates was to get the returns, after that Champlain was to take charge. As for Acadia, Richelieu left it in the hands of Charles de la Tour, but he gave to Sieur de Razilly a special commission to form a company to rebuild Port Royal. This Razilly undertook to do, and to Charles de la Tour he gave a section now New Brunswick, and to Charles de Menou, seigneur d'Aulnay, went the seigneur of Port Royal, a division of authority which caused much friction, particularly after d'Aulney's death in 1636.

In 1633, Champlain set out from Dieppe with three vessels with a number of colonists, artisans, arms, and provisions and landed at Quebec to take over control from Emery de Caën. This expedition is noteworthy for two reasons: Richelieu forbade any Huguenot to be admitted into Canada and the Jesuits came in to oust the Récollets, for, as Garneau puts it, "occasion had been taken from the abeyance of the French domination to exclude the Récollets, though these friars were very popular in the colony because it had long been thought that the presence of a mendicant order in a new missionary field was more burdensome than useful. The Récollets in vain petitioned the Government to let them remain."[65]

This conflict between the Récollets and the Jesuits went on as the Récollets continued to enter and carry on their work. Parkman writing of this period some years later states: "The Jesuits had long exercised solely the function of confessors in the colony, and a number of curious anecdotes are on record showing the reluctance with which they admitted the secular priests, and above all the Récollets, to share in it. The Récollets of whom a considerable number had arrived from time to time, were on excellent terms with the civil power, and were popular with the colonists; but with the Bishop and the Jesuits they were not in favour, and one or two sharp collisions took place. The Bishop was naturally annoyed when he was trying to persuade the King that a curé needed at least six hundred francs a year, these mendicant friars came forward with an offer to serve the parishes for nothing; nor was he, it is likely, better pleased when, having asked the hospital nuns eight hundred francs annually for two masses a day in their chapel, the Récollets underbid him, and offered to say the masses for three hundred. They, on their part, complain bitterly of the Bishop, who, they say, would gladly have ordered them out of the colony, but, being unable to do this, tried to shut them up in their convent, and prevent them from officiating as priests among the people. 'We have as little liberty,' says the Récollet writer, 'as if we were in a country of heretics.' He adds that the inhabitants ask earnestly for the ministrations of the friars, but that the Bishop replies with invectives and calumnies of the Order; and that when the Récollets absolve a penitent, he often annuls the absolution."[66] This sounds very much like the treatment the Huguenot pastors got from the Catholic clergy in France. Bishop makes an interesting remark: "Bibliographers comparing the text of this volume (the *Voyages* of 1632) with that of 1619 make a curious observation. The whole story of the Récollets first coming to Canada is omitted; everything in their favor is removed and the praise of the Jesuits substituted. The Abbé Laverdière, the Great Canadian editor of Champlain, concludes roundly that the Jesuits tampered with Champlain's manuscript. Such a supposition rouses plenty of problems, and authors so treated by their publishers make frightful outcries. The natural explanation is that Champlain made the alterations himself. He welcomed the rich and zealous Jesuits to Canada."[67]

The year 1633 brings to an end a century-long effort on the part of the Huguenots to establish a colony in Canada which would be financially desirable and provide a land where they had religious freedom and yet could remain loyal to the King of France, for it cannot be too often repeated that the Huguenot had an intense love of his country and a strong loyalty for his King. In Canada, wherever the Huguenots had established themselves the monks moved in, built a monastery and, producing papers from the King of France, they restricted Protestant worship until when they became strong enough they commanded the original settlers to become Catholics or leave the community in a few days. This many of them did, going to New England.

Nevertheless, even after they had been forbidden to land, this prohibition didn't last too long "owing to the necessity of the colony which depended on its communication with France— communication by that time altogether in the hands of the

Protestants since the entire French marine was manned by them. They were, however, kept under rigid restraint and forbidden to exercise their religion or remain in the colony without special licence."[68]

Champlain did not live very long to see what development there would be in Canada. Struck down with a paralysis during the autumn of 1635, it took from him the use of his limbs and he died a short time after at Quebec on Christmas Day, 1635. His death was deplored particularly by Indians because he had always been their friend. His passing brought to a close an era of exploration carried on almost entirely by individuals, and as we have pointed out more than once, these persons were French Protestants who were impelled both by commercial and religious motives. With the closure of Canada to these Huguenots the Government of France began to play an active part, but it is not making an exaggerated statement to point out that, if Roberval, Coligny, and de Monts had not carried on their explorations, there is little likelihood that there would have been any opportunity for any French Government or any Jesuit Order to take over because other nationalities, particularly the English, were close by and would have inevitably moved north as they moved south and west.

"Canada ceased to be a mission. The civil and military powers grew strong, and the Church no longer ruled with individual sway. The times changed and the men changed with them. It is a characteristic of the Jesuit Order, and one of the sources of its strength, that it chooses the workmen for its work, studies of its members, and gives to each a task for which he is fitted best. . . .

"Before the end of the seventeenth century the functions of the Canadian Jesuit had become as much political as religious; but if the fires of his apostolic zeal burned less high, his devotion to the Order in which he had merged his personality was as intense as ever. While in constant friction with the civil and military powers, he tried to make himself necessary to them, and in good measure he succeeded. Nobody was so able to manage the Indian tribes and keep them in the interest of France . . ."[69]

But no matter how powerful the Catholics were, it is an incontestable fact, for it is admitted by the Roman Catholic historian Charlesvoix in his annals of 1690, "that the most distinguished officers of New France were Protestant. Here are the names of the best known: de Louvigny, de Clermont, de la Mothe, Colombot, des Marais, de Villiers, de Lusignan, le baron de la Houtan, le sieur d'Argenteuil, Desnon Deignat, controller-general of the Marine, les sieurs de Bonrepos, de la Brosse, Dejardins, St. Martin, d'Aberville, all Calvinists giving a very good example." [70] Salone, another Roman Catholic writer, would also agree: "Up to 1628 New France is, as Old France, under the rule of the Edict of Nantes. Catholics and Protestants are given equal rights. Only is this equality broken in favor of the former when the royal wishes reserves for them the conversion of the natives. But in compensation from all points of view it appears that in the colony the Calvinistic element plays the leading role. In the beginning, the great majority of those who near or far exercise sane authority there are Huguenots. If after the withdrawal of de Monts, the viceroys and their irremovable representative, Champlain, belong to the Roman Church, the largest number of the associates and business agents were always Protestants." [71] And in another place he voices the same opinion: "What a pity that he (Louis XIV) had such a short-sighted view that he didn't conceive the immense empire that he could have founded in America, that he didn't have the far-sightedness of a Talon or of la Galissionniere! What a pity indeed that he was possessed of such a fatalism that he could not tolerate the presence of Huguenots in some distant area of the Mississippi!" [72]

This importance of persons of Huguenot belief in Roman Catholic-controlled situations is understandable if we refer to our discussion of the type of person a Huguenot was and why he was a Huguenot. We need to be reminded that he was a Humanist who turned to the Bible to get his inspiration and learn the meaning of life. In other words, he was a thinking person who, because of his religion, had a keen zest for life for it had a purpose, and this made him an individualist who resented dictation. Besides, he usually belonged to the middle artisan and commercial class with a considerable admixture of nobility; hence it was a natural thing for him to give leadership. Without question Richelieu's prohibition of Huguenots to enter Canada after 1633 was as much the cause of the loss of Canada by the French to the English in 1763 as the loss of the Huguenots by France in 1685, at the time of the Revocation of the Edict of Nantes. Had the Huguenots been allowed to settle in Canada, she would have flourished both as a colony and as a commercial enterprise because a splendid type of French citizen would have been willing to emigrate to enjoy religious freedom. He would have been comparable to the Puritan and other religious refugees who went to the English colonies during the latter part of the seventeenth and all of the eighteenth centuries.

But those who emigrated went for a different reason : "Two thousand settlers, largely from the northern and western provinces of France, *were sent out* (Italics mine) to Canada in the decade after 1663, many of them veteran soldiers who were induced to become colonists by special concessions. Colbert, through priests, told the people that their prosperity, their subsistence, and all that is dear to them depend upon a general resolution, never to be departed from, to marry youths at eighteen or nineteen years and girls at fourteen or fifteen. Bachelordom was penalized, while early marriages and large families were rewarded. Ship-loads of carefully selected poor or orphaned royal wards were sent out to provide wives in a land where white women were rare. Thus was established the French-Canadian tradition of early marriage and large families, one of the strongest forces in the remarkable vitality of this people. Though liabilities in the mother country, large families were assets in the expanding economy of New France, which was an agricultural rather than an industrial society, and had land to spare." [73]

It is interesting to note that although it is part of the French-Canadian legend that the colonists from the first were most interested in agriculture and had a flair for it, this can hardly have been the case because in the first twenty years of the colonies' life only one-and-a-half acres were cleared and even in 1754 almost a quarter of the population was urban.[74] The Protestants retired in the winter to the towns where true to their backgrounds they carried on commerce and were called 'hivernants'. The Roman Catholic Church opposed this move and encouraged their adherents to go into the country where they made less money but where they could own their land and be master of it. Hence they were known as 'Habitants', a name they still bear.

Religious Backgrounds of Prominent Frenchmen

FRONTENAC

In all probability Louis de Buade Comte de Frontenac et Palluau came from Huguenot stock for there is a record[1] which states that Louis' grandmother was buried the 30th day of May, 1618, in the church after having been received again into the bosom of the Church after having been absolved of her heresy. Presumably the family was considered Protestant by the Huguenots. Furthermore, Antoine de Buade, Louis' grandfather, was a Councillor of State under Henry IV, who always surrounded himself with Huguenots. His children were brought up with the Dauphin, afterwards Louis XIII, and Louis de Buade was named after his godfather Louis XIII.

Costain, in his *White and Gold* describes Louis de Buade, the Comte de Frontenac, in the following words :

"There now appears on the scene the leading character and the most colorful actor in this drama which was being enacted against the backdrop of Canadian solitudes. The Comte de Frontenac has been accepted as the greatest in the long list of governors who for various periods controlled the destinies of the colony. He was a man of positive qualities, a curious blending of strength and weakness—in fact one of the most contradictory of men to attain such a degree of fame. He came to New France at a time when a strong hand was badly needed at the helm. If this record reviewed at this late period, seems rather lacking in solid achievement to deserve the acclaim which has been accorded to him, there can be no doubt that he had in full degree the strength which was needed and that he brought the colony through a period of desperate crisis." [2]

This is also the point of view of Garneau and Parkman, but not of a recent biographer of Frontenac. [3] With the latter, Frontenac can do nothing commendable and when he accomplishes something which obviously commands approval he is damned with mild praise. On the other hand, the book would appear to be an apology for the Jesuits; there is never a word of real criticism for them, always a satisfactory explanation for any unusual situation.

Louis de Buade was born in Béarn; he was a Gasçon with all the flamboyancy of the Gasçons. A born soldier he started early for the wars for he was only fifteen when he served in the Netherlands under Maurice d'Orange. Father Charlesvoix, who had no reason to be kindly disposed to him, said, "He had a heart much greater than his birth." At twenty he was appointed Colonel of the regiment in Normandy and when twenty-seven he was made a *Marechal de camp*. Ofter wounded he sustained a broken arm which left it crippled.

Brave, audacious, and cool though he might be, he was a great egotist and was often haughty, quarrelsome, boastful, and resented opposition in any form. Yet he had great charm and was a clever letter writer.

He fell deeply in love with Anne, the daughter of Sieur de Neuville, a girl of sixteen, with great vivacity and charming manners. Her father was wealthy and the Comte was very much in debt. It has been suggested that this was his interest in marrying Anne. However that may be, the father first agreed and then opposed the marriage. But Louis de Buade and Anne de la Grange-Trianon were married in 1648 by a Gretna Green priest at the church called St. Pierre aux Boeufs.

The marriage was not too successful although a son was born

to them who meant little to either his father or mother and who grew up to be a soldier and died fighting in the French army. The young wife left her husband and associated herself with the Duchess of Montpensier until dismissed when she set up a salon with one Mademoiselle d'Outrelaise which drew all the great people and the wits of the court. These two were called *Les Divines* and they carried on until the death of the Comtesse nine years after her husband in New France.

Little is known of the middle years of Louis de Buade, Comte de Frontenac, except that he lived far beyond his means, which of course was not unusual for nobility in those days. In 1669 he became involved in the Venetian War with the Turks when he was given an appointment by Turenne. Records of his involvement are contradictory; some say he was in command, others that his arrogance got him into difficulties. He couldn't have been too much of a failure or else he would not have been appointed Governor of New France in 1672 by Colbert who was always willing to appoint a Huguenot if there were no religious complications.

It is not our purpose to give a detailed account of his ten years in Canada other than to point out some of the highlights of those years. Again quoting Costain: "The success of the Comte de Frontenac in Canada can be traced to his capacity for understanding people. It did not matter that he was haughty and arrogant in manner, that he was sure of himself in everything, that he could be as unyielding as Laval of his rights and prerogatives. He saw into the hearts and minds of those about him and knew how to make them respect and obey him. The inhabitants of the colony, who had become accustomed to mediocrity in the post, sensed at once the different mettle of this imperious nobleman."[4]

First of all, he impressed the colonists by calling together the Three Estates of Canada for which he was criticized by Colbert. His method consistently was to act first and seek approval later, one which got results but one which frequently backfired on himself. Realizing that the success of the colony depended to a great extent on satisfactory relations with the Iroquois Indians, he went to Cataraqui with a display of force and magnificence which amazed the tribesmen and again to their astonishment built a fort in a short space of time. Here he unfurled the *drapeau blanc*, actually the flag of the Huguenots. (This flag has since become the official flag of the Province of Quebec.)

The building of this fort provided a great bone of contention since it was built contrary to the orders of Colbert—who was thousands of miles from the situation—and the fur merchants of Montreal who were fearful of losing their control of the fur trade. Frontenac was opposed to Laval, the bishop, of whom Garneau wrote: "He was persuaded that it was impossible for him to err in his judgments because he acted for the Church, a belief which took him far afield and he undertook to do things which would have been considered outrageous in Europe."[5] The Governor of Montreal, Perrot, because of the fur trade was an opponent of Frontenac. Their relations see-sawed back and forth until Perrot finally won out because supported by Duchesneau, the Intendant, who was also at odds with Frontenac. Charges and counter-charges went back and forth to Colbert about who was profiting by the fur trade. Frontenac was accused but it has never been fully proved that he encouraged these *coureurs de bois* to do business with the Indians from which he was reimbursed. According to the ethics of those times, it would be strange if Frontenac did not profit by his position in like manner to the clergy. In all fairness, judgment should be according to the standards of those times and not ours; otherwise few would escape harsh criticism.

Like all Huguenots, Frontenac was interested in exploration, possibly for financial reasons as for extending the French empire in America. In Cavelier de La Salle he found a kindred soul. Michelet says, "Cavelier was a Norman, a son of Rouen, in whom had entered the heart of the great discoverers from Dieppe, some old Normans, forerunners of Columbus and de Gama, a Genius, strong and capable, calculating, shrewd, patient, and intrepid, he had undergone two baptisms without which one could accomplish nothing; he had ennobled himself, had become Cavelier de

La Salle; he studied under the Jesuits and he studied them. With these two acquisitions he went to America, and seeing at first glance that they would be of little help for him, that they would be a hindrance, he turned to the Récollets and to Frontenac, who, curiously enough, was not a Jesuit. Still quite young, he went to Versailles, explained to Colbert his bold and simple plan to descend the great river to penetrate the depths of America. The Jesuits maintained that he was mad. Then, when the thing was realized, they maintained that they had known all about it, that he had stolen the idea from them."[6]

The mention of the Récollets who had been ousted by the Jesuits in 1633 requires the statement that "through the influence of Talon, the King was induced in the year 1668 to sign a decree permitting the Récollets to return to Canada and reinstating them in their former possessions. Père Leclerq, Récollet, says they were very much wanted. 'For thirty years,' to quote his words, 'complaint was made·in Canada that consciences were being burdened; and the more the colony increased in population, the greater was the outcry. I sincerely hope that there was no occasion for it, and that the great rigour of the (Jesuit) clergy was useful and necessary. Still the Frenchman likes liberty and under all skies is opposed to restraint, even in religion!'"[7]

Frontenac backed La Salle in his explorations into the basin of the Mississippi and the possession of Louisiana. Father Hennepin was among those who accompanied de la Salle on his explorations and who has left an account of them in which he makes rather extravagant claims for himself such as being the first white man to view Niagara Falls; also, that it was he, rather than La Salle, who discovered the mouth of the Mississippi.

Frontenac continued to fight now with Laval, now with Duchesneau. Each accused the other of trafficking in the sale of furs; besides, Frontenac persisted in the sale of brandy to the Indians which the Jesuits and Sulpicians strongly opposed. Frontenac's argument was that if the Indians didn't get it from the French they would get it from the English, and that drink wasn't any worse for them than for the white man.

The squabbling was finally brought to an end when both Frontenac and Duchesneau were recalled by Colbert. This meant that the one man—Frontenac—who could keep the Iroquois Indians under control had been removed and Canada soon fell upon evil days. His successor, La Barre, was unsuccessful in dealing with the Canadian situation now and Laval, who after triumphing over Frontenac and getting himself appointed as Bishop, failed to succeed in revoking the edict which secured parish priests in their posts. Denonville, who followed Frontenac as Governor, was a good soldier, a devout, conscientious Catholic and very loyal to the King, but inept when it came to matching wits with the Indians. The result was that the French were badly beaten and although Denonville got along well with the Church and the Intendant, he was recognized as a failure and in 1689 Louis XIV recalled him and sent back Frontenac, now seventy years of age.

Frontenac may not have covered himself with glory during his first term of office but it cannot be gainsaid that he was eminently successful in his second. Upon his arrival he organized three forces and sent them into English territory on successful expeditions. Sir William Phipps in command of a naval squadron for the English approached Quebec and demanded its surrender. Although Frontenac was in no position to defend the city he put up such a bluff that Phipps withdrew. Frontenac had gambled and won and Canada was temporarily saved for the French. Louis XIV was so delighted with Frontenac's success that he had a medal struck to celebrate the event.

Frontenac then tried to consolidate the different sections of New France until the Peace of Ryswick in 1697 assured to France all the lands in America that had been granted by previous treaties. On November 28, 1698, Frontenac died. "He was in his 78th year; but in his body as strong as it is possible to be at that age, he exhibited all the firmness and all the liveliness of spirit of his best years. He died as he had lived, loved by many, esteemed by all, and with the glory of having almost without any help from France, sustained and increased even a colony open to attack from every direction, and which he found on the verge of ruin."[8] Father Goyer, a Récollet, delivered the funeral oration: "I will not seek to dry your tears," he said to the weeping congregation, "for I cannot contain my own. This is a time to weep, and never did people weep for a better Governor."

These two statements, the first by a Jesuit and the second by a Récollet, surely speak for themselves. Thus ended the life of a man who apparently came from a Huguenot family and who was never regarded as a Roman Catholic by the clerical party. At best he was considered a Jansenist, a name which bore as much approbrium as Huguenot. Certainly he fits into our category of being a Huguenot-Catholic for, like Champlain, he always preferred the Récollets to the Jesuits. It is significant, too, that he has never received much recognition by French Canada although in his understanding and control of the Iroquois he parallels Champlain. In any event he can be labelled *un politique*.

ANTOINE DE LAMOTHE-CADILLAC

Antoine de Lamothe-Cadillac in his attitude to the Jesuits and the Church of Rome was as much a Huguenot-Catholic as Frontenac. He belonged to a good family in Languedoc, joined the army, and in search of adventure came to Canada in 1683. At that time he was twenty-three years of age and a very vital, ambitious, and personable man. He soon won the friendship of Frontenac because these two Gascons were much alike for both of them made religion a means to an end. Both were enemies of the Jesuits for they saw in them more searchers for gold and land than for souls.

In 1694 he was put in command at Michillemakinac and for several years fought with the Jesuits, they contending that he was making money out of debauching the Indians and he retaliating by accusing them of lack of co-operation. So long as Frontenac lived he had a friend at court, but when he died in 1698 the

Jesuits got a hearing. Going to France, de Lamothe persuaded Jerome de Pontchartrain to allow him to set up a fort at Detroit in 1701 and this time he was able to get terms that put him in complete charge, much to the chagrin of the Jesuits. Soon thereafter he was sent south, where he held the Miami Indians within bounds and was governor of Louisiana from 1712 to 1717. He was recalled because of his quarrelsome disposition and died in 1720.

RENÉ ROBERT CAVELIER, SIEUR DE LA SALLE (1643–1687)

René Robert Cavalier de La Salle is included in this study because he fits into our category of Huguenot-Catholic. Quite consistently the Huguenot-Catholic was one who would not cooperate with the Jesuits but had no compunction about working with Protestants.

La Salle was born at Rouen in 1643 of a noble and wealthy family. When fifteen years of age he joined the Jesuit Order to fit himself for the mission fields and two years later took the vows of poverty, chastity, and obedience. After three years he was sent to be a teacher but was not successful because of his impatient personality. Nor did he fit into the rigid rules of the Order. At twenty-four he was given permission to resign from the Order.

When he joined the Order, he gave up his property rights to his brothers, but now when he requested them to be returned his brothers demurred and offered him a small yearly income. It seems strange that his parents did not come to his relief seeing that they were wealthy, and it has been suggested that he was ignored because of his connection with the Jesuits. An older brother had joined the Sulpicians in Montreal and it was from them that La Salle was given a grant of land when he came to Canada. Here he built himself a house and studied a number of Indian languages.

The following is a Roman Catholic version of his early life. Note that there is no definite claim to his being a Roman Catholic: "In his youth he displayed an unusual precocity in mathematics and a predilection for natural science; his outlook in life was somewhat

puritanical. Whether or not he was educated with a view to entering the Society of Jesus is a matter of doubt, though some religious
order he must have joined subsequently, for to this fact is assigned
the forfeiture of his estates. The career of a churchman was definitely abandoned when, after the receiving of a feudal grant of
a tract of land at La Chine on the St. Lawrence from the Sulpicians, seigneurs of Montreal—perhaps through the influence of
an elder brother who was a member of the order of that place—
he came to Canada as an adventurer and trader in 1666." [9]

But exploration was in his blood, and he sold his land and with
the money equipped an expedition. With him went Dolbier de
Casson until the latter showed that he was more interested in
missions to the Indians than he was in exploration. La Salle went
on his own and was away two years during which time he went
as far as the Ohio River. On his return he met Frontenac, a man
after his own heart, and these two decided to create a western
empire by seizing control of the Mississippi. In the meantime
Frontenac had built a fort at Cataraqui, much to the displeasure
of the Montreal fur traders and officialdom. La Salle went to
France and secured some money with which he and Frontenac
equipped an expedition. Two Récollet fathers, Luc Buisset and
Louis Hennepin, accompanied La Salle along with Henri de
Tonty, an adventurous young Italian who became La Salle's
Lieutenant.

It is not our intention to give the details of La Salle's adventures
because they were fantastic. He overcame impossible difficulties
such as erecting block-houses at Niagara, building the first vessel
on the upper lakes, building Fort Crececoeur, and making an
expedition to the mouth of the Mississippi. He named that country
Louisiana. Always opposed by officials in Montreal, he had the
support of Frontenac and Du Lhut, the latter another interpid
explorer and a Huguenot.

La Salle returned to France where he enlisted men and supplies
to reach the mouth of the Mississippi by sea in order to establish a
fort there and seize the Spanish forts in the vicinity. He met with

misfortunes and landed in Texas instead of the mouth of the Mississippi. Realizing his hopeless plight he tried to work back to France by way of the Mississippi. A quarrel broke out and La Salle was shot in the head and dropped dead. Although there was a Friar in the party he does not say anything about La Salle's religion as a Roman Catholic. Like other Huguenot-Catholics he was bitterly attacked by the Jesuits and his contact with the Church was through the Récollets.

DANIEL GREYSOLON, SIEUR DU LHUT

Daniel Greysolon, Sieur du Lhut (du Luth, Dulhud, Duluth), who has been called the King of the woodsmen, was born at St.-Germain-en-Laye of a family known to be Protestant-Reformed. He became an official in the King's bodyguard and came to Canada in 1676, going to Three Rivers where some of his relatives had located. Du Lhut is remembered for his ability to win the confidence of the Indians. His motto was: "I fear not death, only cowardice and dishonour." He is remembered also for his explorations as he opened up the country west and south of Lake Superior. In 1680, four Frenchmen, one Indian guide, and he discovered the area of the Brulé River and the St. Croix. Establishing a trading post at the mouth of the Pigeon River, he founded a settlement which later was named Duluth in his honour.

His ability to deal satisfactorily with the Indians is shown in his conference with the Sioux and Assissiboin tribes who were forever at war. He secured their friendship towards the French which made them allies against the Iroquois during the years 1684 to 1687. At various times he was in charge of the forts at Lachine, Cataraqui, and MacKinac. He spent his last years at Cataraqui and died in 1709. Thus another Huguenot had made his contribution to Canada.

RADISSON, GROSSEILIERS, SIR GEORGE CARTERET

Although 1633 marks the close of the active participation of the Huguenots in Canada there continued to be in France an appreciation of Huguenots or men of Huguenot families as leaders when there was a specific job to be done that required courage and initiative. Richelieu and Colbert both regarded Huguenots highly and opposed them only when political exigency demanded it. The Jesuits in spite of their emphasis on missions had such a keen interest in the fur trade that they were constantly embroiling themselves with the governing bodies in Canada. Mason Wade writes: "Missionary activity was not the primary purpose of the French in coming to America, and at first it was not their dominant concern, despite the claims of most French-Canadian writers; for New France was frequented by explorers and traders for nearly a century before the first missionaries came. . . .

"There is little truth, however, in the traditional opposition of a spiritual-minded New France to a materialistic New England. The French were first of all explorers and exploiters of the natural resources of the New World; and the great missionary effort of the seventeenth century was not unrelated to the necessity of winning the support of the Indians, whose goodwill was vital to the fur trade."[10]

With this idea in mind that the motivating force in the seventeenth century was still the fur trade and the money to be made from it, let us turn to two men who are alternately praised for their initiative, bravery, and cleverness and derided for their willingness to serve the highest bidder. These men were Pierre Esprit Radisson and Medard Chouart, better known as des Grosseilliers.

Pierre Esprit Radisson was born in St. Malo about 1630 and came with his parents when fifteen yars old to Three Rivers where he was captured by the Indians, adopted into a Mohawk family, and well treated. Escaping he got back to France by a Dutch vessel sailing from Manhattan. Returning to the colony he became a *coureur de bois* along with Medard Chouart des Grosseilliers, born at Charly-sur-Marne in 1618, whose first wife was a Martin of the Plains of Abraham and his second in 1653, Marguerite Hayet, a half-sister of Radisson and a widow. In 1660 Radisson and Grosseilliers returned to Quebec with a wealth of furs but instead of approval they were arrested and fined.

Before they broke with France, because of this unfair treatment, they went to Paris but received no assistance and consequently returned to America, this time to Port Royal, Nova Scotia, where they encountered a sea captain, Zachariah Gillam, who agreed to take them to Hudson Bay by boat. But the season was late and the captain was afraid of the ice when he reached the Frobisher Straits. They returned to Boston and here they arranged for two ships to take them north; but one was wrecked and the other turned back. On their return they were faced with a lawsuit.

At this point they met Sir George Carteret who along with them was responsible for the establishment of the Hudson's Bay Company. And this is how it happened : let us turn to Sir George Carteret :

"He was one of the St. Ouen's de Carterets, and his uncle, Sir Philippe, was Seigneur of the manor . . ."[11] "George now dropped the 'de' from his name lest he should be thought a Frenchman . . . (not clear when, but apparently as a midshipman)."[12]

"Royalism became his religion, a simple, almost doglike, devotion to the crown. . . ."[13] "In November 1643 he landed at Mont Orgueil . . . and George regained the Island without striking a blow. He ruled it for the next eight years; but it was no easy task. The religion of the island was Calvinism; so the sympathies of the people were with the Puritan Parliament . . . In 1642 he aided the Duke of Vendôme, an illegitimate son of Henry IV, to defeat the Spaniards in raising the blockading of La Rochelle. Further exploits were rewarded by the French appointing him Supt. of the King's Shipyards . . . About Carteret's family we know little. Even Baptism Registers fail; for those born in Jersey were baptized in one or other of the Castle Chapels, and both these registers are lost; those born in France were baptized in Huguenot temples. Pepys, however, names nine . . . (there were three sons and six daughters)."[14] "Additional evidence is the following record : Lovis Carteret, daughter of the Right Honble.

Sir George Carteret, Vice Chamberlaine to his Majesty. (See C.J. VIII 358–9. Passed 8 May, 1662."[15]

These last paragraphs are the most substantial evidence that this family was Huguenot for it was something to have one's children baptized in Huguenot temples in France in the mid-seventeenth century; as a rule, the Huguenot Society recorded only Huguenot persons.

When Charles II was restored to his throne, George Carteret was rewarded by being made a baronet and granted "a certain island and adjacent islets to be known as New Jersey" and made one of the proprietors of the Carolinas. While on business in the American Colonies he came in contact with Radisson and Grosseilliers who agreed to join forces with the English. (There is some doubt as to whether Sir George came to America or his nephew). They then proceeded to London arriving there in 1665 after being captured by a Dutch war vessel and put ashore on the coast of Spain. Radisson and Grosseilliers were maintained in Oxford and Windsor and given forty shillings a week from the Royal purse.

On June 3, 1668, the *Eaglet* and the *Nonsuch* started for Hudson's Bay, the former, on which was Radisson, was disabled while the latter with Grosseilliers got as far south as James Bay and returned home with a valuable cargo of furs. Henry Hudson had been in the bay previously but his purpose was not to engage in the fur trade but to find the north-west passage to the Orient.

On May 2, 1670, the Hudson's Bay Charter was signed giving wide powers to eighteen men among them Sir George Carteret and Prince Rupert, but no mention was made of Radisson and Grosseilliers which probably explains why they in 1675 bolted for France where they were well received by Colbert. They carried on with the French until 1684 when they were again taxed contrary to their rights. This time Radisson returned to London for good and took an oath of fidelity to the Hudson's Bay Company. Grosseilliers returned to Three Rivers where he died in 1690. Radisson acquired some wealth and a pension from the English

Crown and died in 1710. He married three times : his first wife was Mary Kirke, daughter of Sir John Kirke, of a Huguenot family; his second wife was Margaret Godet, daughter of Lord Preston's spy in the Court of Louis XIV; and of his third wife we have no name. Radisson's name occurs among the denizations : "S.P. Com. Car II. Entry Book 67. 1687, Dec. 16 . . . Peter Esprit Radisson." [16] Obviously, he was among those escaping after the Revocation.

All evidence points to the fact that Radisson and perhaps Grosseilliers, for he married his half-sister and did not hesitate to oppose the Jesuits—had a Huguenot background. His association with Sir George Carteret, his marriages with Protestant women, his mention in the Huguenot record, and the fact that he has never received a commendable word by historians of that period would indicate his Protestant faith. Modern historians are more sympathetic. Douglas MacKay in his *The Honourable Company* has this to say :

"So far as the Hudson's Bay Company is concerned, Radisson did a first-rate job for which he was underpaid—not an uncommon incident in any company's history.

"Grosseilliers and Radisson had provided the initial idea and most of the know-how, without which there might never have been an English company on Hudson Bay. . . .

"Their remarkable journeys on two continents left a permanent mark on the fur trade itself. For all the men of their time in the old countries and the new, it was Radisson and Grosseilliers who showed up the overland trail from the St. Lawrence to Hudson Bay. For that alone they would be remarkable. But they were also the first men of their time to demonstrate the practicability and later the superiority of the great sea route both from the St. Lawrence and from England to the shores of Hudson Bay. Before Radisson and Grosseilliers, Hudson Bay was there for the taking. After them there was no question of the merit of the Hudson Bay route and the advantage it gave to the Hudson's Bay Company." [17]

MARQUIS DE MONTCALM

Marquis de Montcalm was born at Candiac near Nimes in 1712 and entered the army in 1721, becoming a captain in 1727. He served on the Rhine, in Bohemia, and in Italy, repeatedly distinguishing himself. In 1756 he was made Marechal de Camp and sent to Canada to command the French troops. In 1759 when defending Quebec against General Wolfe he was mortally wounded. Montcalm's background is definitely French-Protestant. It was his mother who persuaded his father to abjure his religion. The following excerpts are found in the Parliamentary Library of Quebec:

.... "Jean de Montcalm, fils de Guillaume, seigneur de St. Verans, de Tournemine, de Viala, de Cormes, devint aussi seigneur de Candiac par héritage de son oncle, Gaillardet de Montcalm. Il est juge-mage et sénéchal de Nimes, et commissaire du Roi aux Etats du Languedoc, en 1528. François de Montcalm, son fils, est capitaine de galères. C'est l'époque de la Reforme et des guerres de religion, et malheureusement (sic : a Catholic said this . . .) plusieurs des Montcalm deviennent partisans du Calvinisme. Honoré de Montcalm, fils de François, est l'un des chefs Protestants du Midi, et succombe dans un combat singulier près de Lodeve, en 1574.

.... "Madame de Montcalm, Marie-Thérèse-Charlotte de Lauris, mère de notre héros, était douée d'un grand coeur et d'un grand esprit. Fervente catholique elle avait eu le bonheur de faire partager ses croyances à son mari, et de lui faire abjurer le calvinisme dans lequel il était né. Et la forte éducation qu'elle donna à ses enfants, s'inspira des principes religieux qui fais la règle de sa vie."[18]

.... "On sait qu'à la fin du 16ᵉ siècle un grand nombre de gentilshommes du Languedoc, entrainés par l'exemple du Prince de Condé, avait embrassé la Religion Réformée. Les Montcalm étaient de ce nombre et des plus ardents. Par de récentes alliances, ils tenaient encore au Parti Protestant dans les Cevennes, lorsque

Louis Daniel abjura l'hérésie pour revenir a la foi catholique abandonnée depuis plusieurs generations. Quant aux Lauris-Castellane, ils comptaient parmi les familles les plus invoilablement attachées au catholicisme et à l'Ordre de Malte".[19]

JACQUES RENÉ DE BRÉSAY, MARQUIS DE DENONVILLE

Jacques René de Brésay, Marquis de Denonville, was the first of this family to come to Canada. After Frontenac's recall LaBarre was made Governor-General of Canada. He had been head of the faction which had been opposed to Frontenac and La Salle fared badly at his hands. La Barre and his friends wanted to monopolize the fur trade of the upper lakes, but when he became Governor in 1682 he was unable to control the Iroquois and he was recalled in 1685 to be replaced by the Catholic de Denonville. It was the latter's task to humble the Iroquois and this he did. He built, in 1689, Fort Denonville, on the site of Fort Niagara as one means of holding them, but instead of intimidating them, he angered them and the massacre of Lachine, 1689, must be regarded as one of the unhappy results of his administration. He was recalled in 1689. De Denonville, however, has always been regarded as a man of ability and courage.

It was then that Frontenac perhaps another Huguenot was sent back by Louis XIV as Governor because of Frontenac's experience in dealing with the Indians.

SIR FREDERICK HALDIMAND

Sir Frederick Haldimand was born in the Canton of Neuchâtel, Switzerland, in 1718, of Huguenot descent. After serving in the armies of Sardinia, Russia, and Holland, he entered British service in 1754, and subsequently was naturalized as an English citizen. During the Seven Years' War he served in America, was wounded at Ticonderoga in 1758 and was present at the taking of Montreal in 1760. After various commands in the colonies in 1778 he succeeded Sir Guy Carleton (afterwards Lord Dorchester) as Governor of the Province of Quebec and continued until 1784. His measures for the defence of the Province during the period of alliance between Old France and the American Revolutionists were eminently successful; his arrangements for resettling the United Empire Loyalists were a model of efficient organization.

Canada owes its first public library to Haldimand. Founded at Quebec in 1779 and stocked with several thousand volumes purchased in England, it was the nucleus of the present Quebec Literary and Historical Society Library.

Haldimand had much to do with the framing of the Quebec Act of 1774, and he befriended the Ursuline nuns by securing exemption for certain dues in return for their care of the sick. Granted the seignory of Sorel, he became a general in 1776, was knighted in 1785 and returned to London. He died at his birthplace in June, 1794.[20]

JACOB MOUNTAIN

The first Anglican bishop of Quebec was Jacob Mountain, a descendant of the Huguenot Montaignes, who escaped from France to England probably before the Revocation. It is not known for certain who the original Montaignes were, although there is a strong tradition that it might have been Montaigne, the famous French essayist. It is known, however, that the family settled near Norwich, and one of the children was baptized in 1681. Jacob's father died in 1752 and the Mountains eventually located at Norwich where Jacob attended the Cathedral School. When fifteen he left school and went into a counting house but disliked business and went back to school. Graduating from Cambridge in 1774 he stayed on as Fellow until 1783. He had various church appointments until in 1793 he was made Bishop of Quebec.

He spent the rest of his life as Bishop of Quebec during which time he was instrumental in establishing the Church of England in Canada. Although considered to be the state church, the support from England was spasmodic, largely because the British Government did not want to disturb the Roman Catholic Church in Canada for fear of alienating the French-Canadians and driving them towards the United States. It is interesting to note that during the period immediately following the conquest of Canada by the British, the Roman Catholic Church was given financial support by the British Government. There was even a fear that it might be considered the state church. Jacob Mountain fought this strenuously and finally won out. Unfortunately, however, he opposed giving the Church of Scotland any state recognition, thereby creating much bitter feeling against him. To Mountain the Church and State were one. Millman states: "He was an alert guardian of the interests of his Church, an assiduous public servant, a model husband and father. A sense of duty was one of his marked characteristics. Time after time he urged the government to take steps in accordance with his wishes for the church, knowing full well that he was laying himself open to misunderstanding and indeed wearying the secretaries of state with his continual pleas. Yet to the end of his days he never courted popularity by swerving from his convictions."[21]

He died in 1825 and is buried in the chancel of the Cathedral in Quebec. One of his sons, George J. became a bishop in 1836.

Other French Protestant clergy were Reverend David Francis de Montmollin, a native of Switzerland, who was commissioned to the Parish of Quebec by Governor Carleton in 1768, and Reverend Legère Jean Baptiste Noel Veyissiere, a native of France and a former Récollet who seceded from the order, joined the Church of England and began his ministry in 1768 at Three Rivers. There was the Reverend John Doty, who arrived from Schenectady in 1777 and eventually built a church at Sorel— "The first English church within the boundaries of the present province of Quebec."[22]

SIR GEORGE PRÉVOST, 1769–1816

Sir George Prévost was the eldest son of Major-General Augustin Prévost (who served under Wolfe), by his wife Anne, daughter of Chevalier George Grand of Amsterdam and of Huguenot descent. He entered the British Army and served during the Napoleonic Wars in the West Indies, and was made military governor of St. Lucia, 1798–1801, where he was so successful in dealing with the French population that he became Governor of Dominica. In 1808 he was appointed Lieutenant-Governor of Nova Scotia, where he was a successful administrator and in 1811 he was transferred to Quebec for Lower Canada and later in that year was made Governor-General of Canada. He conciliated the French-Canadians and prevented them from joining the Americans. As Commander-in-Chief of the British forces in Canada he was not successful and was personally responsible for the humiliating defeat at Sackett's Harbour and Plattsburg. Recalled to England he died before he was to face a court martial. In 1789 he married Anne, the daughter of Major-General John Phipps, R.E.

JOLY DE LOTBINIÈRE

Joly de Lotbinière is a distinguished family in Quebec and stems from a Joly ancestor who came from Switzerland to settle in County Lotbinière, P.Q. Henri Gustave Joli was the son of the second daughter of a descendant of Marque de Lotbinière who, having no sons, left his seignieuries, Rigaud, Vaudreuil, de Lotbinière, to his daughters. When Joli came to Canada he inherited the seignieury of Lotbinière from his mother and changed his name to Joli de Lotbinière. In due course he became premier of Quebec, then a member of the Federal Cabinet, and finally, Lieutenant Governor of British Columbia. His grandson, Edmond Joli de Lotbinière, the owner of the present seignieury, is second secretary to the Governor-General at Ottawa. (Edith Greenwood.)

Huguenots in the Maritimes

The Huguenots can take credit for establishing the first settlement in Nova Scotia. Roberval, at Port Royal (now Annapolis Royal) in 1540 made the first effort, although it was not successful. In 1604 de Monts and Poutrincourt made the first real settlement which, although captured and burned by the English in 1613, was rebuilt in 1635. From then on it became a Roman Catholic settlement.

In 1662 La Tour was given by Cromwell a grant of territory in Acadia extending from Lunenburg to the River St. George in Maine, including the whole coast of the Bay of Fundy on both sides and one hundred leagues inland. He sold his rights in a short time and retired into private life, dying in 1666. Descendants are the D'Entrements, Girourds, Porliers, and Landrys.

In 1710 after many years of belonging, now to France, now to Britain, Acadia was captured by Colonel Frances Nicholson in command of a New England force. He renamed Port Royal Annapolis Royal after the reigning monarch, Queen Anne of Great Britain.

Paul Maserene, who became Lieutenant-Governor in 1740, was a French-Huguenot, who, with his parents, had been driven out of France after the Revocation. "His whole life was spent in the military service of England, and he proved himself a most efficient officer, rising by his merit, unaided by patronage, to the rank of Major-General. He assumed the administration of affairs in Acadia when serious difficulties and dangers were imminent, and showed his capacity by the manner in which he discharged the duties of his position. It was well that at such a crisis in the history of the country, the reins of government were in strong hands."[1]

The first Huguenot settlers came to Nova Scotia following the year 1749. They came at the request of Lord Cornwallis, who "after the sad experience of the Cockneys, requested the Lords of Trade to send out more suitable settlers, preferably German farmers. And so they came in hundreds each summer for the next three years, poor people from the Rhineland, most of them, but with a strong proportion of 'Swiss'. There were some Swiss in fact, but the early chroniclers were hazy about European divisions and many of the immigrants they wrote down as 'Swiss' were actually French : Protestants from Montebéliard in Lorraine, near the foothills of the Alps. These are said to have comprised about one-third of the continental immigrants. But they came with the folk who called themselves *Deutsche*, and the English settlers knew them all as 'Dutch'—hence Dutchtown, the north suburb of Halifax in colonial times, and Dutch Village on the isthmus."[2]

In 1753 the Huguenots along with the Germans removed to Lunenburg where the government assisted the settlement with a system of bounties. In 1754 there were two hundred and fifty German-speaking and fifty French-speaking families in the settlement. Although the Germans were Lutherans, the French were Calvinists. Because the Church of England clergyman, Mr. Moreau, was French, the French-speaking settlers worshipped in the Anglican Church until, as the years went by, the French-speaking people moved to St. Margaret's Bay, to Tatamagouchi and River St. John. According to J. B. Brebner[3] the Huguenots became Anglicans in 1758 in order to be able to vote for the assembly.

The Palatines, Swiss, and French were sent out because they were supposed to be Protestants who could offset and perhaps undermine the prevalent Roman Catholicism of the Acadians who insisted on retaining their allegiance to France. Besides, emigration from the British Isles was very hesitant.

In Lunenburg a difficulty arose because there were three languages and three confessions and it was unsatisfactory to have all of these worshipping in one church. In 1759 the Lutherans and Calvinists (Huguenots) established separate congregations. A Lutheran Church was built in 1771. In 1779 the Reformed families seceded and sixty of them organized a Reformed Church and one of their number, the Rev. Bruin Romcas Comingo, became their pastor. He was commonly known as Brown, and was born in Leuwarden in the Province of Groningen in Holland in October, 1723, and came to Nova Scotia in 1752. He came as a woolcomber but became a fisherman in Chester. Ordained as a minister he was a pastor at Lunenburg for half a century and died in 1820, aged 96 years.

There is a record of some French families who lived on the

Hammond River, having come there from settlements on the Petitcodiac River and the Isthmus of Chignecto. Their names were : Tibideau, Violet, Robicheau, Goodin, Blanchard, LeBlanc, and Doucett. Later these settled at Madawaska on the way to Quebec.

In 1782 Sir Guy Carleton made overtures for refugees to be provided with ships to go to Nova Scotia, and in the spring of 1783 some forty-four ships were prepared to transport the Loyalists. Among these refugees were some French Huguenots. In two of DeLancey's companies of soldiers there were three hundred and fifteen men together with women and children. Doubtless many of these were French Huguenots the same as the DeLanceys who after arrival took an active part in locating the *émigrés*.

Esther Clarke Wright, who has given these Loyalists careful study, states that there were about eighty Huguenot families, many from the New Rochelle and Staten Island Huguenot settlements.[4] Most of these settled in Queens County. In Sunbury County, Maugerville became a centre. The following names of families have been provided by Mrs. Wright in a personal letter : Allair, Ansley, Aymer, Babbitt, Barbarie, Beardsley and Beaty, Bedell, Beebe, Belyea, Beyea, Bulyea, Bettle, Billopp, Bourn, Boyer, Britney, Brundage, Burditt, Caleff? Carre, Chadeayne, Chaloner, Chidister, Chillas, Cohee, Coombe, Cougle, Crozier, Dalziell, DeBow, DeBlois, DeForest, DeLong, DeMill, DePeyster, Devoe, Dibble, Dingee, Ebbett, Eccles, Evarts, Foshay, Frazee, Ganong, Gaunce, Gerow, Gesner, Gidney, Gua or Guiou, Guthrie, Guyer, Hait or Hoyt, Harbel, Haycock, Harned, Heddon, Heustis, Hewlett? Hilyard, Innis, Joslin, Jouet, Kinnear? Lamoreaux, Leferge (Lefurgey), LeRoy, Lester (some of them), Losee, Mabee, Mersereau, Micheau, Morrell, Mowry? Napier, Nase? Ness, Odell? Parlee, Perrine? Pettit, Pugsley? Purdy, Quereau, Rouse? St. Croix, Sarvenier, Sayre, Secord, Segee, Sipprell, which possibly was Siple or Supplee, Sturdee, Stymest, Theal, Tisdale? Vail, Valleau, Weyman.

There were more than thirteen hundred men, women, and

children who went by ship to Canada and many more came by their own means. Some, however, returned to the United States after the close of the Revolutionary War and some two hundred left New Brunswick, which in 1784 was separated from Nova Scotia. These moved on to Upper Canada influenced by John Graves Simcoe who, when made Lieutenant-Governor of Upper Canada in 1792, encouraged officers that had served under him in the Queen's Rangers to come to Upper Canada and serve as members of his Council.[5]

The settlers who came from the town of Montebéliard were from a section of the domination of the Duke of Württemberg which had been annexed by Louis XIV after the Treaty of Nimeguen in 1679. Shortly after this they prepared to emigrate to Nova Scotia in response to the investigation which had been made by the British Government offering liberal terms to those who would settle in the Province. They came down the Rhine, took shipping at Rotterdam, landed at Portsmouth only to find themselves destitute. The British Government put them in four vessels, two for South Carolina and two for Halifax. Two hundred and twenty-four persons came to Halifax and went to Lunenburg.

After the peace of 1763 Colonel DesBarres, a countryman of theirs and a son of one of their Protestant ministers, who had entered the British Military service, and who had served at the taking of Louisburg and Quebec was, it was said, one of the officers into whose arms Wolfe fell. Afterwards, he was successively Governor of Cape Breton and Prince Edward Island. He obtained a grant of land at Tatamagouche, where he induced a number of settlers to locate. Accordingly, eleven of them moved their families from Lunenburg about 1771, among them the Langille family—David, his son John James, and his brother Matthew.

Here after many hardships they did well but DesBarres would not sell them the land and so they moved in 1785 to land in River St. John, then known as Deception River. These settlers spoke a corrupt dialect of French, but with a German tone and accent like the inhabitants of Alsace.

Because settlers did not come into Cape Breton it became part of Nova Scotia again. Following the American Revolutionary War, there was a great influx of refugees. Esther Clarke Wright[6] estimates that between fourteen and fifteen thousand Loyalists came to New Brunswick which had been separated from Nova Scotia in 1784, but of this number only a small proportion were Huguenots, perhaps one hundred families and not all of these remained.

The Dauphiné family, David and Jean Dauphiné, emigrated to Nova Scotia sailing from Helvoot Roads in 1752. They were among those sent out by John Dick and came from Montebéliard which was once part of the Kingdom of Burgundy and close to Switzerland. From the end of the fourteenth century until 1793 it belonged to the House of Württemberg. From 1733 to 1793 the Duke of Württemberg was a Roman Catholic and in a predominately Huguenot country such as Montebéliard this caused religious persecution and political unrest, which led to emigration down the Rhine River to Holland and embarkation for America.

This family whose name has been spelled Dauphnee, Dauphinee, Dofine, includes the following children of Jean Dauphiné (b. 1726) and his wife, Maria Elizabeth Bauvard (b. 1732, d. 1799, ten days after her husband), who were married in 1753;

Maria Eliza m. George Emounod in 1772.
James Christopher, 1756, m. Sarah (Sally Phillips) Veinot in 1790.
Jean Christopher, 1757, m. Mary Elizabeth Bouteiller in 1776.
Joseph, 1759.
Marie Catharine, 1761, m. John Christopher Jean Pierre in 1779.
George Frederick, 1753, m. Barbara Sartees in 1787.
John George, 1764, m. Sarah Veinot in 1783.
James, 1767, m. Susan Catharine Jolinus in 1791.
Anna Judith, 1770, m. Peter James Veinot in 1791.
Jean Pierre, 1773, m. Mary Elizabeth.

In 1753 Jean and his family with other Foreign Protestants moved from Halifax to found the town of Lunenburg. A prominent member of the family was Capt. John Dauphinee who was one of the founders of Hubbards. He and his brother Frederick settled on what is known as Dauphinee's Point where a saw mill was built and a brigantine made regular trips to the West Indies for rum, molasses, and tobacco. Capt. John was also a captain of the Halifax Regiment of Militia, No. 1. He died, aged 56, in 1846.

The Langille Family originated in the town of Montebéliard and came out to Nova Scotia in 1752, landing at Halifax, later going to Lunenburg. David and his son, John James, and his brother Matthew were the first to come. They settled on the French River, but as they could not own the land they went to the River John in 1785 along with George, the son of John James, where they were joined in 1790 by other settlers, including George Langille, the only son of Matthew. John James had five sons, George, David, James, Joseph, and Frederick. Frederick moved to the United States while the others stayed in the vicinity of River John.

Other Huguenot families who settled at River St John at that time were Perrin, Patriquan, Gratto, Tattrie. All were from Montebéliard except the Perrins who were silk manufacturers at Locke, Touraine, France.

The Mabee Family is widespread, the name appearing as Mabile, Maby, Maybee, Mubie. The Huguenot ancestor was Seigneur Pierre Mabille de Neve, born about 1550, in the Province Anjou, France, fought under Coligny and during the massacre of 1572, escaped to Holland where he lived and died at Noorden. He had two sons, Gaspard and John. Gaspard was one of the signers of the Leyden petition in July, 1621, which was sent to Sir Dudley Carleton, British Ambassador in Holland, asking permission to emigrate to the New World. Being in the Dutch Navy, he had previously made several trips to the Americas.

John Mabille came to America and settled at Schenectady while a son of Gaspard—Pierre—married and settled in New

York City where he died in 1665. His son, Caspar, who was the grandfather of Frederick, who came up to Canada, lived at New York and later at New Rochelle, where his son, Simon, married a granddaughter of Ambroise Sycar (Secord).

Frederick was born in New York in 1735 and married Lavinia Pelham in 1765. After the close of the Revolutionary War he, his wife, and seven children, went to St. John, New Brunswick, but in the fall of 1792, along with Peter Secord, a cousin, who had travelled to the Niagara district left New Brunswick and travelled to Turkey Point in the Long Point district where they settled. Frederick died in 1794. Mrs. Mabee then married Sg. William B. Hilton and they settled on land given by Governor Simcoe in the Township of Charlotteville and here they died, the husband in 1817 and the wife in 1822. Pelham, a son, had four boys and six girls.

The Raddall Family of whom Thomas Raddall, the author, is one of the few survivors, had as its ancestor one who fled from Brittany to Cornwall at the time of the Revocation. There he married a Cornish woman and founded the English family of this name, which was originally spelled Raddal with emphasis on the last syllable. In Canada, Thomas and his son, Thomas Jr., are located at Liverpool, Nova Scotia.

The Lamerieux Family, pronounced Lumoree or Lamoroo, came first to Acadia and sometime about 1816 came on to Ontario County, in Upper Canada. James Lamerieux is a son of the first ancestor in New Brunswick.

Two brothers, Mersereau, of Huguenot stock moved from New York State to New Brunswick, one settling in the Fredericton area and the other farther north in the Mirimichi River District.

One of the best-known families in the Maritimes is the Ganong, originally Guenon. The family originated in the Province of Saintonge in the vicinity of La Rochelle. Jean Guenon sailed from Amsterdam on April 2nd, 1657, and landed at New Amsterdam (New York) and settled at Flushing, Long Island. Thomas Ganong was a Loyalist who left May, 1783, and came to New

Brunswick, settling on a farm at Kingston, King's County. Descendants have married Secords, Ryersons, Sissons, Kiersteads, Macdonalds. James Harvey Ganong and his brother, Gilbert White, founded the Saint Croix Soap Manufacturing Company and the Ganong Brothers Candy Company. Dr. Howard P. Whidden, a past Chancellor of McMaster University, married Katharine Louise Ganong, whose son is Dr. Evan Whidden of Acadia University.

The Berton Family originated at Chatelerault, in the Province of Poitou, France. Pierre Berthon de Marigny and his wife Marguerite came to Narranganset colony, Rhode Island, between 1681 and 1685. There were forty-five families in this colony among them was Ezechiel Carre, a minister, and Pierre Ayrault, a physician, with Pierre Berthon de Mariguy, as head of the expedition.

This colony had been well equipped and for five years did very well, but owing to disputes over ownerships, they disbanded some going to Boston, some to New Rochelle, some to South Carolina, and the largest number to New York, Pierre Berthon, among the latter. Here Peter Berton was born in 1729. He became a New York merchant, was interested in shipping and master of a ship from 1756 to 1770. Declaring himself a Loyalist he was persecuted and sought refuge on Long Island. In 1683 as Captain of a company of thirty-one men, fifty-one women, twenty children, and thirty servants, he sailed in the 'Summer Fleet' of fifteen vessels carrying two thousand exiles for St. John, N.B.

Landing at Parr Town, Peter Berton went up the St. John River to 'Oak Point', where he gave land for a church, built in 1792. From there he removed to St. John. Thirteen children had been born to him and his wife, Ann Duncan, one of these being George (1774–1828), of whom the following notation was made in the family Bible—still extant—"He appears a fine straight Lad well maid a Good Complection Square Shouldered—for further Particulars Inquire of the Nurses". His son, George Frederick Street Berton, was born in Fredericton in 1808, married Delia Hooke.

214 | THE TRAIL OF THE HUGUENOTS

Their son, William Street, born 1835, married Lucy Fox, whose son, Francis George, went to the Yukon in 1898 and married Laura Beatrice Thompson. Pierre Berton, the author and columnist, is a son born in the Yukon, at Whitehorse, in 1920.

The Hue Family in New Brunswick came from the Parish of St. Mary, Island of Jersey. Jean Hue who married Marie Le Brun was the earliest ancestor known. Of their ten children Philippe had a son, Stannas Edward, who came to New Carlisle, Gaspé, about 1880. He married Alice Harriet Hamon and when she died, he married her sister, Eliza. They lived at Paspebrac, P.Q., then Montreal, and finally Kentville, N.S. Their descendants are scattered throughout New Brunswick, Nova Scotia, Newfoundland, Connecticut, and two are in Ontario; Stannas Edward, at Maple R.R. 1 and Rev. Canon L. C. Swan, St. George's Anglican Church, St. Catharines.

The Hamon Family would appear to have located in the Island of Jersey. Descendants are found in Bath, England, Quebec, New Brunswick, and one, Ivy, who married Mr. Le Grand living at City View, Ontario.

The Des Brisay Family came early to Canada when Jacques René Des Brisay Marquis de Denonville was made Governor-General of New France, a position he held until 1789. Following the Revocation another branch of the family went to Ireland where they occupied an important place in Dublin society. In 1769 Captain Thomas de la Cour Des Brisay, Royal Irish Artillery, was appointed Lieut.-Governor of St. John's Island (now Prince Edward Island) who had sixteen children, one of them, General de la Cour Des Brisay was at one time in charge of the British forces in Nova Scotia. Another descendent was the Rev. Theophilus Des Brisay who was a Chaplain in the Royal Navy and later Rector of St. Paul's, Charlottetown, P.E.I. Two present-day members of the family are Alexander Campbell Des Brisay, Chief Justice of British Columbia, and A. W. Y. Des Brisay, B.Sc., D.I.C., Ph.D., P.Eng., Lieut-Col., retired.

The Embree Family goes back to the earliest settlement of

Flushing, on Long Island, and is of French Huguenot stock in Normandy, the original form of the name being d'Embrée. There is early mention of two brothers, Moses and Robert. John Embree (1697–1769) was born at Flushing and later moved to La Rochelle. Col. Samuel Embree (1746–1800) was a son of John Embree and Elizabeth Lawrence and became Commander of the King's Light Horse Guards who left White Plains in 1775 and settled in Amherst, Nova Scotia. He had a brother, Joseph, who also came to Nova Scotia and settled at Westchester. Samuel married Sarah Hyatt, was given a grant of land by George IV and a yearly pension. They had four children : Elisha, Thomas, Israel, Mary, who intermarried with several of the Huguenot families of the Maritimes.

Huguenots in Ontario

Huguenot is almost an unknown word in Ontario. Proof of this can be found by reference to the Bibliography of Canadiana as published by the Toronto Reference Library in 1934 where not a single item is found ; and by searching the index in the Archives at Ottawa where one item appears and that has to do with Quebec City. The Legislative Library in Toronto has a few listings and a complete set of the publications of the London Huguenot Society. Of the many Proceedings put out by various United States Huguenot Societies, none are to be found.

And yet there are a great number of persons in Ontario who have a fierce pride in their Huguenot ancestry; one has only to give them an opportunity to declare it when he discovers what frustration these people have had over the years, never having been able to give recognition to it. Often the French ancestry is hidden in names which have been translated or changed into other racial forms. In many cases an Anglicized pronunciation has brought forth an Anglicized spelling. For instance, *Le Quesnel* is now spelled *Connell* : or translation was resorted to : *Keffer* was originally *Tonnelier* which was translated in the German *der Küfer* and then spelled *Kieffer*. *DeWitt* was originally *de Blanc* and then translated into the Dutch form. *Guérin* became *Wearing* and *DuLaux, Loucks*; Ramsay, *Ramazay*. Furthermore, the situation is still more complicated when the original French ancestor escaping to some European country married a woman of that area and learned a new language so that when he came to America he consciously or unintentionally passed himself off as a native of the country whose language he then spoke.

However, there are two rough and rule of thumb measures that can be used to discover persons with a French background : if the name appears to be French, that is : the emphasis is on the last syllable and the name resembles a French word and that person is Protestant, in all probability there is some Huguenot blood in the ancestry. Another means is the shape of the head and the colour of the eyes and hair. In France there were two main types : the southern Mediterranean and the northern Norman. The southern is perhaps the more noticeable in that the face is long and narrow, with eyes and hair black or dark brown. The stature is not tall while hands and feet are small. This is particularly true of women. Then too this group is quite vivacious with quick wit, keen minds and eyes possessing a concentrated look which almost amounts to a stare. The Norman type is quite tall, not fleshy, with heads narrow and hair more Teutonic fair. Emotionally they are less volatile.

It is remarkable that the foregoing characteristics are dominant even after several intervening mixtures with other races. However, not all Protestant French ancestry in Ontario was Huguenot in origin. Some of it goes back to Norman times when William the Conqueror brought over many French barons. Colonel Thomas Talbot is one example and the Massey family is another. The Talbots de Malahide were one of nine great houses which survived the Wars of the Roses. Richard Talbot, the founder of the house, who crossed the Irish Channel in 1172 in the suite of Henry II, a son of Lord Talbot of Eccleswell, is mentioned in the Domesday Book. Settling in Ireland, nine miles north of Dublin, this family retained its ancestral estate for some seven hundred years. Colonel

Thomas Talbot was born here in 1771 and in 1791 came to Upper Canada with Lieutenant-Governor John Graves Simcoe. In 1803 he was granted five thousand acres in the township of Yarmouth where he established what came to be known as the Talbot Settlement.[1]

Another well-known Canadian family is the Massey which is said to have come from Normandy with William the Conqueror. In the seventeenth century some members of it went to New England and Massachusetts. Daniel Massey left Watertown, N.Y., in 1808, and came to Northumberland County. There were two sons, Jonathan, the father of Levi Massey, and Daniel, the father of Hart A. Massey. This is the branch that began to manufacture farm implements at Newcastle, Durham County. Rt. Hon. Vincent Massey, Governor-General of Canada from 1952–1959 and his brother, the actor, Raymond Massey, are descendants.

With the exception of a few who came into Ontario in the late eighteen hundreds and since World War II most of those who claim Huguenot blood have ancestors who migrated from 1776 on.

The Niagara District

It is of interest to note that three at least of the five persons to flee to Upper Canada that we have any record of were Huguenots. William Canniff states: "In 1776, there arrived at St. George, in a starving state, Mrs. Nellis, Mrs. Secord, Mrs. Young, Mrs. Buck, and Mrs. Bonnar, with thirty-one children, whom the circumstances had driven away."[2] Of these we know that Mrs. Nellis and Mrs. Secord and probably Mrs. Bonner (Bonheur) and Mrs. Young (Le Jeune) were Huguenots, even Mrs. Buck (le Bouc).

The first settlers in the Niagara Peninsula were soldiers disbanded from Butler's Rangers. It should be noted that General Haldimand, who was Governor and Lieut.-Colonel Arent Schuyler de Peyster, who was moved from Detroit to Niagara to take over the upper posts in May, 1785, were both French Huguenots, the former from Switzerland and the latter from a Loyalist family in New York State.

The Bay of Quinte District

In all probability the greatest number of persons with French Huguenot blood came into Upper Canada in 1784 and settled in and around Kingston and the Bay of Quinte. This was so because of the situation that existed in New York City following the close of the War. Carleton, who was Commander-in-Chief in 1782, found he had a large number of Loyalists who had lost all their property and his problem was what to do with them.

Having learned that there was a German by the name of Michael Grass (Kress) who had been a prisoner and confined at Fort Frontenac during the French War, he consulted him as to whether people could live there and when Grass spoke favourably of it he was asked if he would conduct some of the Loyalists there. Replying in the affirmative, he was given five vessels and together with Captain Van Alstine shepherded a considerable number of these Loyalists in the late Spring of 1783 to Sorel, Quebec. Leaving the women and children in temporary quarters, Grass proceeded to Cataraqui where he consulted with Major Ross who advised him to return to Sorel before winter set in and make arrangements for the transportation of their wives and families in the Spring.

This he did and by the end of July, 1784, this company of people who were Palatine Germans, French Huguenots, and English Quakers and Puritans were settled on lands in the Kingston and Bay of Quinte area. Major Edward Jessop, of Huguenot background, settled his Huguenot families in Edwardsburgh and Augusta and in the Bay of Quinte. These troops were not regular soldiers but volunteers who had espoused the royal cause at the commencement of the Revolution. Grass located the Germans in Kingston township while most of the Quaker English took up land in the Bay of Quinte.

The Ruttan Family were Huguenots who fled from France

after the massacre of St. Bartholomew in 1572 and went to England, then back to Holland where they amassed a large fortune. In 1734, Abraham Ruttan emigrated to America and settled at New Rochelle, N.Y., but baptism records in existence in the French Church in New Paltz, N.Y., show that Abraham Ruttan and Marie Petillion were on this continent in 1675. William, born 1757 and Peter, born 1759, were either grandsons or great grandsons of the original Abraham. Another Abraham remained in the United States, but the two older boys came to Canada. Peter, in 1778, accompanied Joseph Brant from New York State to Canada on a tour of observation and these two became such fast friends that Peter named his son Joseph Brant Ruttan.

When the mission was completed, Brant presented Peter with a handsome brace of pistols, which at his death came into the possession of his nephew, Sheriff Henry Ruttan, whose descendants now have them. Brant also peeled from a birch tree a piece of bark and on it recorded the services rendered by Ruttan which the latter presented to the proper authorities and was granted later that tract of land in Adolphustown that terminated on Ruttan's Point.

Both Peter and William held commissions in the British Army and when the war was over both left for Canada with the Van Alstine band of Loyalists. One of them brought two black slaves, a man and a woman, who proved a wonderful help. William also settled at Adolphustown, married an Irish girl, Margaret Steele, who had crossed the ocean with her parents.

In the hungry years of 1788 in order to get some food William, who had some money saved from the sale of his commission, sent two men to Albany during the winter months for four bushels of Indian corn which they carried on their backs through forests without roads. As the Ruttans possessed a cow, her milk, plus the precious corn, with roots and berries from the woods, provided enough nourishment to keep eight persons alive until the following harvest.

Peter W., eldest son of William, married Fanny Roblin (who

was said to have been the first white child born in Adolphustown, her parents having been married in New York previous to September, 1783). This couple acquired a grandfather clock (now in the possession of Mrs. Lyons of Montreal) and it is recorded that the whole neighbourhood (within hearing) guided their household arrangements by the prompt blowing of the dinner horn at the stroke of twelve. Peter served in the War of 1812.

Henry, fourth son of William, served in the War of 1812, was seriously wounded, and made a Major in 1816. In 1820 he was elected to the House of Assembly and eventually in 1838 was Speaker of the House. (Mrs. Harris L. Walsh, 65 South Dr., St. Catharines, Ont.)

The Condé Family has a very distinguished ancestry since it can be traced back to the Codet branch of the House of Bourbon in France. It originated with Louis I de Bourbon, Prince de Condé, 1530–1569, Protestant leader and general who commanded the Huguenots in Wars of Religion. Another branch of this family was Conti and both of these branches played important parts in the history of France and in the history of the Huguenots. Descendants emigrated to Scotland during the French Revolution and one of them, Malcolm Condie, came to Canada in 1842 and settled in Smiths Falls. Later he lived in Montreal where he took an active part in the Protestant Church life of that city. After farming for some time in Chateauguay County, he retired to Lancaster, Ontario, where he died. Descendants of this man are scattered throughout the United States and Canada. (D. A. Condie, Cornwall, Ont.)

Ontario is indebted to the van Egmond family because of Col. van Egmond who was born the 10th of March, 1778, and baptized on May 19th of the same year, Count Anthony James William Gisberg Lamoral in the high and free Goure of the Dominion. His lineage goes back to Egmond, Count of Lamoral, prince of Gavre (1522–1568) who was born in Hairaut, the younger of two sons of John IV, Count of Egmont. In 1544 Egmond married Sabina, sister of the Elector Palatine Frederick

III, and from then on had a very distinguished career in Flanders both as a general and administrator for he was appointed a stadtholder of Flanders and Artois. Along with the Prince of Orange he opposed King Philip of Spain in his effort to convert the Netherlands into a Spanish dependency. Eventually because of his opposition he, although a Roman Catholic, was beheaded along with Horn in 1568. Thus he is credited with beginning the famous revolt of the Netherlands and he became the theme of Goethe's *Egmont* (1788).

The father of the man who came to Canada was John Arnold James Gisbert Lamoral, Count of Egmond and Lord of Gaure, Colonel of the Regiment of Venati in the service of the Region and Drossard of the Region between the Meuse and the Waal. Mary Josephine Ludovica Aloom of Aulzon and Jonkerstein was his mother and he married Martha Dietz. Their family consisted of five boys and three girls: Constant, the eldest, Leopold, Edward, William, August, Louisa, Susan, and a Mrs. Helmer, whose christian name is unknown.

The Colonel was an officer in Napoleon's army and one of his sons, thought to be August, was born on the march to Moscow, as at that time it was the privilege of the officers to take their wives along on long marches.

Because he refused to fight against Wellington and his officers, he was imprisoned and wounded, but he escaped when his wife visited him with one of his small sons. His wife, Martha, was masculine in appearance and her husband walked out of prison in her clothes, leaving his wife behind. She was soon released.

Having previously taken her household possessions to Germany she joined her family and they emigrated to Pennsylvania. Not liking the region they chose they came up to Canada where they met John Galt at Doon in Waterloo Country. Because Colonel Van Egmond had a sizeable fortune he agreed to build the road from New Hamburg to Goderich. In return he was given thirteen thousand acres of land between Mitchell and Clinton

Along this route he built seven hotels and grew the first wheat in Huron County.

His sons went into business for themselves. Constant built a flour mill and started the village of Egmondville. The house which he built is still standing. Leopold built a sawmill; William, a hotel; and August, a woollen mill.

The Colonel in some way became involved in the Mackenzie Rebellion, was arrested and died in prison, one day before a pardon was given. His wife, Martha, lived for another twenty years.

The Mowat Family, for our purpose began with Magnus Mowat born 1624, the last Mowat of Buchollie. In 1651 he married Jean, daughter of Alexander Sinclair of Latheson. David, son of Magnus, died in 1711. Oliver his grandson was born in 1746 and married Janet Nicholson. They had four sons and four daughters, John, the third son being born in 1791. John fought in the Peninsular War and went with his battalion to Canada in 1814. In 1815 he was given two hundred acres of land near Kingston and he then sent for his sweetheart, Helen Levack in Scotland, who had waited ten years for him. Her family—Le Veque—had been Huguenots who fled to Scotland after 1572. This couple had five children, the eldest being Oliver, later, Sir Oliver Mowat, Another son, Rev. John Bower Mowat, D.D., became Professor of Oriental Languages at Queen's University, of which their father had been one of the original trustees. Sir Oliver Mowat, born July 22, 1820, married in 1846, Jane, daughter of John Ewart, of Toronto. He was a lawyer, member of the Coalition Cabinet in 1864; Premier of Ontario, Minister of Justice, Leader of the Senate, Attorney-General, Postmaster-General of Canada, Vice-Chancellor of Upper Canada, Lieutenant-Governor of Ontario. He died in 1903 at Government House, Toronto. (W/c Ralph Manning, R.C.A.F. Staff).

The McGowan Family originated with Alexander Sinclair, a younger son of the 12th Earl of Caithness who quarrelled with his father and adopted the name of McGowan. He married Isabella Levack (Le Veque) in Edinburgh, was a tailor and came to Canada as an officer in the army. In 1843 he sent for his wife and children and in 1855 went to New York where he died in 1868. A daughter, known as Ida Vernon, became a noted actress (W/c Ralph Manning, R.C.A.F. Staff).

The original name of the Nelles Family is said to have been 'Né-lis' and that it fled about 1685 to the Rhine Palatinate where three sons, William, Christian, and Johannes were born at Heidelberg, Germany. In 1700 they, with their parents—who perished in the voyage—sailed for America and settled for months on Governor's Island, later being transferred to Governor Hunter's 'Tar Camps' on the upper Hudson River. During the next ten years they moved on, William and Christian came to the Mohawk Valley by way of the Schoharie Creek. Johannes went down the Susquehanna to William Penn's Settlement near Gettysburg, Pa.

Wilhelm (William) Nellis and Christian Nellis were pioneers at Palatine Mohawk Valley, N.Y. in 1720. Christian married Barbara Klock and William, Magdalene Klock, daughters of Hendrick Klock, a pioneer Dutch Indian trader.

William Nellis and Margaret Klock had five sons and one daughter. The second son, Hendrick William (1735–1791), came to Canada with Sir John Johnson; was captain in Butler's Rangers; Major in Indian Dept. N.E. (List 1786, Niagara Stamped Book). He with his sons were the first settlers in Grimsby, later going to York on the Grand River where his house is still standing in very good condition. (Mrs. Basil M. Mundy, Thornhill, Ont; Mrs. C. Duff Nelles, Scotland, Ont.)

The Valleau Family originated in Geneva, Switzerland, with Anthony Valleau. Isaac, the next known member, was born in 1608 on the Isle of Re on the west coast of France and became the Sieur de la Pree. His son, Isaac, born in 1638, became a merchant at St. Martin's and married Susanna Descard. In 1685 they escaped to New York and settled in New Rochelle where the old home is still said to be standing, built in 1700 and known as the Drake homestead. In succeeding generations there was an

Isaac until 1751 when Peter was born in Bergen County, New Jersey, who was loyal to the British Crown and who established the family in the Bay of Quinte district. He married Jannetie Lazier, widow of Andrew Labriskie, and with his two sons, Hildebrand and Cornelius, left New Jersey and coming to Quebec by boat went up the St. Lawrence River until they reached Adolphustown where they took up land and remained eleven years. Then they moved to Sophiasburg where five generations of Valleaus have lived.

The Ryerson Family was of Dutch Huguenot origin. Martin Reyerzoon and his brother, Adrian, came to New Amsterdam in 1647. The name was abbreviated to Ryertz, later Ryerse, and about 1700 anglicized to Ryerson. Col. Samuel Ryerson was a captain in the New Jersey Volunteers during the Revolutionary War and in 1783 having his property confiscated he went to New Brunswick and drew lands according to his rank as captain. In 1794 he decided to go to Upper Canada but first went back to Long Island. Travelling by foot he reached Niagara where his old friend, General Simcoe greeted him and gave him a large tract of land. He brought his family in 1795 and located at Long Point. His son, Egerton, was a prominent educationist in Ontario.

The Gosselin Family came from Dieppe, France, where Jacob G. and his wife Martha Chauvel lived and were members of the Reformed Protestant Religion. About 1620 they fled to Holland where they became members of the French Protestant Church in Amsterdam (L'Eglise Wallone d'Amsterdam). There were four children born in Holland. One son, Jacob, baptized March 31, 1627, went to England and married in the French Church, Threadneedle St., London, Sarah Gooris (also a Huguenot), April 1, 1655. Jacob, baptized November 24, 1661, was one of the sons who became a silk weaver and lived in Soho, London, and Canterbury. About 1699 he emigrated to America and settled at Newton, Long Island, where two children, Judith and Josse (Joseph) were born. This was the period when the name was changed to Gorsaline. Joseph's grandson, John, came to Canada about 1689 and married Jane Cronk (Cronkheyt) of Dutch parentage from Dutchess County, N.Y., and settled at Sophiasburg. He served in the War of 1812. His son, Reuben, who married one of the de Mille sisters (Huguenot family) was a farmer first near Belleville, later at Bloomfield. A descendant is Brigadier R. M. Gorsaline, a retired medical military officer who married Beatrice Marjorie Sparks, a direct lineal descendant of Nicholas Sparks, the founder of Bytown (Ottawa). (Brigadier R. M. Gorsaline, 22 Downing St., Ottawa.)

The following families are found in the Bay of Quinte district and are said to be Huguenot in origin : Ackerman, Bastedo, Bongard, Burdett, Barton, Blanchard, Buis, Canniff, Conger, Corby, Collier, Doxsee, Denyes, Dafoe (Defoe, DeVaux), Denike, Dulmage, Demille, DuColon, Dulyea, Flagler, Fox, Gerolomy, Goodonier, Huyck (Huyghens), Huff, Lazier, Mosure (Mosier), Pilchard, Pruyn, Pearsall, Parliament, Parrott, Purdy, Ruttan (William, Peter, Abraham), Redner, Ransier, Stickle, Striker, Saylor, Thiely, Toby, Trumpour (Paul and Haunts) Vanderwater, Vandervoort, Volleau, Valentine, Vrooman.

The Hardy and Ellis Families are two well-known families in Ontario, both of which have the Sturgis family as ancestors. Thomas Hardy was a Covenanter who after the battle of Bothwell Bridge escaped to Ireland where the family remained about a hundred years after which they came to America and settled near Harrisburg, Pa. The Ellis ancestor came from Ireland where he was a weaver, although the Ellis family is said to have had property in Flintshire, Wales. He settled at the 'Big Bend' of the Susquehanna River in Pennsylvania.

The Sturgis Family is said to have come from Wales to America. The first known Sturgis is Anthony who took title to land in 1687 for the entire block of Third and High Streets, Philadelphia. His son, Cornelius, married Elizabeth Millard, whose father was a Huguenot living in Philadelphia in 1696, thus bringing Huguenot blood into the family. His great-grandson, Thomas, born 1723, had a son, Amos, born 1751, who with his son, William, came to

Upper Canada and in 1801 leased two farms for nine hundred and ninety-nine years in Mount Pleasant from Joseph Brant of Brant's Ford, situated south of Brant's Fording Place (Brantford). Along with them came the Ellis family and founded Mount Pleasant named after the Ellis property in Wales. The Ellis family founded the Barber-Ellis Company.

Captain John Hardy during the Revolutionary War was an officer in the 84th Regiment while Captain Amos Sturgis fought for the Colonial forces. However, other members of the Sturgis family fought for the Colonies, but after the Revolution desired to return to the Crown and they all came to Canada together.

The Hardys, the Ellises, and the Sturgises intermarried. One of the Hardy and Sturgis descendants became Premier of Ontario— Hon. Arthur Sturgis Hardy; one a Senator—Hon. A. C. Hardy; and one a Judge—A. D. Hardy. Members of the Sturgis family have entered political and professional life in the United States, among them Dr. Samuel B. Sturgis, M.D., Honorary President, Pennsylvania Huguenot Society and Honorary President General of the National Huguenot Society.

The Secord Family is perhaps one of the best known in Canada, owing to the exploit of Laura Secord during the War of 1812–15. Ambroise Secord (Sycar) (1631–1712), the first-known ancestor, was a French Huguenot who fled from France some time after the Revocation to New Amsterdam with five grown children. In 1688 his eldest grand-child was baptized in the French church at New Amsterdam. In 1689 he became one of the founders and proprietors of the French settlement at New Rochelle, N.Y., where his will, written in French, is to be found in the Records. There is no information of his wife having reached America.

Daniel Sr. (1672–1742) lived at New Rochelle and inherited part of his father's estates. His son, Daniel (1698–1765) lived also at New Rochelle until late in life he seems to have moved to Cortlandt Manor, N.Y., where his son, Peter (1726–1818), lived before the Revolution.

Peter was a Loyalist and went to Niagara early and joined

Butler's Rangers, with whom he fought during the Revolution. At the close of the war he received several grants of land as a reward for his services to the Crown. First settling near Niagara, he later moved to Charlotteville, locating finally on the Talbot Road. His son, Captain David, served during the War of 1812 and lived at Charlotteville.

James, a brother of Peter, also fought in the Revolutionary War, and his son James married Laura Ingersoll.

The Tremaine Family is an example of a family, probably originally French because the crest suggests the name Trois Mains, which is first known in both Devon and Cornwall. The name of the ancestor was John de Tremain who married in the early part of the thirteenth century. Tremayne is situated on the banks of the Helford estuary in the parish of St. Martins-in-Meneage, Cornwall.

Descendants of this ancestor figured prominently in the Church and State life of succeeding centuries. One branch of the family went to France about 1540 and took part in the religious wars, returning to England during the reign of Elizabeth I; however, many of this family were killed in France near Montreau where a plaque is to be found.

About 1830 Richard Nicholas Tremain came to Canada when ten years of age with his parents (Michael) from St. Ives, Cornwall. Settlement was first made near Belleville; later they pushed on to Perth County, east of Listowel. Here Michael was born in 1855, and the 'e' was dropped because it was thought to suggest a French and therefore a Catholic background. (Clifford Tremain, Hespeler, and Glenn Tremain, Hamilton.)

The Wearing Family is interesting because of the change in name. Originally Guérin, the 'Gu' was changed to 'W', a phonetic change characteristic of both Spanish and French. This family came to Ontario in 1895, two members achieving professional recognition: Joseph, became a judge, and Thomas, Dean of Theology, Colgate University, Rochester, N.Y.

The Bogardus family tie in with the Reverend Evarardus

Bogardus who married in 1638 a Dutch woman, Annette Jans Webber, born in Holland. She was first married to John Roeloffson in 1628 and they came to America in 1630. The Bogardus family consisted of William, Cornelius, Jonas, and Peter. William married Wyntie Sybraut in 1651 and they had a daughter Annetzie who married Jacobus Brower in 1682. Eleven children were born to them; the youngest one in 1720 married John Drake who was the ancestor of the Drake family who came from New Jersey and settled in Jerseyville, near Brantford, about 1810.

Sir John Bourinot (1837–1902) was born in Sydney, Cape Breton. A great Canadian, he will always be remembered by his *Practice and Procedure of Parliament,* and for being one of the founders of the Royal Society of Canada. His family originated in Normandy and escaped after the Revocation to the Channel Islands. About 1812 John Bourinot came to Sydney, Cape Breton, was Lieutenant-Colonel, Vice-Consul for France in Canada, and represented Cape Breton in the House of Assembly at Halifax. Later he became a member of the first Senate of Canada. His son John became Chief Clerk of the House of Commons and exerted a wide influence on Parliamentary Procedure. An eminent historian and journalist, he was a great friend of such persons as Sir Gilbert Parker, Martin Griffin, John Reade, Duncan Campbell Scott, Archibald Lampman, and William Wilfred Campbell. His son Arthur S. has nobly carried on the traditions of this family by his many contributions in the fields of prose and poetry.

The following families are a few of the many who settled in the Niagara Peninsula after 1776:

Laurence Lemon (Le Moigne, Lamont) Loyalist from Pennsylvania, who settled in Bertie township. He married Mary Wilson, a Loyalist from New Jersey, a native of Ireland.

Samuel Van Wyck had ancestors who were some time seigneurs of Wyk in Holland, lost their high estate during the Spanish wars and fled to New York. After the Revolution Samuel settled in York County, later going to Niagara where he settled near the Falls.

William Pew (De Pieux?) came from Wales to Pennsylvania, then to New Jersey, and settled in Stamford in 1797.

Misener (Meissener) Family settled on Chippewa Creek in 1789.

Lundy (Lundi?) William and his brother Samuel were Quakers in Pennsylvania who came to Canada in 1786 and got a land grant at Stamford.

Fralick, John served in Butler's Rangers, came from New Jersey of 'Dutch' blood and settled at Stamford. His son was Robert Fralick.

Philip Chesneau DeLatre, a Lieutenant-Colonel in the British Army, came to the Peninsula in the Twenties. In 1836 he was President of the Niagara Harbor and Dock Co. and had a residence in Niagara called 'DeLatre Lodge'.

The Corwins were Norman French.

The Louks (Loucks, De Laux) Family originated in France and from there went first to Holland and then to Vermont. About 1788 William Louks came to Upper Canada and settled in Norfolk. The Honourable Ellen Fairclough, Postmaster-General, is a direct descendant.

The Guillet Family went from France in 1685 to Jersey and then to England. Jacques Louis Guillet made this migration. The family in the eighteenth century returned to Jersey and in 1832 John came to Canada, settling in Cobourg. The Guillets and the Thoreaus were intermarried. Jacques Thoreau had a daughter Jean T. whose descendant Marie married Charles William Guillet in 1796, and it was their son John who came to Canada in 1832. Edwin C. Guillet, the Canadian historian, is a grandson. A son of Jacques Thoreau, Philippe T., was the ancestor of the author and philosopher, Henry David Thoreau.

The Deeth Family name was originally de Ath but has had such variants as Deeth, Death, D'Eath. Coming to England from Flanders late in the fifteenth or early sixteenth century, they settled at Dartford, Kent. They were of the family of Count Leopold de Ath, of Ath, Heinault, Belgium. All records of this family are to be found in the records of the Established Church of England, the earliest being that of Stiles D'Eath, who was married to Mary Marsden on May 4, 1858. Later members became baronets. Thomas Death, born in London, came to Canada with his wife Charlotte in 1831. His son William married Martha Bassingthwaite and lived in Toronto. (Ruth Deeth.)

The Decew (DeCou) Family came originally from Saintonge district of France. Leuren (Larence) desCou signed a petition in 1654 where he lived in the salt marsh areas near Sandtoft in Lincolnshire, a Huguenot settlement founded about 1630. Isaac and his brother Jacob are thought to have come to America in 1676 and to have bought land from William Penn and finally settled in and around Trenton, New Jersey. A descendant also called Jacob came to Canada in 1790 and located in the Niagara district but later moved to Burford. He was granted land as a Loyalist.

The Cody (LeCaudey) Family has its roots in the Isle of Jersey, the first known ancestor being Guillaume (1480–1568). In 1668, a descendant, Phillipe, was born in the parish of St. Pierre and in 1692 he married Marthe Le Brocq of Guernsey. In 1692 a son, Phillip, was born in Beverly, Mass. It is probable that this family left the Isle of Jersey about the time many Huguenots were coming to Massachusetts for they came there as early as 1660. The migrations from the United States to Canada were three in number: Phillip from Marcellus, N.Y., to Peel County, Ont., in 1798; his brother Joseph from Marcellus, to Newmarket, Ont., area in 1801; their cousin Elijah Cody from Marcellus who was the great grandfather of the late Rev. Canon H. J. Cody and Ernest W. Cody of London. Col. Wm. F. Cody, better known as 'Buffalo Bill', was also a member of the Cody family.

Essex County

Reference to two large volumes; *Commemorative Biographical Record of the Counties of Essex and Kent* does not reveal many families that have a Huguenot background although it is very evident from many of the names that, in spite of the statements that these families originated in England, Ireland, or Scotland, the real country of origin was France. Quesnell, Desmarais, Clunis, and Loop are typical examples. Let us consider the County of Essex first :

Daniel Dutot was a Huguenot refugee who escaped from France to the Isle of Jersey where he acquired wealth through cattle raising. His wife was Catharine Lecauteur, also a refugee, and they had five children, among them John, who married Mary Anne Nicolle, also of Huguenot stock. In Jersey John was a gardener and spoke both English and French and came with his family to Quebec in 1862. From there they went to the County of Perth and settled in Tilbury West township. Of their five children, John became a farmer in Tilbury West; Mary Anne married Lorne Smith; Elizabeth, born in Canada, married James Bailey; and James, who became a leading farmer in Perth County, married Mary A. Halliday, and they had six children : Mary Charlotte, Elizabeth Maud, Grace Mildred, Ruth Lillian, Susan Jane, and Alfred Nickle.

The Gauthier Family in Canada stems from Jean B. Gauthier of Quebec who left there for Sandwich, Essex County.

The La Belle Family is descended from James S. La Belle who came from France and settled in Two Mountains, Quebec. A grandson, Oliver, became a pastor of the French Evangelical Church of Montreal.

Frederick Bouteiller, a Huguenot, was born in 1740 in Mont-béliard, France, was married in 1765, and died in 1785. His grandson, Pierre Antoine, was born in 1793 in France, married Catharine Dormoy, and in 1838 came with his family to Detroit. He bought farming land on the Grand River Road and became the ancestor of the American family.

The Gosnell family came from the County of Cork in the south of Ireland and contrary to the religious beliefs of the people of that area were Protestants in religion.

Of French origin, the Dauphin family was brought to Canada

by John Dauphin who served against the American forces when they invaded English territory along the Detroit River.

The LaMarsh family whose first known representative was Samuel LaMarsh came from France to Quebec, then to Kingston, and finally to Gosfield township, County of Essex. He fought in the war of 1812 and drew a tract of two hundred acres in the Colonel Talbot grant.

Daniel Van Horn was born in New Jersey in 1794, the son of Cornelius Van Horn, who came from Holland to New Jersey before the Revolutionary War. Daniel came to Kent County in 1825 and is said to be the first fruit grower on the River Thames and also one of the pioneers of Kent County.

Henry Van Allen of Holland ancestry was born in Long Island in 1763, married Winnifred Rapelgie, and their fifth child was born in 1798. Coming to Canada in 1818 they settled in Burford. Their son, Daniel Ross, was born in Burford and in 1833 he came to Chatham where he died in 1902.

The Huff Family have Abraham as ancestor in New York State. Leaving there he came to Prince Edward County and his son, Solomon, settled on an island in the Bay of Quinte where he acquired eleven hundred acres. Paul, Solomon's son, was born on Huff's Island in 1797 and with his wife came to Lambton County in 1845.

The Van Velsor Family was U.E. Loyalist in Nova Scotia where James was given two hundred acres of land. His son, William, came to Elgin County where his son, Dr. Daniel James, was born in 1835. The latter practised medicine in Blenheim.

The Malott (Marlotte) Family was French. Three brothers, Peter, Theodore, David, and two sisters, Catharine and Delilah, made their way from Maryland to Detroit in 1783. Captain William Malott was born in 1822 and became interested in marine pursuits. Of the original three, Peter married Mary Jones, who as a girl had spent ten years as a prisoner of the Indians.

The Laramie Family trace their ancestry to Alexander Laramie who came to Colchester South in 1843. Later he was a sailor and married Sarah Richardson.

The Perriss Family came to Ontario from Kentucky. Joseph and his bride, Christina Hahn, who had been a prisoner of the Indians, located in Colchester South township.

George Bedell was born in 1814, son of David Bedell who came from Staten Island to New Brunswick and from there to the County of Wellington.

The Dusty Family is of French descent. Samuel was born in St. Catharines. His son, James Donald, was a pioneer peach grower of Point Pelee.

It is interesting to note that two important places in Essex County, Maidstone and Colchester, are places in England where the Huguenots settled in large numbers.

Kent County

The Charteris Family came to Canada from Dumfriesshire, Scotland, the first known ancestor being Charles George, born in 1828. The family is known to be French coming from France during the reign of George II. James VI is said to have slept on the Charteris estate on his way to England; the bed on which he slept is now in Edinburgh museum. Dr. C. R. Charteris was born in Chatham township in 1865.

Stephen Parnell Sturgis, born in St. Catharines in 1852, settled in Brant County, thence to Camden in 1872.

The Bergie Family originated in Switzerland and came to Canada from Montgomery County, Pennsylvania, to settle in Waterloo County in 1850. They were members of the Mennonite faith.

Francis Xavier Goulet was born in 1791 in St. Jacques, Montcalm County, P.Q. In 1811 he came to Amherstburg and served in the British army during the War of 1812–14. Following the War he came to Raleigh township where he was given two hundred acres of land by Colonel Talbot.

Red River Colony of Lord Selkirk

About two hundred people were recruited in 1817 mainly from the Cantons of Bale, Berne, Fribourg, Solothurn, Neuburg, Geneva, and Valois, and by religion were Reformed Church and Lutheran. Mostly musicians, watch makers, and cooks, they knew little or nothing about agriculture and consequently had a difficult time at Red River. This was a settlement of Scots brought out by Lord Selkirk. Because he had aroused the animosity of the North West Company, his settlement was destroyed and Governor Semple, of the Hudson's Bay Company, was killed. On his way back to the Colony Lord Selkirk learned at Montreal of the attacks by the North West Company agents and the death of Governor Semple. He thereupon engaged over a hundred men of two disbanded Swiss mercenary regiments, the 'de Meurons' and the 'de Wattevilles', to be his soldier colonists and protect his Red River Settlement.

The soldiers did not fare much better in the Colony than the other Swiss, and after a few years most of the Swiss moved southward to Pembina, North Dakota. A few, however, went to the area which is now Hay Township in Western Ontario where they or their descendants founded the towns of Berne and Zurich. By 1849 only two Swiss families were left in the Red River Settlement.[3]

PART FIVE

Some Conclusions

1. In general, the term Huguenots is meaningless to most Canadians; consequently, they have no knowledge of them having existed elsewhere.

2. Huguenots in other parts of the world are entirely unaware of the parts Huguenots have played in the explorations of Canada, and of the number of persons now living in Canada who have a Huguenot ancestry.

3. The only historical data that exists concerning the discovery and development of New France come from persons whose purpose was to tell a story that would benefit them either as explorers or missionaries. In most cases such story tellers if not opposed to, were unfavorable to Calvinism, as it was known; consequently, only one side of the story has been told and even that has been edited, some of it twice, in order to delete anything derogatory to the Roman Church. This matter of editing has been freely admitted by French historians. Even Garneau's first edition, published in 1845 and generally accepted as the best and most unbiased history of early Canada, has been changed in later editions so that any facts critical of the Roman Catholic Church no longer appear.

4. Since there is no history of Huguenots in their relation to Canada, Protestants have accepted without question the Roman Catholic version. Canadian historians have never bothered to make a study of the early days of New France to learn if Protestantism ever played a major role, or any role, in fact, in its discovery.

5. It is quite reasonable to assume that, had it not been for such Huguenots as Roberval, Coligny, Chauvin, Pontgravé, de

Monts, and even Henry IV, it is very doubtful if France would have had any interest in New France and it would have become an English Colony. In all probability, if Huguenots, who were the best sailors and soldiers of France, had been allowed to migrate to Canada after 1633, England would have scarcely been able to conquer Canada in 1759.

6. In spite of strong and often repeated statements, it is not difficult to prove that the motivating interest for the first hundred years was the spirit of exploration and the money to be made from the fur trade. Missionary zeal was either absent, or at least secondary. And this was just as true of Champlain as of de Monts.

7. Explorers who were non-Roman Catholics never fared very well at the hands of early historians. Such persons as Roberval, de Monts, Radisson, LaSalle, and Frontenac are either severely criticized or lightly passed over as having contributed little.

8. What archival data concerning the first century of New France exists, should not be considered as sacrosanct. As pointed out above, because of the purpose for the writing of the letters, strong bias entered in; therefore, what data is still extant should be read with open-mindedness. This is not to consider them incorrect, but it does mean that they should be checked by other facts before being accepted as the final word.

9. In Canada, today, as in many other countries, there are a great number of persons who are intensely proud of their Huguenot ancestry. However, Canada is perhaps unique in that there is no Huguenot Society in existence.

10. Canada is unique in another way. Frenchmen do not hesitate to assimilate, but this has not taken place in the Province of Quebec where every effort has been expended to prevent assimilation, and where Roman Catholicism is a controlling factor.

In general, the Huguenots who left France were of a superior type, many of them belonging to the nobility and more coming from the highly skilled artisan class. For this reason French culture and artistic ability have been scattered throughout the world.

PART SIX

Vestiges of Huguenot Families in the Province of Ontario

BRIEF BIOGRAPHICAL SKETCHES

Huguenot Family Name	First Known Migration	First Known Ancestor	Person(s) Providing Information
Amour	Scotland		Amy Armour Smith, Stuart Armour, Hamilton, Ont.
Barron	Ireland		Mrs. Alice Pilant, Brantford, Ont.
Bethune, Le Béthune	Scotland		D. B. Shutt, Guelph, Ont.
Boyer	New Brunswick		R. B. Inch, Mt. Allison Univ. N.B.
Berlanquet, Berlinquette		George Berlanquet	Mary J. Berlanquet, Moffat, Ont.
de Bordeaux	Holland to Germany, to Canada 1951	Isaak de Bordeaux	Walter Bordeaux, London, Ont.
Bièler	Canada	Jean Henri Merle d'Aubigné	Mrs. Andre Bieler, Kingston, Ont.
Bigneys	Nova Scotia	Charles Frances d'Aubigné (1817–1878)	Mrs. T. F. Bulmer, Kingston, Ont.
Bordervijk	Holland to Canada	Catharina Witovet	Jantien Walma Witovet, Orillia
Clements (Empeys)			Norris Woodruff, Hamilton, Ont.
de Courcy Dean	Ireland	Mrs. Josephine Dean, Thomas de Courcy	Ruth T. Rushton, Rev. de Courcy Rayner, editor, Presbyterian Record, Toronto, Ont.
Evel, Eveleigh Evelley	Devonshire, Eng. (D'Eveille)	Thomas Evel's son came to Hamilton 1871	J. Guy Evel, Hamilton, Ont.

Huguenot Family Name	First Known Migration	First Known Ancestor	Person(s) Providing Information
Le Furgey	Azores to Maritime Provinces, PEI		Mrs. C. B. Barwise, Charlottetown, PEI
Le Gresley	Channel Islands		Miss Ethel McKague, Bowmanville, Ont.
Fites, Francis		Martin Fite	Eva S. M. Griffin, Mrs. Gerald Galbraith, Gorrie
Hogan	Ireland (original name Mullette) then to Penn.	George Mullette	Mrs. Frank Thorpe, Port Credit, Ont.
d'Hougard Huggard	Southern Ireland	John William and Henry Irwin Turner, came to Canada 1911	Mrs. H. I. Turner, Toronto, Ont.
Lods	From Hericourt, France to Montreal and Namur after Franco-Prussian War		Emile A. Lods, Macdonald College, P.Q.
Molyneux	Canada c. 1819	Wm. Molyneux	Miss Myrtle Stephens, Toronto, Ont.
Lavis, Plaunt	Scotland	Francis Xavier Plaunt, a first settler in Renfrew	Mrs. C. E. Thompson, St. Thomas, Ont.
Perigoe	Sussex, England		I. H. Perigoe, Toronto, Ont.
Powell	Pennsylvania	Roxanna Powell, M. Edward Dales	Silas A. Salter, Toronto, Ont.
Pilant	Prussia, Missouri, Ontario	Frederick William Pilant	Richard Pilant, Brantford, Ont.
Quereau	Nova Scotia c. 1685, exiled to U.S. in 1755		Eleanor Quereau, Rochester, NY
de Munck	Possibly a German family that married into Lere and Bastwick Huguenot family		Mrs. R. M. Rogers, Toronto, Ont.
Martin	Ireland (Riverstown)	John, Abraham, Robert, Thomas	Esther M. Brodie
Le Lacheur	Guernsey	James L. Lacheur	Ralph S. LeLacheur, Guernsey Cove

Huguenot Family Name	First Known Migration	First Known Ancestor	Person(s) Providing Information
Mainguy	Channel Islands		Miss A. Cecilia Pope, Toronto, Ont.
de Niord de Nord	England		W. A. Brent, Hespeler, Ont.
Sissons Sisson	England (Hull) to Canada 1831, Penetang	Jonathan Sissons	Prof. C. B. Sissons, Newcastle, Ont.
Trieux	Pennsylvania, early 1600s, in c. 1784, Waterloo, Que. then Essex Cy., Ont.	Abraham Truax	Dr. F. G. Truax, Toronto, Ont.

NAMES OF FAMILIES SAID TO BE OF HUGUENOT ORIGIN

Brebner (le Brabaner)
Confort (Comfort)
Collins
Costain
Crommelin
Cunard
Currie
Currelly
Dalhousie
De Grassie
David
Dupuy
Dysert
Desbarres
Eccles

Farmer
Finch
Fleming
Found (Fownes)
Grierson
Jevons
Maynard
Pequenat
Pidoux
Sampson (Feuilleteau)
Silcox
Tanner
Verity (Verité)
Zeller (Sellaire

ADDITIONAL

Huguenot Family Name	Place of Origin	Date and Place of First Migration	Names and Dates of First Known Ancestors	Dates and Place of Second Migration	Migrated to Canada
Battelle	France	Liverpool, England	Arthur Battelle, Fred Battelle		1890
Bréhaut (Burhoes)	Channel Isles	Guernsey 1331		Prince Edward Island 1798	1798
Condie Condé	France	Scotland	Alexander Condé	Went to Canada then back to Scotland for 7 years	
Du Cas	France	Sweden		Estonia	1946
Durand	Montpillier, France	Nimeguen, Capet, Westphalia, Milan, Bruges	John Durand, a son Francis Guillaume	Norwich, 1744, Canterbury	
Jowsey	France	Northumberland, England	John and Isobel Jowsey		1816
Larrobie, Larrobée	France	Isle of Wight	Greenleaf Larrobie	Rhode Island, U.S.	
La Hogue	France	Channel Isles	Margaret La Hogue	Ireland (?)	1830
Medill	France	Belfast, Ireland	Christmas Medille, b. 1796–1888		1819
Prestige	France	England			c. 1885
Provins	Provins, France	England		N. Ireland	
Rambo, Rambeau, Rimbault (?)	France	Sweden	Peter Rambo	Philadelphia 1669	1832
Richard	Paris, France		Bedard Lods(z)		1874
Rimbault	France	England 1570	Eduard Francis Rimbault		
Runions, Runyan, Runyon, Roguin, Rougnion	Poitou	Jersey Island	Vincent Rognion, m. Ann Boutcher in N.J. 1668	Elizabethtown, N.J. 1664	
Toutin de Villeseauve	Anger, France				1904

FAMILY NAMES

Locations in Canada	First Ancestors in Canada	Other Facts of Interest	Person(s) Providing Information
Montreal, Napanee	Fred Battelle	Wealthy family in England	Mrs. Irene Stringer, Coe Island Lake, Bancroft, Ont. Mr. Sterling Walker, c/o Higgs & Co. Ltd., Charlottetown, P.E.I.
Near Smith Falls	Alexander Melville Condie	First "ice cream" was made when Louis Condé was entertaining Louis XIV. Some salt fell on some cream in the ice and then covered with sherry. Louis XIV named it "Ice Cream"	Mrs. Stella Schaefer, 71 William St. W., Smith Falls, Ont.
Toronto			D. H. Pooles, 127 Midland Av., Toronto R. W. Scringeour, 1114–4th St., N.W., Calgary
Quebec City, Eardly Twp.	Thos. Jowsey (1801– 1872), m. Rosannah Merrifield, 1826		R. Philip Smart, Picton, Ontario
Eastern Twp., Sherbrooke, Quebec Seaforth	Roland Larrobee, b. at Livermore Falls, Maine Margaret La Hogue, m. Finlay Ross	Brothers Aaron and Myron lived in Boston, Mass. Both buried in Egmondville Cemetery	Mr. Marjorie Rothwell, 116 Oakdale Ave., Merritton, Ont. Finlay A. Ross, 1517 Dougal Ave., Windsor, Onterio
New Brunswick, Ohio, Bruce Penincula North shore of Lake Superior, Lumber camp, Toronto	Christmas Medill, m. Hugh Carroll, Thomas Medill	A brother Joseph Medill founded *Chicago Tribune*	Mrs. E. M. Stewart, 30 Norwich St. E., Guelph, Ontario James Prestige, Peterboro, Ont.
Near Napanee	Samuel Provins 1802–1882		Florence Provins, 151 Aberdeen St., Fort Erie, Onterio
Port Huron, Caledonia, Ontario	Mary Rambo, m. Snider at Caledonia, Ont. William and brother Jed Rambeau		Sara Scrase, Detroit, Mich. Mrs. Victor Simpson, R.R.1, Port Colborne, Ontario
Ottawa	Martin Lodz Richard Victor Rimbault	Bedard Lods founded French Protestant Church in Ottawa One ancestor wrote "Abide with me"	Mrs. A. A. H. Richard, 195 Patterson Ave., Ottawa Mrs. Victor Rimbault, 139 Briscoe St., London, Ont.
Cornwall	Henry Runions, m. Abigail Lynch	Damon Runyon is a family connection	Miss Mary C. Runians, 53 Carfree St., London, Ont.
Montreal	August Bingamin Toutin	Original castle in France still stands	Robert S. Toutin, 8 Lake Ave. S., Stoney Creek, Ont.

MORE EXTENDED BIOGRAPHICAL SKETCHES

Huguenot Family Name	Place of Origin	Date and Place of First Migration	Names of First Known Ancestors and Dates	Date and Place of Second Migration	Date of Migration to Canada	Location in Canada	Ancestors in Canada	Other Facts of Interest	Person(s) Providing Information
Achtzehnter	France	1680 Friedrichsdorf	Theodor Achtzehnter		1952	P.E.I., Chatham, Ont.		Belonged to group that left after Revocation	Thos. Achtzehnter, 143 Park St., Chatham
Adolph	France	As a child to Switzerland	Henri Adolf	Returned to France as member of Imperial Swiss Guards. Escaped to Italy, Switzerland, then Pennsylvania		New Dundee, Waterloo Cy.	Henri Adolf	Married in Switzerland, clever musician, spoke several languages	Miss Ruth W. Adolph, R. R. 2, Collingwood, Fred Adolph, to Sheldon Block, Calgary, Alta.
Ames Eymes	France	Kent, England 16th-17th cent.			1926	Vancouver, B.C.	Geraldine (Mrs. S. A. Young) John and Michael Ames		Michael M. Ames, c/o Messrs. Cook & Sons, Colombo, Ceylon
Annett	France	England 1572			1829	Elgin County	Robert Annett (1892)	His son Philip came in 1829	Miss Leapha Annett, Bothwell, Ont.
Arnaud	Bigorre, France Saintonge	Elias Arnaud to England 1685; smuggled in a hamper and went to England in an open boat	Guillem Arnaud Baron of Barbazan		1869	Ottawa, Antongish and Annapolis Royal, N.S.	Elias de Barbean Arnaud	Was Canada's first Trade Commissioner, Chicago, St. John's, Nfld., Bristol, England	John deB. Arnaud, Picton, Ont.
Batiste	Lyons							His ancestors invented the Batiste cloth and it was named after him	
Bellamy Belesme Bellamée Bellamie	Bellesme, France	England c.1575	John Bellamy and son Matthew	New Haven c.1635	1816	North Augusta, Grenville Cy.	Justus and sons Channey Hall, Channey, Channey Jr., Warren M.	Bought 400 acres of land and built saw and grist mills	Herbert J. Bellamy London, Ont.
Bennett	France	Spitalfields, London			1888	Ottawa district	Mrs. Edward Gane	The Bennetts married the Ganes; were weavers	Mary Anne Hanson Bennett, 351 Pleasant Park Road, Ottowa
Bilyea Bulliers (F.) Beljee Belje (Dutch)	France	Holland after 1572	Jan Beljee, b. 1695 m. Helen Wilemse, 1719	Long Island, N.Y.	1783	St. John's River, N.B.	Henry, James, John	Henry came to Ontario in 1848, settling in Middlesex Cy	Miss Leila Belyea, 149 Emery E. London, Ont.

								children	
Blanchard	Cape of the Hague, Normandy; made Huguenots by John Calvin	England 1500	Thos. Blanchard	Boston, Mass. 1610 Braintree, Dorchester	1799	Brockville	Leeds Cy. Founded Greenbush, near Brockville	John and Abigail Blanchard	Arriving in Boston in 1639 same ship: Bellnay, Bissell, Carpenters, Chamberlains, Marshalls, Langtrys (Lily), Coolidges, Mayhau (Mailloux), Taplins, Loverins, (Lavengnes), Leavitts, De la Noye (Delano), Molines (Mollins) Savages (Sauvage)	Bissell, 70 Lonsdale Rd., Toronto Harry D.Blanchard, 224 Oakridge Dr., Toronto
Bobier Bobiar	France	Wexford Cy, Ireland c. 1700	John Bobier m. Hannah Hudson	New York 1848	1849		Hammond, Russell Cy.	Margaret m. Jonathan Watson Benjamin, Hannah, Eliza, Sarah Eliza m. John Kinsella (Huguenot)	There were Bobiers who came from Wexford Cy, Ireland, on Talbot Settlement about 1825	Hazel Watson, Macdonald, Navon, Ontario. Bryson A. Bobier, 10 Kenneth Ave., London
Bouchard	France				c. 1860		Ha-Ha Bay	Elzear Bouchard m. Agnes Colclough	Louis, a son, became French Protestant minister, United Church, Montreal	Mary E Jowsey, 252-11th Ave., Lively, Ont.
Bovaird Beauvert Boisvert Bovard	Lyons, La Rochelle, Paris (late 15th c.)	England then Scotland (one year) 1572	Jacques Beauvert m. Marie le Printemps	Ireland	1840–45		Augusta Twp.	Richard	Escaped St. Bartholemew's massacre in boat in England, then Scotland, Ireland and Canada	Harold Bovoird, 12 Jane St, Grimsby, Ont.
Burgar Bourchault	Cambrai, France	Norwich, England 1595		America 1760	1797		Welland	Peter and wife, Ann Nelson, Joseph and wife, Anna Rowley	Burgar Street and Burgar Recreational Park, Welland, located on original farm and named after them	Gertrude M. Burger, 27, Dickson St., Galt

243

Huguenot Family Name	Place of Origin	Date and Place of First Migration	Names of First Known Ancestors and Dates	Date and Place of Second Migration	Date of Migration to Canada	Location in Canada	Ancestors in Canada	Other Facts of Interest	Person(s) Providing Information
de Brisay		England (?)		Ireland	1769	P.E.I.	Capt. Thomas de la Cour DesBrisay, Lt.Gov. of PEI	Jacques Read DesBrisay, Marquis de Denonville, Gov. of N. France 1685–89, an ancestor Chief Justice of B.C. Alexander Campbell DesBrisay, a descendant	A. W. Y. DesBrisay, Lieut.-Col. retired, Ottawa
Batiste	Lyons	Guernsey Island	John Batiste m. Rachel Major		1880	Elgin Cy.		John Batiste was a silk weaver in Lyons and invented the material Batiste	Ernest Batiste St. Thomas Ont.
de Burgh Bourck	Hungary	France	Hugh de Burgh, England 1685		1847	Halifax	Rev. William Harvey, Heu de Bourck	Served as congregational minister in N.S.; then Quebec; Iowa, U.S.A.; became Presbyterian and served at Brockville	Rev. S. Simpson Black, Uxbridge, Ont. Mrs. J. G. Clark, Toronto, Ont.
Corneille	France	Galway, Ireland			1824	Georgina Twp. York Cy, Ont.	Mary Corneille Shier	A widow she made her home with her daughter the widow of Capt. John Brethour	Mrs. James Quigley, Belleville, Ont.
Calas	Toulouse, France	England	John Calas		1920			Voltaire proclaimed the innocence of John Calas	Mrs. A. A. Magenty 29 Grange St., Stratford, Ont.
Cantelon de Cantillon Cantlon Cantlin	Bavarian Palatinate	1685 England	John de Cantillon	1690 Kilcooly, Ireland	1808	Peel Cy., Goderich Cy., Huron Cy., Ont.	John Cantelon 1800–87; Wm. 1775–1859; John 1778–1874; Peter (Cantton) 1786–1863; Arthur 1793–1877; Rev. David	This family can be traced back to 912 A.D. Four sons and twenty-five grandchildren of John emigrated to Canada where there are 1800 descendants	Leon C. Cantelon, Wingham, Ont.

Surname	Country	Place of origin	Original name	Migration	Date	Place of settlement	Settler / descendant	Notes	Reference
						Prescott, Waterdown	[...]let m. James Fields, 2 sons, Edmund and Fulford	[...]onard came to Waterdown; Fulford to Prescott; Jane, the mother, and daughter Sophia came from St. Germain	Mrs. [...] R. Cureton, Embro, Ont.
Charlton de Charleton	France	Cevennes	Cazalet			Ilderton Ont.	Edward		Mrs. Jean Charlton, Ilderton
Claris	France	Falstone, England			1830	Talbot Settlement Belmont Twp. at Havelock	John, George, and Christopher	First settlers with Silcox, Allsworth families	
Doupe	France	Canterbury England Holland		Iceland					A. Phillips Silcox, Lorne Park James Doupe, Prince Albert, Ont.
Dupère	France	East end of London			1909	Guelph		Weavers in London	Mrs. Anne Cutler, 45 Rose Ave. Brantford
Dupuis	France		Jacobi and Jeremy Dupuis		before 1800	Quebec City, Minda, Que.	Jacobi and Jeremy Dupuis	Original ancestors started a potash business in Quebec City but were forced to leave; Jacobi settled at Minda, where he changed his name to Marcus	Mrs. Dolores Deverell, Stouffville, Ont.
Dutilh	France	Holland	Moise-Dutilh 1634-1708		1953–57	Scarborough, Ont.	C. W. Bagschus		C. W. Bagchus, 1689 Victoria Park Ave., Scarborough, Ont.
Duval	France	Amsterdam, Holland				Bonaventure Island	Capt. Duval	A privateer under George IV. Scarlet coat and bible 1707 in archives, Ottawa	Mrs. Alice Warren, 142 Rachael Ave., Ottawa
Du Vernet	France	Holland after 1572		Went to England with William of Orange	1800	Louisburg, N.S. Greenville, S.C.		Leaving military service one branch took land at Gagetown; another went into the church, and other professions	E. A. Du Vernet, 37 Hartfield Cresc., Toronto
Dumbrille Domville	France	Etchingham, Sussex			1852 (John)	Maitland, Ont.	Richard Dumbrille and wife, Martha	A landscape gardener who planned grounds of Spencerwood at Quebec. Dorothy Dumbrille, the writer, is a descendant	Dorothy Dumbrille

Huguenot Family Name	Place of Origin	Date and Place of First Migration	Names of First Known Ancestors and Dates	Date and Place of Second Migration	Date of Migration to Canada	Location in Canada	Ancestors in Canada	Other Facts of Interest	Person(s) Providing Information
D'Esterre	France	Jersey Island c. 1572		1860					Mrs. P. B. D'Esterre, 39 Arundel Ave., Toronto, Ont.
Falle	France	Channel Islands late 1700s		1860		Gaspé Peninsula Belleville	John Albert Folle	First émigré to Channel Island given grant of land by King of England, still occupied by descendant	John Francis, Folle Carter, 851 Johnson St., Kingston, Ont.
Farrants Le Farrand	France	England	Edward Farrants m. Margot Jane Lack	Michigan 1882	1884	Toronto	Edward Farrants	A member of Toronto Fire Dept. 35 yrs.	Gordon W. Farrants, 439 Douglas Ave. Toronto, Ont.
Fawdry	Nimmis, France	Salford, Oxfordshire, England	Jacques Flaudry 1685	1906		Calgary, Alta.	Herbert Edward	Cornelius, Lydia Marion came 1913	Mrs. Marion Fawdry, 1206 Fairfield Rd. Victoria, B.C.
Ferns	France	Ireland							Mrs. S. Olheiser, 300 Steele St., London, Ont.
Foucar	Proissy, Picardy	Friedrichsdorf, Germany, 1698	Isaac Foucar m. Anne Boulle	1911		London, Ont.	Henri Ernest Foucar	The Foucars played a prominent part in Friedrichsdorf, the settlement in Germany where asylum was offered by Frederick II of Germany in 1786	Dr. H. O. Foucar, 484 Waterloo St., London, Ont.
Forrest de Forêt	France	Scotland			1882	Mariposa Twp.	William Forrest	He married Susan Perrin whose parents (de Perrin) were Huguenots from Wales	Rev. A. C. Forrest, Editor, United Church Observer
Gendron	France			c. 1665		Montreal, Brockville	Mitchell Gendron; sons	Family trade in Ontario was	Edward Phelps, 1777 Lake Shore

246

Surname	Origin	Emigration / settled	Immigrant ancestor & marriage	Descendant / name	Date	Place	Notes	Contact
(continued from previous page)		1665	m. 1780; m. Rebecca Clark Penn. 1725				sons Thomas and Charles, Samuel and daughter Elizabeth	in Indiana and Pennsylvania. Dr. Robert Goheen, Pres. of Princeton University was a descendant	...ouden, Millbrook, Ont.
Gorsline Gosline Gosselin Gosnell	France; Dieppe, Normandy	Amsterdam, Holland 1620; England	Jacob Gosselin m. Martha Chauvel, London, England 1645	Henry Gosnell		Cork, Ireland; Kent Cy., Highgate		Glenn C. Way, 1631 Niagara Ave., Niagara Falls, N.Y. Mrs. Geo. M. Oliver, 334 Boler Rd., Byron, Ont.
Hébert	France; Bolvec, Normandy	1671 England	Hébert, Seigneur de Sainte Marie, Normandy	T. Hébert Lant	1950	Toronto		T. Hébert Lant, 125 Lawton Blvd., Toronto
Huestis	France	United States		Martin Bent Huestis *m.* Victoire Ayrton Johnson		Maritimes (?)	Rev. Dr. Stephen Fulton Huestis, Publisher, Methodist Book Co., Halifax, Rev. Dr. Chas. Hubert Huestis, columnist, *Toronto Star*; Anne Campbell Huestis, poet, member of this family	Doris Huestis Spiers, Cabble Hill, Pickering, Ont.
Huff	France	1685 New York (?)	William Huff	Lt. Paul Huff	1802	Hay Bay	First Methodist Church class met in his home in 1791 and first church built on his farm 1792	Miss Marjorie Huff, 173 Sheridan St., Brantford, Ont.
Le Huguet	France	ersey Island	Abraham le Huguet Elizabeth Palot	Ann le Huguet	1870		Married when 18 Rev. Brenton, Methodist lay preacher. Family names Palot, Renouf, Cabot, Mallet	Clara le H. Brenton 188 Bruce St., London, Ont.
Hulsart	France	1572 England (?)	Raymond de Toulouse	Eliza (Raymond) Hulsart		Richard in Salem, Mass., William in Quebec, John in Norwalk, Conn.	Born in N.Y. City 1811	Mrs. E. V. Bachanan, 776 Wellington London, Ont.

Huguenot Family Name	Place of Origin	Date and Place of First Migration	Names of First Known Ancestors and Dates	Date and Place of Second Migration	Date of Migration to Canada	Location in Canada	Ancestors in Canada	Other Facts of Interest	Persons(s) Providing Information
d'Honoré Honor Honnor	Normandy	Ireland, Wales	Edward, Robert, Gregory, Joseph	New York	c. 1830	Darlington Twp., Essex County	Edward's seven sons all born in Ireland	Edward, James, Frank, Thomas, Joseph, William, Frederick, name spelled 'Honner' all fought in 1837–38 Rebellion	Mrs. Melville Buttars, Pickering, Ont.
Hough	France	Holland	John Hough	Pennsylvania	c. 1783	Lennox Cy.	John Hough m. Catharine Margaretta Alquire 1775		Mrs. H. M. Hough, Sillsville Dr. Robert Grierson, Toronto Miss Florence Swan Fredericton, N.B.
Hue	France	Parish St. Mary, Isle of Jersey	Jean Hue m. Marie Lebrun		c. 1880	New Carlisle Gaspé	Stannas Edward Hue m. Alice H. Hamon; m. Eliza Hamon		
Jacques	France	England	Christopher Jacques 1750 1834		1830	Jarvis, Ont.	Thomas m. Elizabeth Cole	Came to Canada with his mother and stepfather Isaac Bird	A. B. Lemon, Dean Emeritus School of Pharmacy, University of Buffalo
Jaap	France	Scotland c. 1685			1870	St. Marys, Thedford			Alex M. Jaap, Milton, Ont.
Janthur	La Rochelle, France	Brandenburg, Germany	Ganthur		1954		Richard O. Janthur		W. O. Janthur Jasper, Ont.
Jay	La Rochelle	England	Pierre Jay d. 1685	Ancestor came to N.Y. 1686, John Jay, a son	1796	Hastings Cy. near Belleville	John Jay Farley, William Worden Farley	John Jay had a daughter, Mary, who married Col. Farley. Their sons came to Canada	Hazel Farley Trenton, Ont.
Jolly Joli	France	Scotland c. 1572				Elma	Henri Joly was Premier of Quebec in 1878; a member of Laurier's cabinet 1896–1900 and Lt.-Gov. of B.C.		Mrs. E. Etherington, 297 Erie St., Stratford, Ont.
Journeaux	France	Jersey Island					Philip Journeaux m. Betsy Moreaux		Mrs. Neil Lewis 62 Laurel Ave., Ottawa
Kidd	France	England 1709		Cy. of Wicklow, Vale of Avoca, Ireland then to north of Ireland	1812	Wilsey Lake, north of Brockville;	Joseph Kidd		James H. Kidd Woodbridge

248

249

Surname	Origin	Birthplace / origin	Immigrant ancestor	Earlier settlement	Year	Place settled	Married / descendants	Notes	Present descendant
Lamoreaux	France	Bristol, England 1692	Daniel m. Elizabeth Ogden	New York State 1700	1783	Parr Town, N.B.	who married Rowland Barr in 1819; James Lamoreaux m. Martha Cross. He lived to be 111 years of age	J. B. Tyrell and brother William were grandsons of Hester	Thos. Kennedy, 35 Hartfield Rd., Islington, Ont.; Mrs. R. Stuart Fleming, 723 W. Onandaga St., Syracuse, N.Y.
Lapraik	France	Scotland	John Lapraik				William Fairbairn m. Sara Lapraik	John Lapraik was a neighbor of Robert Burns on farm Mossgiel and had some poems dedicated to him by Burns	Dorothea P. E. Druce, 573 Earl St., Kingston, Ont.
Lazier Laslier	Dettingerm Bavaria	1640 New Amsterdam	Jacob Victorian Lazier	1708 Yonkers		Sophiaburg	Nicholas Jacobus Lazier	Connected with Demorest family	Mrs. Margaret Kelsey, R.R.1, Athens, Ont.
Lilliott	France	Sussex, England			1818	Levis, Que.	Richard Lilliot m. Mary Turner of London, England in 1818	Married by Bishop Mountain	Mrs. D. V. Wyatt, 2 Hazelbrae Rd., Toronto
Lamerieux Lamoree Lamoroo	France				1800	New Brunswick (1816 Pickering), Ont.	James Lamerieux	Martha Lamerieux m. Sherwood Palmer	Silas Tool, Locust Hill, Ont.
Langille	Montebeliard, France				1753	Lunenburg, N.S. (1771 River John)	John David Langille	As inhabitants of Alsace they understood German as well as French	Mrs. G. J. Barrett, Lancaster, N.B.
Levan de Long de Longville		Dutchess Cy. N.Y.S.			c. 1780	Woodstock, Ont.			M. J. Guthrie, Guelph, Ont.
Lageer La Guerre	Brittany	Ireland 1692	Michel LaGuerre			Bradford, Ont.	Amelia Long LaGuerre and children, Amelia, James, Katherine, Margaret	Michel was a soldier who married a farm girl and was disinherited and died. His wife came to Canada and joined her own people Longs at Bradford. She later married Drummond of Barrie; a daughter married Maher	Mrs. Winnifred Lageer, Stayner, Ont.

Huguenot Family Name	Place of Origin	Date and Place of First Migration	Names of First Known Ancestors and Dates	Date and Place of Second Migration	Date of Migration to Canada	Location in Canada	Ancestors in Canada	Other Facts of Interest	Person(s) Providing Information
DeLong	France	England c. 1685		Dutchess Cy., New York State	1785 (?)	Prince Edward Cy.	David deLong	David deLong was a surveyor who helped to survey Ameliasburg Twp.	Jack F. DeLong, 125 Wragg St., London, Ont.
Losee					1780s	Prince Edward Cy.	Rev. William Losee	First Methodist Minister to Hay Bay Church 1793	Mrs. H. D. Wightman, John St., Napanee, Ont.
Luard	France	Lincolnshire, England, 1685	Sir Wm. Garsham Luard, K.C.B.		1892	Burford	Arthur du Cane Luard	Listed in Burke's Peerage	Mrs. A. D. C. Luard, Burford, Ont.
Mallard	France	Holland, England 1572		Northern Ireland	1928	London, Ont.			Mrs. John Morgan, 19 Wyatt St., London, Ont.
Manchee	France		Dorion de Monchy		1876		one of the de Monchy girls m. Montmorency after whom the Montmorency Falls is named		Frank C. Manchee, 38 King W., Toronto
Marmont	North o France	Gloucestershire, England c. 1572	General Marmont a Napoleon general		c. 1880	near Brandon Man.	Lindsay Marmont	In England they made cloth, needles and pins	H. E. Taylor, Can. Bank of Commerce, Head Office, Toronto
Marriage	France	England, Essex Cy.			1897		Bernard Marriage	Original family was all weavers	Bernard Weaver, 8 Bellevue Ave. London, Ont.
Martin	France	Ireland							Esther M. Brodie, 98 Edinburgh Ave., Hamilton, Ont.
Meredith	France	Ireland	Henri duc de Montmorenci (Lord High Admiral of France)		1819	Montreal, Quebec, Toronto (1842)	Mrs. Elizabeth (Thomas) Meredith, son, Edmund Allen	Louis Henri le Jeune, second generation from the duc, fled to Ireland, changed name to Younge	Mrs. Jas. O'Reilley 267 Inglewood Drive, Toronto
DeMille	Paris, France	Canada			1798 (?)	Fort Erie, Ont.	Margare De Mille m. Alex Douglas	Their grandson Dr. Wm. Douglas left money to found Douglas Memorial Hospital, Fort Erie	Miss Norah M. Clark, 315 Lonsdale Rd. Toronto
de Monchy	France	Holland	René de Monchy 1670		1953-57	Scarborough, Ont.	C. W. Bagchus		C. W. Bagchus, 1680 Victoria

Name	Origin	Refuge	Immigrant Ancestor	American Settlement & Date	Year	Place	Family Details	Notes	Contact
Morpier Morphy	France	Ireland			c. 1831	Toronto	d. 1762 m. Margaret David Samuel, Henry, George, Thomas, Edward, Andrew	joined Dutch Reformed Church about 1693 Several became prominent lawyers and businessmen	G. A. Barr, Q.C., Regina, Sask.
Manigault	La Rochelle	England	Pierre and Gabriel Manigault	Charleston, N.C. 1690	1869	London	Gabriel Manigault		Anne V. Manigault, London, Ont.
de la Mater	Artois, France	Canterbury	Claudede la Mater	Amsterdam, Holland, then Flatbush Lond Island 1652	1817	Pelham Welland Cy.	Seymour de la Mater, his father Isaac and brother Martin	Many descendants have been educationists	Miss E. Magdalene de la Mater, Fenwick, Ont.
Mercer	France	Holland		England 1688 (Hillborough), Ireland 1690		York Mills	Thomas Mercer (1744-1829)		Malcolm Faulkner
Parrette	France	Ireland			before 1800	Halifax	Mary Parrette m. John Grierson 1853		Dr. Robt. Grierson, Toronto
Paskell Pascal	France	Suffolk, England							F. J. Pascall, 99 Cobourg St. Stratford
Pecunier							Margaret m. James Cope, son of Conrad Cope		M. Moses, Niagara Falls, Ont.
Perchard	France	St. Helier, Jersey Island			1852	Whitby, Norwood, Hastings	François Perchard m. Sousanne Lecouteur	Married by Bishop Mountain	W. Fred Stewart, 2 Clarendon Ave., Toronto
Pettigrew	France	Ireland					William Carson Pettigrew		Mrs. L. A. Macklin
Pickard Picquard	France	England	Picquard	1774 Germantown, Pa.	1810	Niagara Falls, Peel Cy.	James Pickard, Jr., Niagara Falls; Archibald	James fought in Revolutionary War; ret'd to England; died; his two sons given grants in Ontario. Archibald first settled in Brampton	Mrs. F. L. Goodman, 181 Jane St., Toronto

Huguenot Family Name	Place of Origin	Date and Place of First Migration	Names of First Known Ancestors and Dates	Date and Place of Second Migration	Date of Migration to Canada	Location in Canada	Ancestors in Canada	Other Facts of Interest	Person(s) Providing Information
Prieur de la Roche	Paris	England 1887	Léontine Marie Henriette Prieur		1888	Rosseau, Parry Sound District	Léontine Marie-Henriette Crossley (Prieur)	The family possessed a sword given by Napoleon in Russian campaign to an ancestor in 1812	Mrs. L. M. Binglos, 114 Ridley Blvd., Toronto Mrs. L. M. Burgess, Rosseau, Ont.
Peppy Peppin Peppen	France	Channel Islands			1750–60	Harbour Grace Nfld.	Charles Peppy	One ancestor was an admiral of the French Navy and present at the expulsion of Acadians in 1750	Geo. E. Peppy, Glace Bay, N.S.
Perrin Perrine Perin Prine Perine	France		Dan Perrin, b. 1640		1829	Mt. Vernon	Thos. Perrin, Jr., b. Springfield, Mass, 1791	Founded Mt. Vernon, Brant County	Miss Smythe, Mount Pleasant
Le Quesnel (Connell)	Normandy	Ireland 1626		1834		Grenville Cy.	John Connell and wife Elizabeth Levis	Irish changed the pronunciation and spelling of name	Dr. W. S. T. Connell, 37 Claremont Dr., Hamilton
Raymond	Toulouse, France	England	Count Raymond	Plymouth Hoe on "Mayflower" 1620	1867	Guelph	Charles Raymond	Sewing machine manufacturer Ernest Raymond, the author, son of Henry who returned to England	Mrs. D. B. Shutt, Guelph, Ont.
Renaud	France	Holland 1685	Renaud de St. Jean d'Angélie				Mrs. M. Heynneman-Renaud	Quinan Renaud went to Leiden; his brother Philippe to Maastricht	Mrs. H. Renaud 84 Lillian St., Toronto
Robert	France	Guernsey Island			1873	London Ont.	Maring Robert m. Marguerite Gilbert		Minnie E. White
Robinette	France	Saffron Walden, England 1685		Penn	c. 1816	Middlesex Cy.		T. C. Robinette, noted criminal lawyer, descendant	John J. Robinette, Q.C., Toronto
Savigny	France	Hadingtonshire, Scotland, 1572	John Horatio Savigny		1834	Little York (Toronto)	Andrew Blair Savigny	Moved to Montreal 1838 where he became	Mrs. J. F. Julian, Fenwick, Ont. Ruth Savigny

							Johnson	George Bunker (Bunker Hill), member of this family	
Salter	France	Channel Islands			1860	Gaspé Peninsula Belleville	Wife of John Albert Folle		
Segar Seger Sager Seager	Flanders, c. 1600	Norwich, England	Garret Segers m. 1683	Kingston, N.Y. 1640	1784	Richmond Twp., Bay of Quinte	William Sager, b. 1779	Married into the Bradt and Volyear families	Howard T. Volyear 38 Rans St., Buffalo, N.Y.
Standish	France	St. Barthomew's Day 1572			1820	Esquising Twp., Halton Cy.			Mrs. Leslie Young Terra Cotta, Ont.
Terhune	France	Holland 16th Cent.	de Huyn or de Huen In Holland Der Huen. Ter Huen	Long Island, Dutch Settlement, 1642	1833	Vittoria, Norfolk Cy.	Albert and Mary (Van Ryper); Son, Gillian, m. Mary(Roome); grandson Garrett	Family came from Hackensack, N.J. now located at St. George, Ont., Albert Payson Terhune, a relative	Miss Opan Howey 22 Nelson St., Branford, Ont. Helen P. Miles, 656 King E., Hamilton, Ont.
Vaux	France	Cambridgeshire, England			1810	Quebec City, Montreal, Brockville Niagara Peninsula	Thomas Vaux, sec'y of House of Commons, Montreal, 1837 Prof. Vietsch, Edinburgh Univ., Rev. Wm. Wyte Smith		M. H. M. MacKinnon, Hyde Park, London, Ont. Mrs. Katharine Adie, 1113 So. 7th St. Ft. Pierce, Fla.
Vietch La Vache de la Vache	France	Scotland	Sara Vietch b. 1799						
de Villiers	Hertogenbosch, Brabant	The Netherlands	Elizabeth de Villiers m. David Ackerman 1641	1. New Netherland 2. Pennsylvania	before 1797	Prince Edward Cy.	Garret Ackerman m. Hannah Van Houten 1819; m. Jemima Minaker 1837	Wm. C. and Lt.Col. Charles H. are grandsons	Charles H. Ackerman, 380 Park N., Peterboro, Ont.
Volier Vollière	France	France	Pierre Volière			Quebec	Andrew Volyear, 1843–1903 m. Martha Talman	A Volière was blacksmith for Count de Puissaye	Howard T. Voyear 38 Rano, Buffalo, N.Y.

PART SEVEN

References

PART ONE

Religious Upheavals

BACKGROUNDS OF PROTESTANTISM

1. McCabe, James D., Jr. : *From Cross to Crown*, p. 23. Philadelphia, Jones & Company, 1874.
2. Muston, Alexis, D. D. : *The Trail of the Alps; a complete History of the Waldenses and their colonies*; Vol. I, translated by Rev. John Montgomery, in James D. McCabe, Jr., *From Cross to Crown*, pp. 25–6. Philadelphia, 1874.
3. *Encyclopaedia Britannica*, 11th edition, Vol. 5, p. 517.
4. Léonard, Emile G. : *Histoire du Protestantism*, pp. 6–7. Paris, Presses Universitaires de France, 1956.
5. Reaman, G. Elmore : *The Trail of the Black Walnut*, pp. 4–14. Toronto, McClelland and Stewart, 1957.
6. ——, ——, *ibid.*, pp. 4–14.
7. Robinson, James Harvey : *History of Western Europe*, pp. 416–417. Ginn & Co., 1903.

PART TWO

The Trail Begins

HUGUENOTS IN FRANCE

1. Boehmer, H. : *The Jesuits*, translated by Paul Zeller Strodach, p. 133. Philadelphia, Pa., The Castle Press, 1928.
2. Maurois : *A History of France*, p. 116. London, Jonathan Cape, 1956.
3. —— : *ibid.*, p. 122.
4. —— : *ibid.*, p. 142.
5. Guizot : *World's Best Histories*, Vol. III, p. 7. New York and London, The Co-operative Publication Society.
6. Agnew, David C. A. : *Protestant Exiles from France*, p. 2. Private printing, 1866.
7. Kastner, L. E., and Atkins, H. G. : *A Short History of French Literature*, p. 55. New York, Henry Holt and Company, 1907.

8. Baird, Henry M. : *History of the Rise of Huguenots in France,* Vol. I, p. 103. New York, Charles Scribners & Sons, 1879.
9. ——, —— : *ibid.,* p. 164.
10. Guizot and Guizot : *op. cit.,* Vol. III, pp. 149–50.
11. —— : *ibid.,* pp. 151–2.
12. —— : *ibid.,* pp. 162–5.
13. Viénot, John : *Histoire de la Réforme Française,* Vol. I, p. 40. Paris, Librairie Fischbacher, 1926.
14. ——, —— : *ibid.,* pp. 141–2.
15. Guizot : *op. cit.,* p. 166.
16. —— : *ibid.,* p. 175.
17. Bonjour, E. Offler, H. S., Potter, G. R. : *A Short History of Switzerland,* pp. 166–7. Oxford, 1952.
18. Léonard, Emile G. : *op. cit.,* p. 60.
19. Bonjour, Offler, Potter : *op cit.,* p. 167.
20. —— : *ibid.,* p. 168.
21. —— : *ibid.,* p. 169.
22. Maurois : *op cit.,* pp. 152–3.
23. Viénot, John : *op. cit.,* p. 254.
24. Guizot. *op. cit.,* p. 212.
25. Baird : *op. cit.,* Vol. I, p. 400.
26. Maurois : *op. cit.,* p. 153.
27. —— : *ibid.,* p. 172.
28. Guizot : *op. cit.,* p. 393.
29. Maurois : *op. cit.,* p. 172.
30. Parkman, Francis : *The Parkman Reader,* edited by Morison, Samuel Eliot, p. 118. Boston, Little, Brown and Company, 1955.
31. Garneau, F. X. : *L'Histoire du Canada depuis sa découverte jusqu'à nos jours,* Vol. I, p. 103. Quebec, John Lovell, 1845.
32. La Bruyère : *Les Caractères,* p. 277. Paris, Hackette et Cie, 1906.
33. Davis, William Stearns : *A History of France from the earliest times to the Treaty of Versailles,* pp. 180–1. Boston, Houghton, 1919.
34. Smiles, Samuel : *The Huguenots in France,* p. 14. New York, Harper & Brothers, 1874.
35. Zoff, Otto : *The Huguenots,* translated by E. B. Ashton and Jo Mayo, p. 232. New York, L. B. Fischer, 1942.
36. —— : *ibid.,* p. 233.
37. —— : *ibid.,* p. 234.
38. Smiles : *op. cit.,* p. 171.

CHARACTERISTICS OF A HUGUENOT

1. Ripley, W. Z. : *The Race of Europe*, pp. 156–7. Boston, Appleton, 1899.
2. Parkman, Francis : *The Old Regime in Canada*, p. 448. Little, Brown and Company, 1909.
3. Léonard, Emile G. : *Le Protestant François*, p. 11. Paris, Presses Universitaires de France, 1955.
4. *Histoire du Protestantisme, op. cit.*, pp. 19–20.
5. Maurois, André : *A History of France*, translated by Henry L. Binsse and Gerald Hopkins, pp. 147–8. London, Jonathan Cape, 1956.
6. Guizot, M. and Mde. Guizot Dewitt, translated by Robert Black : *World's Best Histories*, Vol. III, p. 165. New York and London. The Cooperative Publication Society.

PART THREE

The Trail encircles Europe and extends to South Africa

HUGUENOTS IN THE BRITISH ISLES

1. Smiles, Samuel : *op. cit.*, p. 85.
2. Smiles, Samuel : *Their Settlements, Church and Industries in England and Ireland*, preface. New York, Harper & Brothers, 1874.
3. ——, —— : *ibid.*, p. 269.
4. ——, —— : *ibid.*, footnote, p. 260.
5. ——, —— : *ibid.*, p. 277.
6. ——, —— : *ibid.*, pp. 273-4-5.
7. Lefanu, W. E. : *Proceedings of the Huguenot Society of London*, Vol. XIX, No. 6, p. 272. 1958.
8. Smiles : *op. cit.*, p. 119.
9. *Proceedings of the Huguenot Society of London:* op. cit., p. 276.
10. Weiss, M. Charles : *History of French Protestant Refugees*, p. 12, translated by Henry William Herbert, 2 volumes. New York, Stringer & Townsend, 1854.
11. Durrant, Will : *The Reformation*, p. 604. New York, Simon and Schuster, 1957.
12. Fleming, Arnold : *Huguenot Influence in Scotland*, pp. 21-2. Glasgow, Wilhelm Maclellan, 1953.
13. ——, —— : *ibid.*, p. 93.

14. ——, —— : *ibid.*, p. 99.
15. ——, —— : *ibid.*, p. 145.
16. ——, —— : *ibid.*, pp. 151–2.
17. Smiles : *op. cit.*, p. 301.
18. Lee, Grace Lawless : *Huguenot Settlement in Ireland*, p. 86.
19. ——, —— : *ibid.*, p. 100.
20. ——, —— : *ibid.*, pp. 76–77.
21. ——, —— : *ibid.*, p. 258.

HUGUENOTS IN THE CHANNEL ISLANDS

1. Godfray, H. M. : The Early Protestant Refugees in the Channel
   Islands, Bulletin of Société Jersiaise, 1927, p. 325.
2. De Faye, W. E. : *Huguenots in the Channel Islands*, pp. 34–35.
   Huguenot Society's Proceedings, London, Vol. XIX, No. 2,
   1954.
3. Smiles, Samuel : *op. cit.*, p. 119.

HUGUENOTS IN CONTINENTAL EUROPE

4. Grant, A. J. : *The Huguenots*, p. 195. London, Thornton Butter-
   worth, 1934.
5. Zoff : *op. cit.*, *The Huguenots*, p. 325.
6. *Chronique de la Colonie Réformée Française de Friedrichsdorf*,
   pp. 8–9. Hambourg-es-Monts, Imprimie, J. G. Stanhaeusser,
   1887.
7. —— : *ibid.*, p. 10.
8. —— : *ibid.*, p. 61.
9. Privat, E. C. : Huguenottisches Leben, Baden-Baden, 1950,
   passim.
10. Grant, A. J. : *op. cit.*, *The Huguenots*, pp. 182–3.
11 Zoff : *op. cit.*, pp. 326–7.

HUGUENOTS IN SOUTH AFRICA

1. Jooste, G. P. : Address, National Huguenot Society, April 24,
   1954, at Washington, D.C., Vol. XXV—Proceedings of the
   Huguenot Society of Pennsylvania, 1954, p. 116.
2. Smiles : *op. cit.*, pp. 184–5.
3. Jooste, G. P. : *op. cit.*, p. 118.

PART FOUR

The Trail Crosses the Atlantic

HUGUENOTS IN THE AMERICAN COLONIES

1. Wilson, Woodrow : *A History of the American People*, Vol. 1,

p. 23. New York, N.Y., Harper & Brothers.
2. Zoff : *op. cit.*, p. 253.
3. Lee, Mrs. Hannah : *Huguenots in France and America*, Vol. II, pp. 95–96. Cambridge, John Owen, 1843.
4. Laux, James, B. : *The Huguenot Element in Pennsylvania*, read before the Huguenot Society of London, 1896, re-published in Proceedings of the Huguenot Society of America, Vol. XXVI, p. 11. 1955.
5. Chinard, Gilbert : *Les Réfugées Huguenots en Amérique*, p. 219. Paris, Société d'Edition "Les Belles Lettres", 1925.

HUGUENOTS IN CANADA
Orientation

1. Wade, Mason : *The French Canadians*, p. 45, ref. 17.
2. Morison, Samuel Eliot : *op. cit.*, Introduction, p. 20.

Huguenots in New France

1. Garneau, F. X. : *Histoire du Canada depuis sa découverte jusqu'à nos jours*, second edition, p. 19. John Lovell, 1852.
2. Baxter, J. P. : *Memoirs of Jacques Cartier*, pp. 304–5. 1906.
3. ——, —— : *ibid.*, pp. 315–6.
4. ——, —— : *ibid.*, p. 323.
5. Garneau, F. X. : *op. cit.*, p. 19.
6. Morison, Samuel E. : *op. cit.*, p. 71.
7. de la Roncière, Charles : *Jacques Cartier*, p. 157. Paris. Librairie Plon Les Petits-fils de Peon et Nourrit, 1931.
8. Charlevoix : *Histoire de la Nouvelle France*, tome 1, p. 32. Paris, 1744.
9. Biggar, H. B. : *A Collection of Documents Relating to Cartier and Roberval*, pp. 178–85. Publications of the Public Archives of Canada, No. 14.
10. ——, —— : *ibid.*, p. 276.
11. Garneau, F. X. : *op. cit.*, p. 25.
12. Morison. *op. cit.*, pp. 82–84.
13. Biggar, H. B. : *op. cit.*, pp. 275–9.
14. Morison : *op. cit.*, p. 79.
15. Biggar, H. B. : *op. cit.*, p. 451.
16. —— : *ibid.*, p. 457.
17. Garneau, F. X. : *op. cit.*, pp. 29–30.
18. Réveillaud, Eug. : *Histoire du Canada*, pp. 27–28. Paris, Grassart Libraire-Editeur, 1884.

19. ——, —— : *ibid.*, p. 29.
20. Garneau, F. X. : *op. cit.*, pp. 33–34.
21. ——, —— : *ibid.*, pp. 34–35.
22. Viénot : *op. cit.*, p. 114.
23. Wade, Mason : *The French Canadian Outlook*, pp. 20–21. New York, Viking Press, 1946.
24. Viénot : *op. cit.*, pp. 109–10.
25. Barnabas, Rev. J. R. : *Huguenots in Canada*. Proceedings of the Huguenot Society of London, Vol. VIII, 1923–9, pp. 622–3.
26. Garneau, F. X. : *op. cit.* pp. 88–90.
27. Morison : *op. cit.*, p. 92.
28. Bishop, Morris : *Champlain*, p. 5. New York, Alfred A. Knopf, 1948.
29. ——, —— : *ibid.*, pp. 5–6.
30. ——, —— : *ibid.*, p. 58, footnote.
31. Duclos : *Histoire du Protestantisme Françoise au Canada et aux Etats*, Vol. I, p. 26. Univ. Paris, Librairie Fischbacher, 1913.
32. Bishop : *op. cit.*, p. 254.
33. Parkman, Francis : *A Half Century of Conflict*, Vol. I, p. 208. Boston, Little, Brown and Company, 1892.
34. Garneau, F. X. : *op. cit.*, p. 143.
35. Letouzey et ané, Editeurs, Les Jésuits et la Nouvelle-France au XVII° Siécle, p. 19. Paris, 1895.
36. Lescarbot, Marc : *Nova Franca*, translated by P. Erondelle, 1609, with introduction by H. B. Biggar, p. xiii. New York and London, Harper & Brothers, 1928.
37. ——, —— : *ibid.*, p. xiii.
38. Duclos : *op. cit.*, footnote, p. 16.
39. Bishop : *op. cit.*, p. 265.
40. Lescarbot : *op. cit.*, p. 14.
41. Garneau, F. X. : *op. cit.*, p. 81.
42. Lescarbot : *op. cit.*, pp. 64–5–6.
43. Réveillaud, Eug. : *op. cit.*, p. 44.
44. Parkman : *op. cit.*, p. 108.
45. Réveillaud : *op. cit.*, p. 45.
46. Garneau, F. X. : *op. cit.*, Tome Ier, p. 47.
47. Barnabas, J. R. : *op. cit.*, p. 622, 1923–9.
48. Morison : *op. cit.*, p. 113.
49. Réveillaud : *op. cit.*, p. 49.

50. Garneau, F. X. : *op. cit.*, p. 47.
51. ——, —— : *ibid.*, p. 48.
52. Réveillaud : *op. cit.*, pp. 53–54.
53. Zoff : *op. cit.*, p. 322.
54. Bishop, Morris : *op. cit.*, p. 229.
55. Viénot : *op. cit.*, p. 110.
56. Parkman : *op. cit.*, p. 267.
57. Viénot : *op. cit.*, p. 110.
58. Bishop : *op. cit.*, p. 167.
59. Viénot : *op. cit.*, p. 62.
60. —— : *ibid.*, p. 66.
61. Garneau, F. X. : *op. cit.*, Vol. I, Chapter II, pp. 156–7.
62. Lart, Charles E. : *The Huguenots in Two Americas*, p. 39. Proceedings of the Huguenot Society of London, Vol. IX, 1909–11.
63. Garneau, F. X. : *op. cit.*, Vol. II, pp. 106–7.
64. Viénot : *op. cit.*, p. 77.
65. Garneau, F. X. : *op. cit.*, p. 141.
66. Morison : *op. cit.*, pp. 246–7.
67. Bishop, Morris : *op. cit.*, p. 324.
68. Lart, Charles E. : *op. cit.*, p. 42.
69. Parkman : *op. cit.*, p. 207.
70. Duclos : *op. cit.*, p. 30.
71. Salone, Emile : *La Colonisation de la Nouvelle-France*, III Edition, pp. 43–44. Paris, Librairie Orientales Américaine, 1906.
72. ——, —— : *ibid.*, p. 457.
73. Wade, Mason : *op. cit.*, p. 32, footnote.
74. ——, —— : *ibid.*, p. 38.

Religious Backgrounds of Provincial Frenchmen

1. Haag : Frontenac et Paluau, Louis de Buade : La France Protestante, 2°. edition, Tome 3, 1881, pp. 342–3.
Buade (DE) seigneurs' de Frontenac et barons de Paluau, en Angenois "Le 30° jour de May 1618 fut ensepulturée dans l'eglise : dame Jehanne *Secondat*, en son vivant femme de noble homme Anthoine de Buade s^r de Frontenac, premier maistred 'hostel et maistre particulier des eaux et forêts, capitaine et governeur pour Sm. des chasteaux de S. Germain, qui avoit esté remise dans le giron de l'Eglise et recules saincts sacrements d'autel par le p. Arnoul de la

Cie et nom de Jésus, par luy absouste de l'heresie, -et
l'extrême onction par M. le curé de ce lieu le 27°. jour du d.
mois de May (Etat-civil de S.G. en Laye)."

2. Costain, Thomas B. : *White and Gold*, p. 332. Toronto, Double-
   day Canada Ltd., 1954.
3. Eccles, W. J. : *Frontenac: The Courtier Governor*. Toronto, Mc-
   Clelland and Stewart, Ltd., 1959.
4. Costain : *op. cit.*, p. 342.
5. *Histoire du Canada*, Vol. I, p. 172.
6. Michelet : *Histoire de France*, tome XVII, p. 82.
7. Le Sueur, William d. : *Count Frontenac*, footnote, p. 72. London
   and Toronto, Makers of Canada Series, Oxford University
   Press, 1928.
8. Charlesvoix, P. : *Histoire de la Nouvelle-France*, tome II, p. 237.
9. *Catholic Encyclopaedia*, Vol. IX, 1910, p. 9.
10. Wade, Mason : *The French Canadians*, *op. cit.*, p. 4.
11. Société Jersiaise, Annual Bulletin, 1951, Vol. 17, p. 53.
12. ——— : *ibid.*, p. 54.
13. ——— : *ibid.*, p. 55.
14. ——— : *ibid.*, p. 63.
15. ——— : *ibid.*, 14 Car. II, No. 64.
16. Huguenot Society Publications, Vol. 18, p. 201.
17. Mackay, Douglas : *The Honourable Company*, pp. 33-34.
    Toronto, McClelland & Stewart, Second Edition, 1949.
18. Chapins, Thomas : *Le Marquis de Montcalm*, 1712-59, p. 2.
    Quebec, 1911.
19. De la Deyte, M. Grellet : *Une Soeur de Montcalm: La Presi-
    dente de Launas*. Nevers, 1900.
20. Pamphlet from Swiss Embassy in Ottawa, Ontario.
21. Millman, Thomas R. : *Jacob Mountain, First Lord Bishop of
    Quebec*, pp. 276-7. Toronto, University of Toronto Press,
    1947.
22. ———, ——— : *ibid.*, p. 40.

Huguenots in the Maritimes

1. Hannay, James. *The History of Acadia*, p. 328. St. John, N.B.,
   J. & A. McMillan, 1879.
2. Raddall, Thomas H. : *Halifax*, p. 40. Toronto, McClelland &
   Stewart, 1948.
3. Brebner, J. B. : *The Neutral Yankees in Nova Scotia*, p. 54.
   Columbia University Press, 1937.

4. Wright, Esther Clark : *The Loyalists of New Brunswick*, p. 159. Privately printed, 1955.

5. ——, —— : *ibid.*, p. 167.

HUGUENOTS IN ONTARIO

1. Ermatinger, C. O. : *The Talbot Régime*, p. 5. St. Thomas, The Municipal World, 1904.

2. Canniff, William : *History of the Province of Ontario*, p. 56. Toronto, A. H. Hovey, 1872.

3. Swiss Embassy, Ottawa : "Swiss in Canada," p. ii, 1955.

PART EIGHT

Appendices

SOME ENGLISH SURNAMES OF FRENCH DERIVATION

The following names of families, of French descent and derivation, have been selected from Barber's 'British Family Names'. Many of our American families can trace through this source French blood, in very many cases known to be Huguenot. Names given in the various chapters are not repeated here. The list will be of interest, whether the American connection can be traced or not. The abbreviations used are these : 'H', for Huguenot; 'Prot. Ref.', Protestant Refugee; 'L', London.

Agnew (from Aigneau)
Alexander (originally Alexandre)
Allard (H.)
Alloth (H., near Vermeil, 1688)
Ames or Eames (Prot. Ref., L., 1618)
Angler (H., Anger)
Annes, or Annies (Prot. Ref., L., 1618)
Arch (H., L., 1618)
Arnold (H., L., 1618)
Arnott (H., Arnaud, L., 1657)
Arundell (H., L., 1618)
Astor (Norman, 1180)
Avery (H., Norwich 1622)

Bailey (H., Belley, L., 1688)
Bain (H., Norwich, 1622)
Baird or Beard (H., L., 1618)
Baker (Becke, Prot. Ref., Norwich, 1622)
Ballinger (Bellanger, Prot. Ref., L., 1688)
Barchelder, or Barchelor (H., Batchelier, L., 1682)
Barr (De la Barr, H., L., 1618)
Barrell (H., Barill, Canterbury ,1622)
Barrett (Norman, Barette)
Bassett (H., Sandwich, 1622)

Bean (Prot. Ref., Bienne, Norwich, 1622)
Beaumont (Norman)
Bellew, or Bellows (Norman, Bellot)
Bellin (H., Belin, Belyn, L., 1618)
Bence (Benson, H., Sandwich, 1662)
Bendon, or Benton (H., L., 1618)
Benn, Bennett, Benny (H., Benedict, L., 1688)
Bevis (from Beauvais, France)
Bezant (H., Beaussaint)
Billyard (H., Dover, 1622)
Bissett (H., Bissot, L., 1618)
Blewitt (Norman, LaBlouette)
Boffin (H., Bovin, L., 1685)
Bogert (H., Boygard, L., 1681)
Bone (H., Bohon, L., 1621)
Bonhill (H., Bonnel, L., 1618)
Bonner (H., Bonnard, L., 1618)
Boosey (H., Bussey, L., 1618)
Bowcher, Boucher, Bowker (H., L., 1618)
Boyd (H., Boyard, L., 1687)
Brade (H., Breda, L., 1688)
Brain, or Brine (H., Breon, L., 1688)
Brand (Prot. Ref., L., 1618)
Brasier, Brazier (H., Bressuire, Norwich, 1622)
Breeden (H., Briden, L., 1681)
Brett (French, LeBret)
Brewer (Brueria in Normandy)
Briggs (H., Bruges, L., 1618)
Brill (Prot. Ref., Brille, Sandwich, 1622)
Brothers (Brodder, Prot. Ref., Sandwich, 1622)
Brown (Norman-French, LeBrun)
Bruce (Brousse, from Breux, Normandy)
Brunyee (Brunne, Prot. Ref., L., 1618)
Bryan (Brionne, Normandy)
Bryant (from Breaunt, Normandy)
Bubier (Norman)
Buck (LeBuc, Prot. Ref., L., 1618)
Buckett (Bouquet, Prot. Ref., L., 1685)
Bull (Bole, Prot. Ref., L., 1618)
Buller (Bolen, Prot. Ref., L., 1618)
Burden (Fr., Burdon)

Burdett (Bourdet, H., L., 1685). Probably ancestry of Robert J.
    Burdett, the humourist
Burgoyne (Norman-French)
Burr (Bure, Belgian, Prot. Ref., L., 1687)
Burt (Norman-French)
Bush (Bosch, Flemish, Prot. Ref., L., 1618)
Bushell (H., L., 1618)
Busick (Boussoe, H., L., 1685)
Butcher (H., L., 1685)
Buttle (Butel, H., L., 1685)
Byles (H., from Bueil, France)
Byron (Norman-French, Biron)

Cade (H., Cadet)
Camp (H., L., 1618)
Campbell and Gamble (Norman-French)
Campion (Prot. Ref., Norwich, 1622)
Cantrell (H., L., 1618)
Capel (LaChapelle, H., L., 1618)
Card (H., Cardes, L., 1681)
Caron (H., L., 1687)
Carry, or Carr (H., L., 1685)
Carter (Cartier, H., L., 1618)
Cartwright (Cauterets, Norman)
Case (H., De la Cuse)
Chaffe (H., LeChauve, L., 1682)
Chamberlain (Chambellan, H., L., 1618)
Chambers (H., Chambray, L., 1618)
Chaplin (Norman-French, Capelen)
Chattin (H., Chattaine, L., 1618)
Cheney (Fr., Chesnais)
Choffin (H., Chauvin, L., 1684)
Churchill (Nor. Fr., DeCourcelle)
Clark (H., Norwich, 1622)
Clements (Flem., Clement, Prot. Ref., L., 1618)
Cloake (H., Clocke, L., 1618)
Close (Prot. Ref., L., 1618)
Closson (Prot. Ref., L., 1618)
Cocker (H., Norwich, 1622)
Cockerell (Fr., Coqueril)
Cockle (Cokele, Prot. Ref., Norwich, 1622)

T.O.H.—9*

Codd (H., L., 1618)
Cogger (Coege, Flem. Ref., L., 1618)
Cole (Flem. Ref., L., 1618)
Colley (H., Colleye, 1618)
Collier, Colwer (Fre., Collioure)
Coppinger (Flem. Ref., L., 1618)
Corbett (Fr., raven)
Corbin (Norman-French)
Corke (H., Corque, L., 1618)
Courage (H., Correges)
Courteney, or Courtinay, or Courtney (H., name)
Coward (H., Chouard, 1688)
Cozens (Cousin, H., 1688)
Creamer (Prot. Ref., L., 1618)
Cross (Prot. Ref., St. Croix, 1618)
Crowley (Fr., Crulai)
Crudge (Prot. Ref., L., 1688)
Cruso (Creusot, Prot. Ref., Norwich, 1622)
Culley (Flemish, Couillet)
Curtis (H., Courtois, Norwich, 1622)
Cushing (Nor. Fr., LeCuchon)

Dagg (Dague, H., Canterbury, 1622)
Dagget (Dackett, Flem. Ref., Norwich, 1622)
Dams (D'Ames, Prot. Ref., Norwich, 1622)
Dangerfield (Dangerville)
Daniel (H., L., 1618)
Danvers (from Anvers, France)
Dennis (St. Denis, H., L., 1682)
Derlyn, Darling (H., Norwich, 1622)
Derrick (H., L., 1622)
Devine (Desvignes, H., Norwich, 1622)
Dewey (Belgian, Prot. Ref., Dhuy, L., 1618)
Dewfall (Duval, Prot. Ref., L., 1687)
Doubdeday (Doublet, H., L., 1685)
Doughty (Daude, H., L., 1687)
Doy (H., L., 1618)
Drake (Nor. Fr., Fitz-Drac, Prot. Ref., L., 1618)
Draper (Drapier, H., Dover, 1622)
Drew (Dreux, H., Norwich, 1622)
Drewry, or Drury (DeRouvray, Nor. Fr.)

Driver (DeRivers, Nor. Fr.)
Drought (H., Droart, L., 1618)
Durrant, or Durant (Durand, Fr.)
Durrell (Durell, H., L., 1687)

Emery (H., L., 1685)
Eve (Prot. Ref., L., 1618)
Everson (Prot. Ref., Flemish, L., 1618)
Ewing, or Ewen (Prot. Ref., L., 1618)

Fabb (H., Fabri, L., 1678)
Fairy (Verry or Ferry H., L., 1618)
Fanning (Norman)
Farjon (Fargeon, H., L., 1685)
Faulkner (Fauconnier, H., L., 1681)
Fawcett, Fassett (Fr. Fossord)
Fear (H., L., 1618)
Fellows, Fellowes (H., L., 1687)
Fenn (Fene, H., Norwich, 1622)
Ferrett (H., Dover, 1622)
Filbert (Fr., St. Philbert)
Finch (Fl., De Vinck, Prot. Ref., L., 1622)
Flowers (H., L., 1618)
Fleury (H., L., 1687)
Foggs, Fogg (H., Foucat, L., 1685)
Foljambe (Nor. Fr., Fulgent)
Forman, Furch (Forment, H., L., 1618)
Fox (Flemish, H., L., 1618)
Foy, Faith (H., L., 1618)
Freeman (Fl., Freyman, Prot. Ref., Norwich, 1622)
Fremont (Fr., Frimont)
Fromant (Fromeau, H., L., 1618)
Frusher (H., Fruchat, L., 1687)
Fuller (Fr., Fouleur)
Furber (H., Foubert, L., 1618)

Gabbett (H., Gabet, L., 1688)
Gaches (H., Gauchez, L., 1688)
Galley (H., Gallais, L., 1687)
Gallyon (H., Gaillen, L., 1618)
Galpin (H., Galopin, L., 1684)

Garrard (H., L., 1618)
Garret (Fr., Garet)
Garrick (Fr., Garrigues)
Gaskin (Fr., DeGascoigge, from Gascony)
German (H., Germon, L., 1618)
Giddings, or Giddens (H., Guidon, L., 1687)
Gifford (Giffard, full cheeked)
Gillot (diminutive of Gill, H., L., 1618)
Gilyard (Gilliard, H., L., 1687)
Gimlett (Gimlette, H., L., 1618)
Glass (H., Glace, L., 1618)
Goacher, Goucher (Fr., Goucher, H., L., 1618)
Goddard (H., Godart, L., 1618)
Godfrey (Fr., Godefroy, H., L., 1681)
Goding (Fl., Godding, Prot. Ref., L., 1685)
Goodenough, Moodenow (Fr., Godineau)
Goodfellow (Fr., Bonenfant)
Goodhew, or Gooehue (Fr., Godeheu)
Gosling (Gosselin, Prot. Ref., L., 1622)
Goss, or Goose (H., Norwich, 1622)
Gower, Gowers (Fl., Prot. Ref., Govaerts, L., 1618)
Grant (Fr., Grands)
Grave, or Graves (Nor. Fr., De la Greve)
Gray (H., L., 1618)
Gruel (H., Gruelle, L., 1628)
Gubbins (H., DeGobion, L., 1618)
Guerin (H., Gueron, L., 1628)
Gurner, or Gurney (H., L., 1618)
Gye (H., Gay, L., 1684)

Hague (H., LeHague, Prot. Ref., L., 1621). From this family
    came the eloquent preacher, Rev. William Hague, D. D.,
    Baptist historian and minister.
Hall (Fl., Prot. Ref., L., 1699)
Hamblett (H., Hamlett, L., 1622)
Hanchett (Prot. Ref., Hansett, L., 1618)
Hardy (Nor. Fr., bold, strong; H. L., 1684)
Harry (Harrye, H. L., 1681)
Harvey (H., Herve, L., 1681)
Hassatt (Prot. Ref., Sandwich, 1622)
Hay (De la Haye, H., Dover, 1622)

Hayes (Hees, H., L., 1618)
Hebbert (Hebart, Prot. Ref., L., 1685)
Herbert (Herbart, Prot. Ref., Canterbury, 1622)
Hewett (H., Heut, L., 1621)
Hidden, or Iddon (Nor., Hidden, Prot. Ref., L., 1618)
Hood (H., Ude, L., 1618)
Hook (H., Hue, L., 1618)
Hooppell (H., Dover, 1622)
Howell (H., L., 1618)
Howes (Fl., Housse, Prot. Ref., Canterbury, 1622)
Howitt (H., Canterbury, 1622)
Hubbard, Hubert (H., Houbart, L., 1618)

Jackman (H., Jacquement, Canterbury, 1622)
Jacobs (Fl., Prot. Ref., L., 1618)
James (St. James, Prot. Ref., L., 1621)
Jarvis (H., Gerveis, L., 1688)
Jasper (Fl., Jaspard, H., L., 1621)
Jay (Jeyen, H., L., 1621)
Jolly (H., L., 1681)
Joy (H., L., 1685)
Joyce (Nor., Joyeuse)
Julian (Fr., Julien)
Juliet (H., L., 1618)

King (Fl. Ref., L., 1618)

Lacy, or Lacey (Nor., Lessay, DeLacey)
Lambert (Fr., St. Lambert, Fl. Ref., L., 1618; General Lambert,
    Governor of York)
L'Amoreaux, Lamoreau (H., L., 1687)
Landers (from Landre in Burgundy)
Lane (Fr., Laigne)
Larter (LaTour, H., L., 1618)
Lawrence, Laurence (Fr., Laurentin, H., L., 1618)
Laws(Prot. Ref., Norwich, 1622)
Lawson (Nor. Fr., Loison)
Laycock (H., Lecocq, Dover, 1622)
Lepper (H., Lepere, L., 1618)
Lessey (H., Lesee, L., 1621)
Lewis (DeLuis, H., Norwich, 1622)

Littlejohn (Fr., Petitjean)
Living (Fl., H., Livain, Norwich, 1622)
Loe, or Low (H., LeLoe, L., 1618)
Lofting (Prot. Ref., L., 1688)
Long (DeLonga, Prot. Ref., L., 1621)
Longfellow (H., Longueville, L., 1685)
Lovebond (H., Lovingsbone, L., 1621)
Lovell (H., Louvel, L., 1618)
Lower (Fl. Ref., L., 1618)
Luce, Loose (Prot. Ref., L., 1618)
Lucy (Louiset, Prot. Ref., L., 1634)
Lumbard, Lombard (H. Lombuart, L., 1687)
Lyon (Prot. Ref., Norwich, 1662)

Mace (H., Mes, L., 1618)
Mackley (Fl., Prot. Ref., L., 1618)
Maitland (H., Mattalent, Nantes)
Major (H., L., 1688)
Male (DeMaisle, H., Dover, 1622)
Marcon (Marquent, Prot. Ref., Canterbury, 1622)
Marlow (Fr., Marlieux)
Marr (H., Marre, L., 1618)
Marshall (H., Marechal, L., 1618)
Martin (H., St. Martin, L., 1688)
Martineau (Fr., Martigne). Family of famous James Martineau,
    Philosopher
Mason (H., Macon, L., 1618)
Massey (H., Macey, L., 1684)
Mate (H., Mette, L., 1618)
Maule, or Moll (H., L., 1618)
Mayhew, or Mayo (H., Mahieu, Mayeux, Norwich, 1622)
Maynard (H., Menard, Dover, 1622)
Mayne (H., Mayne, L., 1687)
Means (Prot. Ref., Minnens, L., 1687)
Mear (H., L., 1618)
Meen (H., Migne, L., 1618)
Mercier (H., L., 1618)
Merritt, Merry (Marit and Meret)
Meyrick (DeMeric, Prot. Ref., L., 1621)
Michell, Mitchell (H., L., 1618)
Miles (Norman French) General Miles of this blood.

Mills (Fl., Miles, Prot. Ref., Norwich, 1622)
Minett (Minet, Prot. Ref., L., 1688)
Minter (Minder, Prot. Ref., L., 1618)
Molineux (Moliner, Prot. Ref., L., 1618)
Money (H., Monnaye, L., 1618)
Munsey, or Monsey (H., L., 1618)
Montague (Montaigu)
Moon, Moen (Fl., Moine, H., Sandwich, 1622)
Moore (Fl., Mor, H., More, L., 1618)
Morrell (H., Morel, L., 1618)
Morriss, Morris (Mourisse, H., Canterbury, 1622)
Moss (Norman-French)
Mott (De La Motte, H., L., 1621)
Mountain (H., Montaigne, L., 1618)
Mouse (H., Mousse, Moze, L., 1687)
Munn (Prot. Ref., L., 1618)
Myhill, Mayall (H., L., 1618)

Neale (DeNeel, H., L., 1687)
Nollett (Fr., Nolleau, H., L., 1687)

Oliver, Olivier (H., L., 1682)
Onions (Angiens, Norman)
Overy (H., Ouvry, L., 1618)
Osborne (Osbern), Osler (l'Oiselor), Norman

Page (H., LePage, L., 1688)
Paine (Fr., Pain, H., L., 1618)
Paley, Pallett (H., Paillette, L., 1688)
Palmer (le Paumier, Fl. Ref., L., 1618)
Parry (H., Parre, L., 1687)
Paskell (H., Paschal, L., 1687)
Pate (Patte, H., Canterbury, 1622)
Paton, Patton, Peyton (H., Canterbury, 1622)
Pattison (Fl. Ref., L., 1618)
Paul (H., St. Paul, L., 1618)
Paulett (Poulet, H., L., 1687)
Peacock (Fl. Ref., L., 1618)
Pear (A., Pierre, L., 1687)
Pears, Pearse (Fl., Piers, Peres, H., L., 1688)
Pearson (Pierrsene, Prot. Ref., L., 1688)

Peberdy, Peabody (Nor. Fr., Pabode)
Penny (Peigne, Peno, Prot. Ref., Norwich, 1622)
Perkins, Peterkin (Little Peter, Fl.)
Perowne (H., Peronnez, L., 1618)
Peters (Peeters, Prot. Ref., L., 1518)
Pettit (H., Petit, 1618)
Phantam, Vendome, Fandam (Prot. Ref., L., 1618)
Phillips (Fitz-Philip, Prot. Ref., L., 1618)
Picard (H., Picard, L., 1621)
Picken, Pickens (Fr., Picon)
Pickett, Pigott (H., Pegot or Pigot, L., 1685)
Pillow (H., Pilot, 1622)
Pinchen, Pynchon (H., Pincon or Pinchon, 1622)
Pinner (Pineur, Prot. Ref., Norwich, 1622)
Plummer (H., le Plumer, L., 1682)
Plunkett, or Plunkitt (Nor. Fr., de Plugenet)
Pollard (H., L., 1618)
Pond (Fl., Pont, Prot. Ref., L., 1618)
Poole (Poule, Prot. Ref., L., 1621)
Porter (H., Portier, Norwich, 1622)
Pott (Fl., Pot, Prot. Ref., L., 1618)
Potter (Fr., Potier)
Poulter (H., Poultier, Canterbury, 1688)
Powell (H., Puel, L., 1618)
Pratt (H., DuPrat, L., 1687)
Prevost (H., Rye, 1621)
Prim, Prime (H., L., 1618)
Prince (H., Prins, L., 1618)
Prue (H., Preux L., 1687)
Pullen, Pullein (H., Poullain, L., 1622)

Quincey (from Quince in Maine; DeQuincey)

Ranney (H., Rene, Renie, Fl., Renaix, L., 1688)
Reason (DeReasne, Prot. Ref., L., 1618)
Reay, Ray (DeRea, Ray, H., L., 1688)
Rebbeck (H., Rebache, L., 1688)
Revill, Revell (H., Revel, Reville, L., 1618)
Ricket (Ricquart, H., Canterbury, 1622)
Robin (H., Robain, L., 1687)
Robinson (Robyns, Prot. Ref., L., 1618)

Roche, Roach (H., de la Roche, L., 1687) possibly the family
from which John Roach or Roche, the American ship-
builder, was descended.
Rogers (Fr., Rogier)
Rose (Nor., Ros, Rose, H., L., 1684)
Roswell, Russell (Rousselle, H., Canterbury, 1622)
Rouse (H., LeRoux, L., 1618)
Rowan, Rowen (H., Rouen, L., 1618)
Rowell (H., Rouelles, L., 1687)
Rowland (H., Dover, 1622)
Rowley (from Norman Reuilly)

Sach (Sac, Prot. Ref., L., 1618)
Sartoris (H., Sartorius, L., 1684)
Savage (Fr., Sauvage)
Seymour, Saymer, Simore (H., 1618)
Seeley (H., Sill, L., 1688)
Seguin (H., L., 1688)
Sherrard (Sheraret, F., Prot., L., 1618)
South (H., L., 1618)
Spear, Speer (Fl., Spiers, Prot. Ref., L.,1622)
Stephens (H., L., 1618)
Sturgeon (H., Lestourgeon, L., 1683)
Summers (H., Somers, L., 1618)
Summerville (from Sommervieux, Nor.)
Symonds, Simonds (H., Simon, L., 1618)

Taber (Taborer, Prot. Ref., L., 1678)
Tardy (H., L., 1688)
Taverner (H., Tavernier, L., 1622)
Terry (H., Terriss, L., 1618)
Thompson (H., L., 1618)
Tibbles (H., L., 1618)
Tiffen (H., L., 1618)
Tolver (H., Tolleve, Norwich, 1622)
Torrey (Thouret, Prot. Ref., L., 1618)
Tree (Tre, Prot. Ref., L., 1618)
Tulley (H., Tulye, L., 1618)
Turnbull (Nor., Tournebu)
Tyron (H., Trion, L., 1618)
Tyrrell, Tirrell (Fr., Tirel)

Valentine (H., 1618)
Valiant (H., Vaillant, 1681)
Vawdrey (H., DeValdarrie, Norwich, 1622)
Vernon (H., L., 1618)
Viall (H., Viel, L., 1684)
Vincent (H., St. Vincent, L., 1618)
Vye (H., De la Fuye, L., 1683)

Walters (Wauters, Prot. Ref., L. 1621)

The foregoing list taken from Appendix of *The French Blood in America*, by Lucian J. Fosdick, Publisher, Fleming H. Revell Co., 1906.

Excerpts from :
> *Memorials of the Huguenots in America*, by Rev. A. Stapleton, A.M., M.S., Huguenot Publishing Company, Carlisle, Pa., 1901.

Excerpts from :
> Pages 50–51.
> Pages 90–91.
> Pages 116–117.
> General List—Pages 149–157.

CHRIST CHURCH RECORDS

In the published records of Christ Episcopal Church of Philadelphia[1] occur the following names of parents of presumed Huguenot antecedents—earliest entries only are given :

Boudinot, Elias, 1738
Boyer, James, 1734
Bonnett, John, 1736
Bruno, John, 1738
Chevalier, Peter, 1721
Couche, Daniel, 1756
Durell, Moses, 1731
Doutell, Michael, 1737
Dupee, Daniel, 1747
Doz, Andrew, Duche, Jacob, 1734
Fleury, Peter, 1731
Garrigues, Francis, 1721

1. Vide Pa. Mag. of Hist. and Biog., Vols. XIV, XV, XVI.

Garrigues, Peter, 1736
Hillegas, Michael, 1760
Hodnett, John, 1737
LaRue, John, 1739
Le Boyteau, William, 1711
LeTort, James, 1709
LeDru, Noel, 1732
LeDieu, Lewis, 1758
LeShemile, Peter, 1741
LeGay, Jacob, 1744
Lacellas, James, 1759
dePrefontain, Peter, 1754
Paca, John, 1758
Pinnard, Joseph, 1733
Purdieu, William, 1738
Trippeo, Frederick, 1713
Renandet, James, 1733
Vidal, Stephen, 1754
Votaw, Paul Isaac, 1747
Voyer, Peter, 1713

The records of St. Michaels Lutheran Church of Philadelphia bear the following names of parents of probable Huguenot extraction—earliest entries only are given :[2]

Remy, Jacob, 1745
Huyett, Frantz Carl, 1747
Remley (de) Conrad, 1747
Ransier, Frederick, 1748
Suffrance, John, 1749
Bouton, John, Daniel, 1752
Bouton, Jacob, 1752
Reno, Peter, 1752
Losche, Daniel, 1752
DuBois, Alex., 1753
LeBrant, John Conrad ("who died on the Rhein"), 1754
Piquart, John Gottfried, 1754
Ozias, Elizabeth (wid.), 1755

The baptismal record of the First Reformed Church of Lancaster city, which was founded in 1731, contains the names of a large number of Huguenot parents, and it is known that Rev. Charles

2. Vide Pa. German Pub., Vol. VII.

Lewis Boehm, who was pastor of the church from 1771 to 1775, sometimes preached in the French Language, which presupposes a considerable number of French-speaking parishioners.[1] From the church records we extract the following names of Huguenot fathers and the earliest entry of children for baptism :

> John Casper Viller, 1733
> Abr. deGaston, 1736
> Melchoir Boyer, 1741
> Jacob Rudisill, 1742
> Jacob Velschang, 1742
> Andrew Beauchamp, 1745
> Melchoir Fortune and David Mich. Fortuney, 1749
> Jacob Fortuney, 1753 (Forteneaux)
> John Ferree, 1745
> Cornelius Ferree, 1745
> Abraham Ferree, 1758
> David Fortunet, 1747
> Peter LaRou, 1749
> John Messakop, 1750
> Henry Racque, 1752
> Peter Bonnett, Lorenz Marquet and DeBeau Rosier; Martin Boyer, 1753
> Abraham DeDieu, 1755
> Jean DeDieu, 1773
> John Jacob Allemand, 1755
> John Jacob Huttier, 1753
> Jacques Calvin Berott, John LeFever, Justice Trebert, 1756
> Jacob LeCrone, Abraham Caupat (Gobat), 1759
> François Delancy, 1760
> John Peter Roller, 1761
> Adam LeRoy, Henry DuKeyness, 1762
> Peter Mumma, 1764
> John Henry Vissard, 1765
> Henry Maquinnett, 1765
> Samuel Gurier, 1766
> Jean Pierre Vosin, 1767

1. "Brand, Elisabeth, daughter of Joseph and Magdalena, born July 28 and baptized August 25, 1771. N.B.—This child was baptized in the French language previous to the sermon which was preached in the same language." Extract from Record.

Conrad Hillegas, 1768
Conrad DuBois, 1770
Joseph LeBrant, 1771
Nicholas Dello, 1773

Besides the foregoing the Doute, Raiguel, Jacques,[1] DuFresne, Dundore, Armeson and Lorah families were members. The Trinity Lutheran Church of Lancaster, which was also founded very early, had likewise a large Huguenot membership. The following is a list of fathers with the earliest baptismal entry of children :

Bernhart Hubele, 1748
Michael Hubele, 1749
Mich. Morett, 1754
Peter Bonnett, 1751
François Moreau, 1755
Jean Mathiot, 1757
George Mathiot, 1764
John Peter Moreau, 1765
Jacques Santeau, 1766
Jean DeMars

Besides the foregoing were the families Marquette, Dillier, Rudesill, Cossart,[2] Bertle and Sponselier.[3]

EARLY MENNONITE AND HUGUENOT SETTLERS

The following list, nearly all heads of families, embraces only such as arrived prior to 1718 in Lancaster county :

Bare[4] Jacob, Jr. (died 1736, Jacob, Jr., Henry, and John)
Baumgardner, Peter
Boyer, Samuel
Brand, Adam
Brubaker, John
Boehm, Jacob
Brenneman, Melchoir, Adam, Christopher, and Christian

1. Jean Jacques, b. 1694 in France and died 1778. He was the ancestor of the Jacobs family.
2. Theopholis Cassart, a printer and publisher, was a prominent citizen about the Revolutionary period.
3. Philip Sponselier was born in Lorraine in 1676, married 1711 his wife Barbara. He came to Lancaster county 1732, died 1752, leaving widow, three sons, and three daughters.
4. Bare—originally 'Barree' Huguenots.

Biere, Jacob
Bowman, Michael and John Wendell
Burkholder, John, Sr., John, Jr., and Abraham
Christopher, Carl
Dondore, Michael
Erisman, Melchoir
Eby, Theodorus, Peter and John
Eshelman, Daniel
Faber, John
Frederick, John
Ferree,[1] John, Daniel, and Philip
Funk, John, Jacob, and Henry
Franciscus,[2] Christopher
Groff, Hans,[3] and Martin
Guth (Good), John, and Jacob
Harnish, Martin
Hershey, Christian
Herr, Hans, and Abraham
Hess, John
Hermau, Christian
Hoover, Ulrich
Hostetter, Jacob
Houser, Christian, and Ulrich
Hufford, Melchoir
Hubert, Hubertson (1709)
Kaigy, Hans
Kauffman, Jacob

1. Sons of Madame Ferree.
2. Franciscus—a noted Swiss patriot who had taken refuge in Alsace. He came to Pequea in 1710.
3. Groff—born of distinguished parentage in Switzerland 1661. Fled as a Mennonite to Alsace where he bore the title of Baron Von Woldon. About 1695–96, accompanied by his brother, he came to Germantown. He was one of the first settlers of Lancaster county, locating at 'Graff's Thal' (Rupp's Lanc. County, p. 133). He was a wealthy and important personage, Earl township being named in his honor (Col. Rec., Vol. III, pp. 420, 673). He founded a great posterity. He was the grandfather of Sebastian and Andrey Groff, noted Revolutionary patriots.

Sebastian Groff (3rd), born in Earl township, Lancaster county, about 1750; delegate to the Provincial Convention 1775; delegate to the Federal Constitution Ratification Convention 1787; State Constitutional Convention 1787; State Senator 1790; died 1792. His brother Andrew was also a man of prominence and member of the Provincial Assembly 1776 and treasurer of Lancaster county many years.

Kindig, Martin, George
Kreitser, Jacob
Larue, Jonas[1]
Lefever,[2] Issac
Leamon,[3] Peter
Landis, Felix
LeBo, John
Landert, Sigismund
Line, John Lochman, Casper
Lighte (Light), John and John Jacob
Meylin, Martin, and John
Mire (Mier, Moyer), Michael, Jacob, Rudy, Abraham, and
    John
Miller, Jacob, Sr., Jacob, Jr., and Martin
Musselman, Henry
Neff,[4] Francis, Sr., Francis, Jr., and John Henry, Sr., John
    Henry, Jr., and Henry
Nissley, Jacob
Newcomer, Peter
Oberholtzer, Martin, and Ulrick
Peelman, Christian
Ream, Eberhart
Royer, Sebastian
Rudy, Ulrich
Shank, John, and Michael
Sower,[5] Christopher
Steinman, Christian, and Joseph
Shultz, Andrew
Schliermacher[6] (Slaymaker), Mathias

1. Larue—a Huguenot and associate of the Ferrees.
2. Lefever—son-in-law to Madame Ferree.
3. Leamon—originally 'Lemont' (Rupp's Lanc. County, p. 516).
4. Neff—Francis and Dr. John Henry Neff belonged to an eminent Swiss Mennonite family, some of whom perished for their faith. They fled to Alsace where they resided before coming to America. Dr. Neff was the first regular physician in Lancaster county (Rupp, p. 125).
5. Sower—the famous German printer who located in Germantown and where in 1743 he printed the first Bible in America in a European language.
6. Schliermacher—Emanated from a notable family and for some time seated at Strasbourg, in Alsace, owing to persecution. He came to Pa. in 1716. Henry Slaymaker, son of Mathias, was born in Strasburg, Lanc. cty. 1730; a Captain in active service 1776, member of Constitutional Conv. 1776, a Justice; succeeded Judge Hubley as Judge of Courts 1784, died

Steiner, Christian
Schnebly, John Jacob, Sr., and John Jacob, Jr.
Stoy, Frederick
Swope, John
Stompher, John
Weaver (Webber), Jacob, Henry, John, and George
Wenerick, Benedictus
Witmer, Benedictus
Woolslegal, John
Zimmerman[1] (Carpenter), Henry, Emanuel, and Gabriel

GENERAL LIST

Note.—The dates following names indicate the time of arrival as derived from official records. The names of counties where immigrant located are abbreviated. Immigrants from Alsace and Lorraine are mostly indicated by brackets.

Ache, John Ludwig—John George and Herman 1752, Leb. Co.; John and George in Cocalico, Lanc. Co., prior to 1756
Alleman, Jacob, Sr., Jacob, Jr. 1741—Stephen 1749 (Lorraine), Dorstius and Peter 1752—John Christian, John Frederick, Christian and Hiram 1753, Jean Jacques 1754 (Lorraine), Lanc. and Leb.
Anganie, Mich. 1736, Dewalt 1746, Theobald 1733, Lanc.–Leb.
Amacher, Mich. 1754 (Lorraine)
Armeson, Pierre (Armishong), 1753, Lanc.
Arnoul, Jean Pierre 1751
Aubertin, Pierre 1739
Anne, Pierre 1744
Aurand, Peter and Herman 1733, John 1733, Berks. Co.

Balliet, Paul 1738, Lehigh, Joseph 1749, Bucks.
Barberat, Jacques 1749 (Lorraine)
Barrett, Baldus 1739
Baptiste, Jean François 1753, Jean 1770, Jean 1771, Jean 1771
Baird, François and William 1754 (Lorraine), Lanc.

1785. His son Amos, born 1755, was Captain in Revolution, member of Congress 1811–14, and later member of Penna. Senate. He held many important offices, died 1840.
1. Zimmerman—Henry, a Swiss, first came in 1698. Returned to Europe and brought over his family in 1706 (Rupp, p. 126). Many of his descendants became prominent men.

Bach, Jacques 1754 (Lorraine)
Bachart, Geo. 1749, Lehigh
Balme, Jacques 1753
Balmas, Pierre 1757
Baldy, Conrad, prior to 1740
Baldus, John Leonard 1749, John Peter 1753
Bar, John 1754 (Lorraine)
Barto (Perdeau), John 1730, Berks., Issac, prior to 1750, Nicholas
    1773
Barre, Jacob, Sr., Jacob, Jr., John Henry, Lanc., prior to 1718
Baron, John Philip 1747—Mich. 1752, Jacob 1753, Jonas 1763
Bashore (LeBaiseur), George, prior to 1733, Lanc., Jacob 1732,
    Daniel and Sebastian 1749
Batillion (Bartillion), George, William, Christian, Frederick, and
    Abraham 1751
Baudeman, Andri 1750, Jean and Issac 1753 (now Butman)
Bauer, John and Thomas 1754 (Lorraine)
Bayer,
Bayard, Bohemia Manor
Bayle, Mich. 1729, Mich. 1749, Andrew, prior to 1745
Bazillion, Peter, John Manwell 1732
Berringer, Elias 1738, Paul 1743, Adam 1748, Henry 1750, Nich.
    and Bartholomew 1754
Berrett, Jos. Berks., prior to 1753
Beaver, Dieble 1741, Geo. Dewalt and John (Alsace), John Geo.
    (Alsace), 1732, Mich., Val and John (Beeber), 1768
Beau, Jacques, Frans Carl 1768
Beaumont, John Geo. 1764
Beauchamp, Jean, Lanc., prior to 1719, Jean 1731, d. in Lanc. Co.
    1749, John Mich. 1732, William 1741 (now Bushong)
Bernetz, John Leonard, John George Carl Elias David, York., prior
    to 1737
Bernot, Jacob 1751
Belle, Jean Pierre 1754 (Lorraine)
Bernhart, John Thomas 1754 (Lorraine)
Bess, Christian 1754 (Lorraine)
Berge, Jacques 1754 (Lorraine)
Berot, Frans Ludwig 1739, York., Hellbart 1751, Berks., Jacques
    1752, Lanc.
Bertolet, Peter and Jean
Bertle, Nich. (Bertolet?) 1732, Lanc.

Bessonett, Richard, Bucks.

Benezette, John Stephen 1731, Phila.

Beaufort, Casper 1775

Benech, Martin and Simon 1732, John Mich. 1751, John Christian 1752

Beggary, Vincent (Peckary), 1753

Beidinger, John Adam and Peter 1736 (Alsace), York., Andrew 1752

Beveneau, Anton 1749, York.

Bigonet, Jeon 1752, Francis 1773 (Bigoney), Mont. Co.

Billet, Bosler, York.

Blocq. Albert, Del, prior to 1677

Bodine, John, *vide* Conewago

Boileau, Issac, Bucks., Jacob, Berks., prior to 1752

Bouchee, Rudolf 1738, John 1749, Gregorius 1753

Bohre, Peter 1750

Borie, Laurens 1766, Mathew, d. Lanc. 1780

Bontaux, John and Joseph 1752

Bourquin, Jean 1773

Bourgeois, Benjamine-

Bouvard, Robert, Cumb., prior to 1740

Bouton, Jean Daniel, 1739, Leonard Nat., Bucks. Co. 1734, George Nat., Phila. 1754

Bonnett, Jacques and fam. 1733, Jean Philipp, prior to 1736, Peter 1737, Lanc. Co., John Mich. 1750, Jean 1753, Henry 1763

Bouchell, *vide* Bohemia Manor

Bouquet, Jacob 1743, Philip 1747

Boschard, John 1739, Adam 1740, Bernard 1741, Fred 1750, John Daniel 1757

Boyer, Alex 1648, Samuel 1710, John Phil. 1731, Gabriel, prior to 1732, James in Phila., prior to 1734, Carlos 1748, *vide* Chap. VII

Bonjour, And. 1754, Lanc.

Boudinot, Elias, Phila., prior to 1731

Boneauvent, Jean 1740, Va.

Bregonier, John Nich. 1740, Md.

Brant, Jos., Lanc.

Brevard-

Brunot, Felix 1732, John in Phila., prior to 1738, John 1752, Felix ?

Buck, Nich. (Lorraine), Mont. Co. 1752

Cacheau (Casho), Jacob, early in Delaware, Samuel, Lanc., prior to 1752, Jacques 1772

Cambourd, Jean 1732
Carmeton, Fred 1742
Cally, Christ (Lorraine), 1754
Carel, Jacques, Sr., Jacques, Jr., Peter and Jacob 1754
Caquelin, Sebastian and sons Jean and Dietrich 1736, Felty ("from
   the north of France") 1752, Lanc.
Carmane, John and Anthony 1756, Leb.
Caffarel, Paul 1753
Cazenove, de, Jean Antoine and Antoine Charles 1780
Cazart, see Conewago
Cellier, John 1727, Pierre 1748
Chapelle, Eberhart 1757, Jeremiah and John Peter 1753
Chamblin, John, York, prior to 1756
Chasseur, Joseph 1764
Chevelier, Philip, Del., prior to 1677, Pierre C., Phila., prior to 1710
Christien, Jean François from Rodan, Alsace, 1736, Christian and
   Peter 1757
Charmeli, Simon 1749
Chartier, Martin, prior to 1697
Choape, Theors 1740
Chars, And. and fam. 1732
Chateau (Shadow), Jean Nich. 1739, Lanc.
Charett- ?
Chedrone (Shetron), Abr. 1749, York.
Clement, Mich., 1738
Clevel (Clewell), Francis and Geo. 1737, Northampton
Claude, Charles 1738, Pierre 1770
Clerq, Henri, Del., prior to 1677
Couvier, Jean Jacques 1754
Cotineau
Cochet (now Gouche, Goshen), Daniel in Phila., prior to 1756, John
   Geo. Deitrich, Francis and Issac 1768, Leb. Co.
Conte, John 1729
Corbo, Jean 1737, Mont. Co.
Compos, Peter 1752
Conrieu, François 1746
Comer, John 1736, Lanc.
Conrad, John Mich. (Lorraine), 1754
Courteur, Joseph 1751
Cossart (Gr. Gossert), J. 1741, Henry 1749, Lanc.
Cossine, Peter and Cornelius, *vide* Conewago

Coshune, Jean, Conewago
Consul, Arenne 1746
Cresson, Issac, Phila., 1728, Conrad prior to 1728
Crespin, Joseph 1753
Creuccas, Jacques 1737
Crownwalt, Jacob (Lorraine), 1754
Cushwa, Issac 1732, Leb. Co.

Darant (Durant), Geo. Peter 1741
Dacier, Daniel 1750, John Mich. and John Martin 1752, Paul 1753
Daron, Mich., York. Co.
Dasons, François 1734, Dauny, Jean Louis, nat. 1732
De Armand, James, Dauphin, prior to 1740, Henry 1756
De Avier, Jean Louis 1732, Lanc.
De Normandy, Andri 1706, Bucks.
De Bran, John 1690
De Bertholet, John Philip 1737
De Mars, Jean 1741, Lanc.
De Belle, Jacob 1738
De Bleame, —? Mont.
De Benneville, Dr. Geo. 1741, Berks.
De Benoit, Humber, prior to 1749
De Cesna, Jean 1718, Lanc.
De Boileau, Issac, Bucks.
De Beau (De Bo, De Bus, Du Bus), Abraham and Philip 1732, Conrad, Lanc., prior to 1737, Christian 1740, Daniel and Jacob 1743
De Dier, Jean, Germantown early, Jean 1770
De Dee, Jean 1712, Oley, Daniel 1750, David and John Geo. 1751, Abraham (Lorraine) 1754, Lanc., Josue, Jean Pierre and Jean, 1765
De Fresne (De Frain), 1731
De France, John, prior to 1740, Dauphin
De Gann, Moris, Delaware, prior to 1677
De Gomois (Degoma), Adam, prior to 1754, York.
De Grange, Andre 1749, John, York. Co., prior to 1750
De Hass, Capt. John, Del., prior to 1660, Geo. Philip 1749, Leb.
De Longschamp, Chas. Julian
De Lage, Pierre Phila. 1736, d. 1766
De Lancy, François, Lanc., prior to 1754
De Long, Jacob 1743, Berks.

De Marcellain, Bucks.
De Morest, Gerrett, Conewago
De Purcell, William, Bucks., 1734
De Pree, Jacques 1764
De Prefontain, Peter, Phila., prior to 1754
De Pui, Nicholas, Minisink, 1697
De Ring, Mat., Delaware, prior to 1677
De Rimley, nich. Francis, Bethlehem
De Remo, Jacques 1750
De Sanno, Frederick, Bucks.
De Turk, Issac 1712, Berks.
De Tar, John, Lanc.
De Tray, Christian 1737, Bucks., Conrad, Nat. Phila. 1662
De Veau, Pierre 1736, Conrad 1754
De Ville, John 1765
De La Barrie (Delabar), Jacob, Bucks., prior to 1745
De La Bach, Val. and Peter, prior to 1757, Dauphin
De La Cour (Dellicker, Rev. Frederick)
De La Camp, Henry, Berks. 1753
De La Grange, Jost. De 1656
De La Planch, Jacques, Berks., prior to 1720
De La Plaine, Jacques, Phila., 1691
De La Noe, Rev. Chas., Phila., prior to 1700
De La Vall, John, Phila., 1682
De La Ware, Issac, m. in Phila., 1735
Decha, Edward 1752
Deschong (Des Champ), Diet. William 1752, Lanc., William and
    Mathias 1753
Deque, Jacques 1773
Dessloch, Geo. (Lorraine), 1754
Demje, Pierre 1773
Deoux, Philip, prior to 1750
Dilloe, Pierre (Dillo) 1736, Lanc., Mich., prior to 1745
Dillier (Diller), Casper 1731, Lanc., Francis 1738
Digeon, Daniel 1742 (Alsace), Northampton
Dinkle, John Daniel 1750 (Alsace), York.
Dispionett, Jacques (Des Bonnett), 1739, to Va.
Douthett, York., prior to 1754
Doz, Anthony 1685, Phila.
Dobler, Nicholas (Lorraine), 1752, Dauphin
Dore, Antoine 1770

Donderman, Jean Pierre 1773
Dondore, Michael (Alsace), Lanc., prior to 1718, John and son Jacob
1741, Berks.
Douay, Conrad 1740
Donatt, Geo., nat. Chester Co., 1734
Duey, John and John Christian 1750, Chester
Doutell, Jacob 1738, Jacob, York. Co., prior to 1746, François,
Lanc., prior to 1750
Doute (DuTay), David and John Geo. 1751, Lanc., François, Lanc.,
prior to 1758
Dracot, Ralph, Bucks.
Drapet, Jean 1750
Dravo, Anthony, Pittsburg
Dupree, Jacob, nat. 1734, Jacob in Phila., prior to 1693, Jacob, nat.
Berks. Co., 762, George, Berks. Co., 1764
Dupree, Danl, Phila., prior to 1754, Christian, Lb. prior to 1749
Durye, Geo. 1733, Berks., Jacob 1739, Samuel, Conewago
Duponceau, Peter, Phila.
Duval, Daniel 1749
Duche, Anthony, Phila., prior to 1700
Dufot, Philip, Sr., Philip, Jr., 1739
Dubrett, Jacques 1763
Duistro, Jean 1740
Durell, Moses, Phil., prior to 1731
Dushane—early in Delaware
Duchand, Francis 1773
Duton, Abraham 1754
Du Simetere, Pierre Eugene 1764, Phila.
Du Corson, Benj., Bucks. Co.
Du Keyness, Henry, Lanc., prior to 1762
Du Castle, Edmund, Phila., 1682
Du Bach, Clement 1734
Du Pont, George 1768
Du Bois, Jean, New Castle, prior to 1694, Solomon 1718, Conrad
1728 (d. 1757), Abraham 1732, Philip —

Eckerline
Emilot, Nich. and Leonard 1732, Lanc.
Escogue, John Peter 1738
Ekore, Phil. 1731

Forney, Abraham, age 64 y., 1734, Christian and Peter 1734, Lanc.,
    Jacob 1752, John Adam 1747
Femme, Geo., Jr. 1753
Ferree,
Fidele, Mich., Mont., prior to 1740
Fiscus, Gerhart (Alsace), 1744
Fleury, Pierre 1732, Joseph and sons Joseph and John 1733, Abra.,
    nat. in Phila., 1743, Adolphe and Geo. 1754
Folquier, Jean Jacques 1754, m. in Phila., 1755
Fontain, Jacob 1751, Dauphin
Fortineaux (Fortney), Jean Henri, nat. 1727, François 1737, David
    1739, Jean, aged 56, and Samuel 1742, Mechoir, d. 1754, Lanc.
Fournier, David, York., prior to 1740
Frentier, Jean 1755
Frenier, Casper 1739, Lanc.
Frank, John Adam (Lorraine), 1754
Frey, Henry, Altheim Alsace, to Phila., prior to 1695

Garragues,
Garton, de, Abraham, Lanc., prior to 1736, Felix 1749
Gasha (Casho ?), Peter 1749, York.
Gashon, Jean 1752, Gannett, John Henry, prior to 1745, Berks.
Gateau, Nich., nat. Phil., 1704
Gallo, Christian 1751, Jean 1768
Gausfres, Jean 1730
Gaigdon, Jean Henru 1763
Gautier, Pierre and Jacques 1753
Gerra, Pierre, and Joseph 1746
Gerard, Nich. 1736, David, d. 1769, Berks. Co., Peter, nat. 1767
Gerardin (also Charetin, Sheradan), Jacob and fam. 1748, Berks.
Gennevine, Leonard, York., prior to 1755
Gehret, Geo. 1737, Frances 1744, Peter 1749, Berks.
Gerber, Christian and Geo. Mich. (Alsace), 1738, Berks.
Gillion, Charle 1738, Pierre 1752
Gilbert, John 1757, John Wendel 1754 (Lorraine)
Gourier, Pierre 1753, Lanc.
Grauel (Crowell L. Dept. Rec), John Mich., Sr. (1683–1753), 1730,
    Berks., John Mich. 1733
Gruwell, John (from France), Delaware after 1700
Grimm, Egideus (Alsace), 1727, Lehigh
Greine, Pierre 1754, Lanc.

GrosJean, Jacques (Groshong), 1756, Dauphin
Granget, Jean 1738, Adrian 1 ⁄67
Grandaden, François and Adam 1749, Lanc.
Grenoble, de, Jacob 1743, Berks.
Gresamere, Casper, Peter, and John Valentine 1730, Mont. and Berks.

Harcourt, Mich. 1751
Haller, Henry (Alsace), 1733, Lanc.
Hathe, Jean Gaspard 1771
Hammand, Erasmus, "from Nancy", 1739
Hasslinger, Geo. (Lorraine), 1756
Hauser, John Henry (Lorraine), 1754
Hauser, Danl. and Nich (Lorraine), 1754, Md.
Hay, John, Sr., John, Jr., 1757 (Alsace), York
Herbein, Jonathan, prior to 1720, Peter and Abraham 1732, Berks.
Heyde, John Jost, prior to 1717 (Alsace), Pa. and Va.
Herring, John Geo. (Lorraine), 1754, Berks.
Heckendorn, Daniel and family (Alsace), 1736, Lanc.
Hoch (High), Melchior and Jonathan (Alsace), 1717, Berks.
Hillegas, John Fred 1727, Leopold 1730, John Adam 1732, Mich. and Peter, prior to 1745, Geo. Albrecht 1746 (Alsace)
Hogar, Antoine 1754 (Lorraine)
Hotel, John 1732
Hobart, Adam 1738
Hodnett, John, Phila., prior to 1737
Hoyer, Franc Carl (Alsace), 1738, Berks.
Hoshier, Laurains, Christian, and Abraham 1741
Hoschar, Theobald, John Peter, and John Henry, 1749
Hoozier, Geo. 1751
Hotman, John 1755, Michael 1753
Horry, William 1727, Martin, nat. York. Co., 1763
Hutier, Jean Jacques, prior to 1751, Lanc.
Hugo, John Daniel 1753
Hubertson, Hubert 1709, Lanc.
Hubert, Geo. 1749, Andrew 1765
Hubele, Joseph and sons Mich. and Barnard 1732, Jacob 1737, John Frederick 1743
Huger, John Christ 1766
Hueling, Lars, Geo. 1750
Huidenbery, Val. (Lorraine), 1754

Huguelet, Abr. and Charles (Lorraine), 1754
Hugett, Francis (Hugus?) 1737, Lanc.
Huyett, Geo., Berks., prior to 1734, Franc Carl 1738, Mich. 1749,
    Peter 1746

Imbert, Andrew 1683, Phil.
Izard, Jean 1770

Jardines, Dr. des, Del, prior to 1680
Jacques, Jean (b. 1696, d. 1778, Lanc.), Abraham 1736, Lanc.
Jacquett, Jean Paul, Del., 1650
Jacquard, Fred 1752, John Peter 1753, John Peter 1768
Janvier, Thomas, Del., prior to 1700
Javin, Pierre
Jeune, C. Jacques 1749, Henri 1751, Lanc.
Joho, John 1739, York
Joch (Schoch), John Jacob, Sr., John Jacob, Jr., Mich. 1749 (Alsace)
Joray (Jury), Jacques 1749, Abraham 1754, Dauphin
douran, Jean 1738
Jommel, Mar. 1750
Jurian, Mathias 1732
Julian, Peter 1764

Kauffman, John Jacob (Alsace), 1737
Keppler, Simon (Lorraine), 1754
Keim, Johannes 1697, Berks.
Kieffer, Casper and Abraham 1748, Mich. and Jacob 1750, Berks.
Klencke, Mich. (Lorraine), 1754
Kuntzelman, John Jacob (Lorraine), 1754

Lambing, Christopher (1720–1810), from Alsace
Lachart, Barnard 1741, John Jacob 1753
Lazelere, Nich. (1691 Long Island, N.Y.), Nich., Jr., to Bucks. Co.
Lantzinger, John (Alsace), 1738
Lanbleau, Jean Jacques 1752
Latz, John Jacob (Lorraine), 1754
Laux, Pierre 1738, Lanc., Peter 1737, Bucks., John Jacob 1754
Laschett (Lawshe), John Jacob age 50, sons John Peter, age 25, and
    Christian, age 18 1736, Lanc., John Wendel 1738, Daniel, in
    Phila., prior to 1752
Lallamand, Jacob 1757

Laurans, Hubert, Del., prior to 1677, John 1736, Henry 1738, Frances
    Peter, d. Lanc., 1758
Laschelles, Geo., *vide* Conewago
Leasure, Abr. (Lorraine), 1754, Dauphin
Levering, Wigard and Gerhart 1685, Phila.
Lingel, Paul and Jacob 1737
Lilou, James, prior to 1750, Cumb.
Linville, Henry, prior to 1740, Berks.
Loresh, Jacob, prior to 1751, Berks.
Lorraine, John, Phila.
Lorange (L'Orange), Henry, Dauphin, prior to 1750
Lorah (Loreau), Phila., prior to 1715, John 1737, John Casper
    1754
Lorie, John Henry and John Melchior 1749, John Peter 153
Lorisen, Geo., Mich. and Gabriel 1738
Lovine, Abraham, *vide* Conewago
La Bar, Peter, Chas, and Abraham 1730, Danl. and Philip, nat. in
    1738, William, nat. 1750
La Belle, Simon, nat. 1762
La Blanch, early in Phila.
La Bert, Michael 1729, Adam 1753
Lapert (Labert?), John 1739
La Cellas, James, Phila., prior to 1759
La Gnau, Batholomas 1754, York
La Mar, Leonard 1741, Michael 1750, John, Nich. and Francis 1754,
    Berks.
La Mott, Jean Henri 1754, York
La Place, Philip Peter 1765
La Pierre, Jean Jacques 1753, Lanc.
La Port, Jean 1777
La Roux, Jonas 1719, Lanc., John, Phila, prior to 1739, George,
    prior to 1740, Dauphin, Abraham, Sr., and Abraham, Jr., in
    Bucks. very early, Abraham, d. York Co. 1757
La Rash, Ludwig (L. Dept.), prior to 1757, Northampton
La Rouse, Ephraim, prior to 1738
La Rose, John Lewis 1740, Lehigh
La Saul, Jacob 1738
La Trine, Anna 1729
La Tour, Herman and Jacob 1749, Lanc.
La Wall, John Michael 1749, Daniel and John Ludwig 1752

Le Beau (Lebo), John, prior to 1718, Lanc., Peter, prior to 1737, John, prior to 1734, John, prior to 1740, John Abr., prior to 1742, John Henry 1765
Le Bot, Albert 1737
Le Boyteau, John early in Phila.
Le Blanch, Joseph, Phila.
Le Boob, Mich., d. York Co. 1780
Le Brant, John Conrad 1751, Lanc., George, Berks. Co.
Le Brun, Ettine 1753
Le Cene, Jean and Paul 1732, Lanc.
Le Colle, Pierre, prior to 1720, Phila.
Le Crone, Daniel, d. Lanc. 1769, Jacob, Lanc., prior to 1757, Jacob, Lanc., prior to 1757, Leonard, York Co.
Le Char,
Le Dieu, Lewis, Phila., prior to 1758
Le Die, Jean 1772
Lemont, Peter, Lanc., prior to 1718
Le Drue, John 1718, Jos. and Noël in Phila.
Le Fevre, Hypolite, Jean and Jacques, in Del., prior to 1685, Issac, Lanc. Co. 1712, John in Mont. Co. 1778
Le Gay (Le Geau?), early in Phila.
Le Maistre, John William, age 58, 1748
Le Moree, Jean Baptiste
Le Roy, John Mich. and George 1738, Jean Jacques 1752, Abraham 1754, Abraham and Adam 1754
Le Shemile, Peter, prior to 1741, Phila.
Le Tort, James, prior to 1787
Le Tellier, Peter, Phila.
Le Van, Abraham, Issac and Jacob, prior to 1725, Daniell 1727, Peter 1748
Le Vassong, John Lewis, 1732
Le Valleau, Chas., prior to 1695, Bucks. Co.

Mackinett, Daniel, prior to 1739, Mont. Co., d. 1744
Marchand, John Lewis and John Geo. 1737
Marti, Laurans and John 1749
Mathiot, Jean and George 1754, Lanc.
Marionette, Jacques 1738
Mallo, John Michael (Alsace), 1749, John Geo. 1755
Marot, Pierre and fam. 1733

Martine, Mich. 1747, Yarra Emanuel 1744, John Theodore, Justus
    and Charles 1753, John Martin 1754
Marett, Mich. 1736, Lanc., Mich. 1737, Albra. 1777
Morett, Jean Dedier and Mattieu 1757, Berks., Etienne 1773
Maier, Adam (Lorraine), 1754
Mallecot, Phillippe 1757
Markie, Marcus 1736, Jacob 1745, Leb.
Marcoe, Abraham, Santa Cruz 1750, Phila.
Markley, John Christman (Alsace), John Jacob 1749, Jean Chris-
    topher 1752
Marquetand, Laurans, Lanc.
Marquard, John Geo. and Martin 1743, John 1750
Marquett, John Henry Lebanon, prior to 1743, Peter 1749, John
    Geo. 1752, John Geo. (2nd) 1752
Marie, Casper 1732
Marree (Marie?) Seb. 1729, James 1730, Christian 1733, Berks.
Morree, Wm., nat. in Bucks. Co., 1734
Mease, Henry, "late from France", 1749
Melfort, John Casper, nat. Chester, 1762
Mercier, Augustine 1773
Mestrezat, Charles Andre,
Meurer, Rev. Philip (Alsace), 1742
Mentjes, François, prior to 1750, Lanc.
Messakop, John 1754, Lanc.
Minuit, Peter, Del., 1738
Mischele, John Geo. and Joseph 1749
Michelot (Mickley), John Jacob 1733 (Lorraine), Lehigh
Missamer, John Mich. (Alsace), Mont.
Millot, Nich. 1749, Berks., Pierre 1749
Morea (Morrow), François, Lanc., prior to 1750, John, d. at Lanc.
    1760, Philip m. at Bethlehem 1757
Moser 1720
Mottier, John Mich. 1749
Molier, Etienne 1773
Monier, Jacques 1770
Monel, Pierre 1768
Montmaton, Gulliaume 1770
Montieth, John, Conewago
Morell, Matthieu, prior to 1770, Berks.
Molan, Jacques, 1752
Molin, Mathew 1752

Moris, Jacques 1749
Monin, Jean Pierre, Sr., and Jean Pierre, Jr. (Lorraine), 1754
Montandon, David 1729, Phila.
Montfort, John, Conewago
Momma, John Conrad and Hermanus (Lorraine), 1747, Lanc.,
    Christian, d. Lanc., 1775, Jacob 1737, Lanc., Leonard 1737,
    Lanc., Peter 1748., Laurens, d. Lanc., 1752
Muni (Le Moyne), Jacob, Sr., Jacob, Jr., Conrad, Andrew and
    Christopher 1750, Dauphin
Mylander, John Daniel (Lorraine), 1754

Naudin, Elie., Del., 1698
Neron, Lorie 1750
Noble, Anthony, Sr., Anthony, Jr., 1734
Noël, Enas and Joseph, with families, 1736, Killian 1738, John, m.
    at Bethlehem, 1746, Philip prior to 1740, Jean prior to 1750,
    in York Co.

Oberlin, Martin and John Adam (Alsace), prior to 1730, Lanc., Israel
    1752, Lanc.
Ozias, Henry, prior to 1750, Phila.

Paca, John, prior to 1758, Phila.
Pallio, Peter, prior to 1730, Berks.
Palin, Laz., 1738
Paris, Pierre, Issac, Sr., Issac, Jr., 1750, Issac 1750, Pierre, George
    and Nicola 1770
Parat, Cornelius 1734
Paire, Jacob 1736, Lanc., Jacob 1747
Pavon, Jean Pierre 1744
Patier, Louis 1770
Parent, John 1727
Parshing, Nich. 1732
Paushon, John Nich. 1733
Perzonze, John Jac. 1740, Leb., d. 1749
Pierson, Laurans 1738, Lanc.
Perrett, Henry 1777
Perretier, Jean Henri, Sr., and Jr., 1754 (Lorraine)
Perlett, John 1732, John Fred 1751
Perqua, Adam 1749
Pechin, Pierre, and sons Jean Nicholas and Jean Christopher 1754
    (Lorraine), Chester

Pettit, John, York, prior to 1749, Jonathan, Northampton, prior to 1759

Perrine, Thomas, Lanc., prior to 1718

Pershing, Frederick 1749 (Alsace), Westmorland

Pigonie (Bigony-Pigoney), Jean 1752, François 1773, Montgomery

Pievex, Laurans 1739

Pinnard, Jos., Phila., prior to 1703, Pierre, Nicholas 1727, York, Christian, nat. in Chester 1750, Martin 1750, Jean Henri 1757

Picquart, James, d. Lancaster, 1749, Henry, prior to 1744, John Gottfried, in Phila. prior to 1754

Pons, Jacques 1727, Augustus 1728, Abra. 1751, John, Sr., and John, Jr., 1768

Poponet, Pierre Carl 1773

Porreau, Jean Daniel 1773

Pontius, John 1738 (Alsace), Nicholas, Martin, and David 1768, Berks.

Purviance, Saml., Phila., prior to 1693, David (Lorraine), 1754, Dauphin

Purdieu, William, Phila., prior to 1738

Pyatt

Pythau, Jean Guilliaume, 1769

Querrier, John Nich. 1752, Berks.

Qua (le), John and Frederick 1753, Chester

Quepic, Jeania (Lorraine), 1754

Rausier, Fred, Phila., prior to 1748

Raboteau, Chas, Cornelius, Mont., prior to 1750

Rappe, Gabriel 1683, Phila.

Raiguel, Jean Jacques 1754, Dauphin

Rayer (Royer), Sebastian 1718, John Jacob 1729, John Martin 1729, John Mich. 1732, J. Nicholas and Jacob 1749

Raquet, Henry, Lanc., prior to 1752, John Nich. and John Christopher 1764

Ramey, Pierre (Lorraine), 1754

Ranc (Ranck), John, Mich., 1728, John Philip, 1729, Lanc.

Remey, Bartol and son Jacob 1737, Daniel, prior to 1754, Northampton.

Revere, Geo. 1773

Remley (de), Ambrose and Jacob 1741, Northampton, Conrad in Phila.

Renoudet, James, Phila., prior to 1733
Receau, Thomas, Phila., prior to 1716
Retteu, William, prior to 1726, Chester
Renart, John Adam 1741
Reusal, John Peter 1751
Renan, Joseph 1764
Relan, Nicola 1749
Renolle, Daniel 1749, York
Renau (Reno), Claude 1749, Issac, 1751, Peter and Francis 1752, Joseph 1764
Riehl, Simon 1729, Nicholas, Berks., prior to 1732, John Philip 1738, Jonas 1742, John George 1751
Ritner, Abr. (Alsace), 1750 Berks., Laurans, 1754
Ridett, Benj. and John, Conewago
Ribolett, Christian 1733, Abraham, Jacob and John Peter 1749
Richardeu, Pierre and Jean 1754
Riboleau, Nicholas, Phila., 1683
Rochia, Laurans, Delaware, Adam 1752
Roller, John and John Jacob 1750, John Geo. and John Mich. 1753, John Peter, 1752
Ronner, John Rinehart, 1743
Roberdieu, Issac, Phila.
Rosier, Laurans 1732, De Beau Rosier, in Lanc, prior to 1753
Roshong, Adam, Phila., prior to 1733, Henri and Pierre (Lorraine), 1753, Philip 1754
Robinett, Samuel, Phila. 1684
Rosher, Gabriel 1731, Lanc., John 1764
Routte, Daniel, New Castle, prior to 1683
Rottie, Jean Pierre 1754
Rutan, Gerritt, New Castle, 1660
Rubishong, Septimus, Lanc., 1712, Mathias, Lanc., 1732, John, Berks., 1732, John 1734
Rumont, Vernier 1753
Ruhlin, John Geo., Berks., 1754
Rutselia (Rudseill), Philip M., at Conestoga 1734, d. 1754, Weirick 1737, York Co., John Jacob 1752, York Co., Andrew 1749
Rubie (Ruby), Peter 1738, Casper 1748, York

Santee, Issac, Bucks.
Santeau (Sando), Jacques, 1754, Lanc.
Sauvet, Henri 1773

Sanguinet, Jacob 1753
Sauvage, John 1738, Berks.
Sausser (De Saussier), David 1743, John Jacob 1749
Saurian, Philip 1754
Sarijons, Philippi 1754
Sangre, Christian, York, prior to 1738, John Ludwig 1749
Saye, Richard, Delaware, prior to 1686, Bernet 1740
Savoy, Jean, Delaware, prior to 1700
Sallada, Jacob 1749, Peter 1750, Frederick 1751, d. 1770, Nicholas
    1752, Thomas 1764
Scharille, Christian (Lorraine), 1754
Schnellbach, John (Lorraine), 1754
Schendt, Mathew (Lorraine), 1754
Schilling, John (Lorraine), 1754
Schreiner, Adam (Lorraine), 1754
Schuett, Carl. Val Mich., prior to 1734
Schora, Jacob 1753, Nich. and John Adam 1768
Sevier, Philip, 1733
Servier, Jean Jacques 1753
Secore, Mathew 1749
Seiz, Jean Louis 1763
Seubert, John and Andrew (Alsace), 1752
Serieux, Jean 1770
Seyzer, John (Lorraine), 1754
Seal, John Paul (Lorraine), 1751, Dauphin.
Sensinia (Sensiny), Jacob, Lanc., prior to 1737, Christian, d. Lanc.,
    1753
Shultz, Ch. Otto (Alsace), 1734
Shuey, Daniel and Ludwig 1732, Leb., John 1748, John Fred 1749,
    John Philip 1764
Showa, Frederick (Lorraine), 1754, John, Sr., and John, Jr., prior to
    1745
Shetron (Chedron), Abraham 1749, York
Sibrick, Guilliaume 1752
Simonett (Simony), Jacques 1727, Lanc.
Sieur, Philip 1752
Sochonet, Henri 1733
Souplies (Supplee), Andre 1684, Phila.
Soloman, Abra. (Alsace), 1739
Soule, John and Francis 1749
Somaine,

Sponselier, Philip (Lorraine), 1732, Lanc., Philip 1754, Geo., nat. York Co., 1761

Spurior, Nich. 1741

Steubesant, John Geo. (Lorraine), 1754

Steg, Albert Otto (Lorraine), 1754

Suffrance, John 1732, Phila.

Sumois (Summey), John Peter, Sr., and sons John Peter, Jr., John Jacob, John, and John Michael 1733, Lancaster

Talman, Jacques (Lorraine), 1754

Thebaut (Tebo), Philip 1714

Thoulozan, Jean 1749

Tien, Jean Henri 1751

Tiesser, Etienne 1770, Etienne 1771

Torson, F. Christopher 1752

Tomel, Paul 1750

Tournay, Daniel 1740, Peter 1741, John 1750

Trasbart, Nicola 1736

Travenger, Peter, nat. Lanc. Co., 1727

Transue, Abr. 1730, Mont. Co.

Trippeo, Fred, prior to 1713, Phila.

Trego, Pierre, Delaware Co., prior to 1684

Trevillier, Jos. Phila., prior to 1745

Trebert, Justus, Lanc., prior to 1755

Trevett, Christian 1739

Trylopare, Jacob (Alsace), 1732

Udree, Henry 1741, Phila.

Urner, Ulrich (Alsace), 1708, Chester

Urffer, Mich. (Alsace), 1765

Ull. John (Lorraine) 1754

Varlet, C., 1773

Valin, Gabrial 1773

Vasqueau (Wesco), Philip 1754, Lehigh

Vassar, Jacob 1751

Vallerchamp, Simon

Rautie, Pierre (Lorraine), 1754

Vandalin, H. Martin 1754

Verdieux, Jacques, York prior to 1755

Vertrie (Verdries), John with fam. to Lanc. Co., prior to 1733

Vidal, Stephen, Phila., prior to 1754

Vincent, Louis 1738

Viellard ("Willer"), Casperius 1732, Lanc., John Peter, Lanc. prior
    to 1733

Vintvas, Jean Pierre 1746

Viersard, Jean Richard 1764

Vielleman, François 1773

Viebert, Geo. 1732

Vishang, Conrad and Philip 1740

Voturin (Woodring), Abraham (Lorraine), 1733, Northampton, John
    1739, York, Nicholas?

Vosin, Jean Pierre 1738, Jean Pierre 1754, Abraham 1768

Voyer, Peter, Phila, prior to 1713

Voshell, Wm., "Delaware near 1700"

Votaw, Paul, Issac and John, near Phila, prior to 1744, John to Va.

Wendling (Vandalin), Peter and Dewalt (Bushweiler, Alsace), 1752,
    Lanc.

Welshans (Velschang), Peter, Abraham, and Joseph 1739, Lanc.

Werley, Dietrich (Alsace), 1736, York

Welle, Jean Pierre 1768

Wiershang (Viershang), Conrad and Philip 1740, Peter 1741, Casper
    1753, Lanc.

Weimer, Barnard 1732 (Alsace), John 1747

Willeman (Vielleman), Alphonse (Lorraine), 1754

Willard, Christian and Martin 1749

Addenda et Corrigenda

BY MILTON RUBINCAM

President, The American Society of Genealogists;
Former Editor, *National Genealogical Society Quarterly*

Dr. Reaman asked me to check the proofs of his book in order to eliminate so far as possible genealogical errors that may have crept in. In order to avoid the cost of re-setting whole paragraphs, and, in one or two cases, whole pages, it was decided that I should prepare the *Addenda et Corrigenda* Section. It should be emphasized that the stories of glamorous ancestry, the product of wishful thinking, were accepted by Dr. Reaman *in good faith*, based upon the books he consulted and the family traditions related to him by present-day descendants. There is no guarantee that we have caught all errors, but the most glaring ones are set out below.

Page 103. In addition to the Huguenot colony at Friedrichsdorf, in Hesse-Homburg (the Province of Hesse-Nassau, named in the text, did not exist until 1866), there were Huguenot settlements in the landgraviate of Hesse-Cassel. The first German prince to offer asylum to the persecuted Huguenots was Landgrave Charles of Hesse-Cassel by his decree of April 18, 1685. As a result, there were French settlements at Cassel, Karlsdorf, Mariendorf, Schwabendorf, Hertingshausen, and other places in the prince's dominions. (See Rudolph Schmidmann, "Die Kolonien Réfugiés in Hessen-Kassel und ihre wirtschaftliche Entwicklung im 17. und 18. Jahrhundert", *Zeitschrift des Vereins für hessische Geschichte und Landeskunde*, Band 57, 1929, pp. 115–224.)

Page 112. It is not clear why John C. Calhoun, the great American statesman, is included in the section on South Carolina Huguenots. Through both of his parents he was descended from Scottish families; I have been unable to find any Huguenot connections, although he may indeed have been descended from Huguenot families. His parents were Patrick Calhoun and Martha Caldwell. (Charles M. Wiltse, *John C. Calhoun, Nationalist, 1782–1828*, 1944, pp. 12, 22. Originally his name was Colquhoun, a very old Scottish family.)

Page 115. Pierre Baudoin, the progenitor of the famous Bowdoin family, was *not* descended from Baldwin I, Count (not Prince) of Flanders in 862. With one possible exception, no American colonial family can trace its pedigree in the male line that far back, because of the dearth of documents covering a thousand-year period. The possible exception is FitzRandolph of New Jersey, for which family there is a fairly well-established descent from the ancient Counts of Brittany. Temple Prime's *Some Account of the Bowdoin Family* (1894) begins with Pierre Baudoin, with no fancy claims concerning his origin.

Page 119. Henry Hudson was not the discoverer of the river that bears his name. The real discoverer was the Florentine navigator, Giovanni da Verrazano, in 1524. (See John Bakeless, *The Eyes of Discovery. America as seen by the first explorers*, Dover Publications, Inc., New York, 1961, p. 204.)

Page 124. General Richard Montgomery, the American soldier who unsuccessfully attempted to detach Canada from the British Empire in 1775, was *not* descended from Gabriel, Comte de Montgomery (Montgomerie), who slew Henry II of France in a tournament in 1559. He was sprung, instead, from a well-known Scottish family, being the "third son of Thomas Montgomery, M.P. for Lifford, grandson of Alexander Montgomery of Ballyleck and descendant in the eighth generation of Alexander the poet". Alexander Montgomery, the poet laureate of King James I, was born about 1546 as a son of John Montgomery, 4th Laird of Hessilheid. It will be observed, therefore, that there could be no possible connection with the 16th-century Comtes de Montgomery in France. (See B. G. de Montgomery, *Origin and History of the Montgomerys*, 1948, pp. 208, 216.)

Page 127. Capt. Nicholas Martiau, the Huguenot settler in

Virginia, was ancestor not only of General George Washington, as stated in the text, but also of General Robert E. Lee and Queen Elizabeth II. For the connecting links, see two articles, "History of York County [Virginia] in the Seventeenth Century", *Tyler's Quarterly Historical and Genealogical Magazine,* vol. 1, April 1920, pp. 247–248, and "Queen Elizabeth's American Ancestry and Cousinship to George Washington and Robert E. Lee", by Anthony R. Wagner, *The Genealogists' Magazine,* London, England, vol. 8, Sept. 1939, pp. 368–375, reprinted from the *New York Genealogical and Biographical Record,* vol. 70.

Page 130. In the list of Huguenot families in Lancaster County, Pennsylvania, De Haas should be investigated before acceptance. In this case the "De" is probably not the French noble particle "de", but the Dutch definite article. "De haas" means "the hare" in the Dutch language.

Page 132. Gen. Daniel *Roberdian's* name should be *Roberdeau.* An excellent family history is Roberdeau Buchanan's *Genealogy of the Roberdeau Family* (1876). Although I have not had occasion to investigate it, his mother's descent from the Scottish Earls of Glencairn (*not* Glencavin, as given in the text) appears, on the surface, to be well established.

Page 134. The claim that the Zeller family was founded by Clothilde de Valois Zeller, of Huguenot origin, is a pleasant day dream. There is an implication in *The Compendium of American Genealogy,* vol. III, 1928, p. 641, that "Lady Clothilde de Valois" belonged to the former French royal house of Valois. This is nonsense; in spite of this statement and that in John A. Zeller's *A Brief History of the Zeller Family* (1945), p. 13, CLOTHILDE DE VALOIS ZELLER NEVER EXISTED. My friend, Dr. Albert H. Gerberich, the leading authority on Pennsylvania German genealogy, informs me that "Clothilde de Valois' " real name was *Anna Catharina,* and her maiden surname is unknown. She died at Tulpehocken, in Berks county, near the Lebanon County (Pennsylvania) line, in 1749.

Pages 134–135. Dr. Reaman's statement on the noble origin of the Rapalje (Raparlier, etc.) family is derived from Charles Kingsbury Miller's *Historic Families of America: William Almy, of Portsmouth, Rhode Island, 1630—Joris Jansen de Rapalje, of Fort Orange (Albany), New Amsterdam and Brooklyn, 1623* (1897), pp. 91–92. My friend, Dr. Herbert F. Seversmith, the distinguished authority on Long Island genealogy, whose monumental *Colonial Families of Long Island, New York, and Connecticut* will shortly go into its fifth volume, is a Rapalje descendant. He informs me that he knows nothing of the ancestry of Joris Jansen Rapalje; the ancestry set out in the text may very well be true, but documentary evidence must be produced to support it. Another friend, John Insley Coddington, now Editor of the *National Genealogical Society Quarterly*, investigated the records of Amsterdam two years ago. He found the following marriage record in the Église Wallonne d'Amsterdam, Marriages 1584–1639, Gemeente Archief, Amsterdam, vol. DNB 1001, p. 132: "1624 espouse le 21 de janvier JORIS RAPORLIE de Valencienne et CATHERINE TRIKO".

Pages 216–217. Richard Talbot of 1172 could not have been "a son of Lord Talbot of Eccleswell", who was "mentioned in the Domesday Book", compiled nearly a century earlier, in 1085–86. In fact, Richard Talbot's ancestry is unknown and there was no "Lord Talbot of Eccleswell", although there were Talbots seated at Eccleswell. "Talbot" is a personal nickname, and there is no certainty that the early persons so called were all of one family. (See *The Complete Peerage*, Revised and Enlarged, vol. XII, 1953, p. 606; *The Encyclopaedia Britannica*, 1962, vol. 21, article "Talbot"; Anthony Richard Wagner, *English Genealogy*, 1960, p. 66.)

Page 220. The claim that the great French princely House of Condé was the parent stock of the Condie family of Canada and the Conde family of the United States (the latter reported by Stephen Elmer Slocum, Ph.D., in his article, "Genealogy of the Conde Family in America", *New York Genealogical and Biographical Record*, April 1928) is unsubstantiated. Printed histories of the House of Condé throw no light on the connection. Condé is the name of some 20 villages and two towns in Frace; hence, at the time surnames were adopted, unrelated families named Condé could have originated in any of these localities. Research must be made to establish the true origins of Malcolm Condie, the 19th-century Canadian pioneer, and Adam Conde, the 18th-century American settler.

Pages 220–221. The noble origin of the Van Egmond family of Canada must also be considered questionable. Investigation in the Netherlands should be undertaken either to verify it or to repudiate it. The historic family of the Counts of Egmont (Egmond), mentioned in the text, is extinct in the male line. The *Nederland's Adelsboek* for 1961 does not list any family bearing this title, nor is a patrician family named Egmond listed in the index to the first 39 volumes (1910–53) of the *Nederland's Patriciaat*.

Pages 220–223. It is disillusioning to read the contribution by a descendant that "The McGowan Family originated with Alexander Sinclair, a younger son of the 12th Earl of Caithness who quarrelled with his father and adopted the name of McGowan". Nothing could be further from the truth; all one has to do is to consult Sir James Balfour Paul's authoritative work, *The Scots Peerage*, vol. II (1905), pp. 356–357. It is there shown that Sir James Sinclair, 8th Baronet and 12th Earl of Caithness (1766–1823), married Jean Campbell, by whom he had nine children, including the following sons. John, Lord Berriedale (1788–1802); *Alexander, 13th Earl of Caithness (1790–1855)*; Lieutenant-Colonel James (1797–1856); Patrick Campbell (1800–1834); Eric George, R.N. (1801–1829); and John (1808–1861). It is true that the 12th Earl of Caithness had a "younger son" Alexander, as stated in the text, but he was the second and oldest surviving son, succeeding his father as the 13th earl in 1823. He married Frances Harriett Leigh, and had children, of whom his son in time became the 14th earl. Alexander, the 13th earl, never settled in Canada, and certainly *never* changed his honored name of Sinclair to McGowan.

Page 224. Albert Winslow Ryerson, in *The Ryerson Genealogy* (1916), p. xi, casts doubt on the French Huguenot background: "There is a tradition in the family that the Ryersons were of French Huguenot origin and that they sought refuge in Holland on account of religious persecution. Yet the family seems to have been of Dutch ancestry before the days of the Huguenots. That they espoused the Protestant cause and were also sympathizers and supporters of the Walloons and Huguenots, is true."

INDEX

Names found in the Biographical Sketches and the Appendices are not included in the Index.